Praise for *Educating in Christ*

"In anxious times, this practical book is good news for parents, teachers, and catechists who introduce Catholic faith and morals to children and young people. Gerard O'Shea offers a way forward that is Trinitarian, Christ-centered, and yet fully attentive to the needs of the child. Inspired by the Catechesis of the Good Shepherd, he is faithful to living tradition and Church teaching on catechesis, while sharing fresh, creative insights and approaches. The wide range of themes provides not only a strong spirituality but accessible formation in faith at all age levels."

—MOST REV. PETER J. ELLIOTT, Auxiliary Bishop, Catholic Archdiocese of Melbourne; Episcopal Vicar for Religious Education; Director of the John Paul II Institute for Marriage and the Family, Melbourne

"If you regard the objective of religious education as the formation of a Catholic heart, memory, intellect, and imagination, then you will consider *Educating in Christ* an indispensable text. Drawing on ideas from Maria Montessori and Sofia Cavalletti, it explains how to hand on the faith at different stages of a child's development. It is aimed at the education of saints who will know, love, and serve Christ. The anthropology is Trinitarian and Christocentric, and the pedagogy includes the insights of the saintly teachers from across the Christian centuries. Every Catholic teacher should read and apply it."

—TRACEY ROWLAND, St. John Paul II Chair of Theology, University of Notre Dame, Australia

"I am often asked how my book, *The Way of Beauty*, which describes the principles of Catholic education at higher levels, might be adapted for younger children. Now I know where to send those inquiring! This wonderful book provides the answers—and much more besides. Balancing the natural and the supernatural, the theoretical and the practical, and combining the best of traditional methods with modern educational theory and psychology (with great prudence), Gerard O'Shea describes how a mystagogical catechesis, rooted in the study of scripture and the actual worship of God, lies at the heart of Catholic education. Then he describes how teaching methods and curricula should reflect these principles for children of different ages. Every Catholic and educator should read this book."

—DAVID CLAYTON, Provost, Master of Sacred Arts, Pontifex University; author of *The Way of Beauty*

"Rooted in the Church's sacramental traditions, informed by classical virtue theory, and drawing upon the best of modern developmental psychology, O'Shea's work is a gem. As both an academic and father of eight, I heartily recommend this practical, credible, orthodox, organized, and hopeful guide to educating our children in the faith."

—RYAN N.S. TOPPING, Vice President and Academic Dean of Newman Theological College, Edmonton; author of *The Case for Catholic Education*

"This masterful work is a much-needed addition to the literature of Catholic religious education. It offers an integrated vision, bringing together anthropology, curriculum guidance, questions of school ethos and teacher formation, analyses of research findings in children's learning—all grounded in a coherent and persuasive account of the aims and nature of Catholic education. With a sure touch, Gerard O'Shea draws upon the well-established educational tradition associated particularly with Montessori and Cavalletti, making treasures from this rich seam available to those in the field."

—PETROC WILLEY, Director of the Catechetical Institute and the Office of Catechetics, Franciscan University of Steubenville

"*Educating in Christ* has come out of the substantial educational and research experience of the author. Gerard O'Shea spent thirty years as a teacher and principal in Catholic schools before serving as a theologian, and more recently as an educational researcher, lecturer, and assistant dean. The text is comprehensive, incorporating strategies to use with children and adolescents as they grow through the different stages of development. It offers guidance to parents and teachers on all the significant areas of religious education: Scripture, Sacraments, moral formation, doctrine, and prayer. Pedagogically, it provides valuable insights into both content and practice. Administrators will find particularly useful the summary of Catholic teaching from the relevant documents of the Church since the Second Vatican Council."

—KEVIN WATSON, Acting Dean of Education, Sydney, University of Notre Dame, Australia

"Gerard O'Shea's new book is an insightful and eminently useful guide for Catholic school teachers, catechists, and home-schooling parents. Drawing upon the pedagogy of Maria Montessori and Sofia Cavalletti, O'Shea provides not only insights into child development and its relationship to religious instruction, but offers practical, easy-to-follow lessons and applications for the teacher. It is a wonderful contribution to Catholic education."

—MICHAEL MARTIN, author of *The Incarnation of the Poetic Word*

"Gerard O'Shea has written an extraordinary book that will serve catechists well in these challenging times. In language both insightful and accessible, *Educating in Christ* engages the question of how today's religious education can lead people into communion with God. O'Shea answers by bringing the movement towards God in religious education into harmony with a reverence for the capacities and potentialities of those we teach. He shows how the content of religious education brings us to the Father, through Christ, in the Holy Spirit—but only when that content moves in the person from body to heart and finally to mind. Drawing on the best insights of educational thinkers from John Hattie to Maria Montessori, O'Shea presents a compelling and comprehensive vision for religious education that will immediately strengthen our formative initiatives. I am excited for my own students to read this outstanding book."

—JAMES PAULEY, Professor of Theology and Catechetics, Franciscan University of Steubenville

Educating in Christ

Educating in Christ

A PRACTICAL HANDBOOK
FOR DEVELOPING THE CATHOLIC FAITH
FROM CHILDHOOD TO ADOLESCENCE

For Parents, Teachers, Catechists
and School Administrators

BY GERARD O'SHEA

Angelico Press

Book and cover design
by Michael Schrauzer
Cover Image:
Stone relief by Kunibert Zinner,
at the elementary school
in Seitenstetten, Austria, 1951
Source: Wikimedia Commons

To my wife, Anne, whose lifelong support and encouragement have enabled me to achieve things I never could have done by myself

and to our children, grandchildren, and all the students I have worked with who have taught me the most that I know

Contents

Abbreviations

CCC *Catechism of the Catholic Church* (1993)
CL *Christi Fideles Laici* (1988)
CSD *Compendium of the Social Doctrine of the Church* (2004)
CRT *Address to Catholic Religion Teachers* (2009)
CSTM *The Catholic School on the Threshold of the Third Millennium* (1997)
CT *Catechesis Tradendae* (1978)
DCE *Deus Caritas Est* (2005)
DV *Dei Verbum* (1965)
EG *Evangelii Gaudium* (2013)
EN *Evangelii Nuntiandi* (1975)
EID *Educating for Intercultural Dialogue in Catholic Schools* (2013)
EO *Ecclesia in Oceania* (2001)
ETCS *Educating Together in Catholic Schools* (2007)
FC *Familiaris Consortio* (1981)
FD *Fides et Ratio* (1998)
GDC *General Directory for Catechesis* (1997)
GE *Gravissimum Educationis* (1965)
GS *Gaudium et Spes* (1965)
LF *Lumen Fidei* (2013)
LS *Laudate Si* (2015)
RDEC *Religious Dimension of Education in a Catholic School* (1988)
RES *Circular Letter on Religious Education in Schools* (2009)
SC *Sacramentum Caritatis* (2007)
ST *Summa Theologica, St Thomas Aquinas*
TCS *The Catholic School* (1977)
VBD *Verbum Domini* (2010)

Introduction

The Great Commission

In dramatic fashion on the Mount of Olives, just before he ascended into heaven, Jesus issued the great commission to his disciples:

> *All authority in heaven and on earth has been given to me. Go therefore and make disciples of all nations, baptize them in the name of the Father and of the Holy Spirit, and teach them to observe all the commandments I gave you. And know that I am with you always; yes, to the end of time.* (Matthew 28:18–20)

Shortly afterwards, St. Paul was to express what would be involved in this with arresting beauty, linking the task directly with Jesus himself. The purpose of passing on the faith, he wrote, is:

> *that Christ may dwell in your hearts through faith; that you, being rooted and grounded in love, may have the power to comprehend with all the saints what is the breadth and length and height and depth and to know the love of Christ which surpasses knowledge, that you may be filled with the fullness of God.* (Ephesians 3:17–19)

Writing nearly two thousand years later, St. John Paul II would recall these words and add his own voice to exhort everyone involved in catechesis to make Christ known and loved:

> *Accordingly, the definitive aim of catechesis is to put people not only in touch but in communion, in intimacy, with Jesus Christ: only*

1

He can lead us to the love of the Father in the Spirit and make us
share in the life of the Holy Trinity.[1]

More recently, Pope Francis insisted that in catechesis we must rediscover
the central role of the *Kerygma:* "Jesus Christ loves you; he gave his life
to save you; and now he is living at your side every day to enlighten,
strengthen and free you."[2]

These quotations can be multiplied until they fill page after page, but
without adding much more to the essential message. In the current climate,
the role of the parent, the teacher, and the catechist is the same as it has
always been — to help those in our care to know and love Jesus Christ.

This challenge was first issued to the apostles on the Mount of Olives
as they witnessed the Ascension of the Lord into heaven. We now refer
to it as the *Great Commission.* The task that faced the apostles can seem
a little remote and even romantic as we look back on what they achieved.
Can we do the same today in the circumstances we face? We know that
it will not be easy. Consider these challenges: a society where relative
peace and prosperity has caused many people to reject religious practices
as a quaint cultural survival; a collapse of respect for the institution of
marriage; a devaluing of life itself both at its beginning and at its end;
sexual license so widespread that the true meaning and value of sexuality seem trivialized and almost inaccessible to most people; a society in
which the wealthy live in extraordinary comfort and the poor are forced
to endure conditions that could be described as slavery; a glorification of
celebrities and a focus on entertainment which distracts from the realities
of life; a fascination for "new age" philosophies to provide answers to
the meaning of life. It may seem that I am painting a gloomy picture of
our society today — but this is not so. I have actually been describing the
Roman Empire at the time of the Apostles. Students of Church history
will be aware that preaching Christ has always been difficult. Moreover,
what makes it possible is the fire of love that we have for Christ; a fire
of the Spirit which drives us to make great sacrifices and to dare great
things for the Kingdom of God. To date, this has always been sufficient
to change the world.

---

1 Pope John Paul II, *Catechesi Tradendae* (Vatican City: Libreria Vatican Editrice, 2013), §5.
[Afterwards CT]
2 Pope Francis, *Evangelii Gaudium* (Vatican City: Libreria Vatican Editrice, 2013), §164.
[Afterwards EG]

This book has been prepared to assist those who have known the love of Christ themselves to pass it on to others. It should not be seen as a set of techniques that will work independently of the person using them. The role of the educator — parent, teacher, or catechist — is to cooperate with Christ and to work in the name of the Church. This must always flow out of their own relationship with Christ, continually renewed through participation in the sacraments, nourished by the Scriptures, attentive to Catholic doctrinal and moral teaching, and made personal through an ongoing dialogue of prayer. The ultimate destiny is communion with the Blessed Trinity, through Christ. To put this in theological terms, the whole process of catechesis must be Trinitarian and Christocentric. This is the greatest cause ever known to this or any other age, and it has the potential to "fire up" our lives with a holy idealism that can make us and others into the saints that the Church now so desperately needs.

Part I
Religious Education for the Human Person

1
Union with God — Our Ultimate Goal

Through Christ, in the Communion of the Holy Spirit, to the Father: Christ and the Trinity

It is a foundational truth that Christian formation works on a human person, a person who is constituted as an image of the Trinity. We can see a number of different ways in which this three-fold mark of the Trinity is manifested. For example, we could look at the organization of the human person as body, heart and mind; or perhaps we could tease out the implications of the desire shared by us all for the true, the beautiful and the good. None of these listings exhausts the meaning of the image of the Trinity in the human person, but all of them contribute analogically to our understanding of who we are. This leads us to one of the most significant issues of genuine religious education — how do we find out who we are? The answer was given eloquently by the Second Vatican Council's document on the *Church in the Modern World*: "Christ reveals man to himself."[1] All contemporary documents of the Church refer to these complementary ways of entering into this great mystery: it must at the same time be Trinitarian and Christ-centered (Trinitarian Christocentricity).

In recent years, I have often found myself in rural communities speaking about strategies for meeting the contemporary challenges of religious education. This has given me the chance to meet many people who have, in their own way, given heroic witness to their faith. During one of these talks, an elderly lady, long retired from her position as a highly respected Catholic school teacher, told me of a struggle she had faced for the whole of her life. "I was always made to feel," she said, "as if all that mattered was

---

1 *Gaudium et Spes* (Vatican City: Libreria Vaticana Editrice, 1965), § 22. [Afterwards GS]

my soul, and that my body was little more than some kind of prison that I had to punish and subdue so that I could leave it behind and become something like an angel. It never really made sense to me. Why did God make us this way if what he really wanted was angels?" She articulated the problem very well. This was certainly the kind of training that many Catholics of her generation had received. It was as if God had made some kind of mistake in putting human beings together with both material and spiritual components, and we would all be better off if we rejected our physical dimension altogether. This approach certainly placed a high value on our spiritual nature — but, in the end, it actually made the doctrine of the resurrection of the body almost incomprehensible. Among many other reasons, it was to address this neglect of the physical dimension of human existence that Pope John Paul II set out to develop and explain a theology of the body — to try to lay to rest this Platonic denigration of the human body and to affirm the goodness of the material creation.

RELIGIOUS EDUCATION AND THE HUMAN PERSON

The General Directory of Catechesis, a 1997 document from the Congregation for the Clergy, makes a valiant effort to bring together in one place many of the insights from Pope John Paul II's massive corpus of authoritative teaching as it applies to education. One of the terms used in this text is "Trinitarian Christocentricity."[2] In fact, the magisterial documents, including the *General Directory for Catechesis* go so far as to say that "every mode of presentation must always be Christocentric-Trinitarian: Through Christ to the Father in the Holy Spirit. If catechesis lacks these three elements or neglects their close relationship, the Christian message can certainly lose its proper character."[3] This may be a complex theological concept, but it really does sum up something very important about how we need to pass on the faith. Namely, that Christian faith is primarily about bringing human beings into relationship with the Blessed Trinity, through Christ. This idea is perhaps more familiar in the Liturgy, where all prayers are addressed to the Father, through the Son in union with the Holy Spirit.

If we take time to examine this process, we will discover that it is an excellent summary of what happens when religious education is working effectively. Sofia Cavalletti, whose insights into catechesis are perhaps

---

2 *The General Directory for Catechesis* (Vatican City: Libreria Vaticana Editrice, 1997), § 99. [Afterwards GDC]

3 GDC, §100.

unmatched in recent history, made this simple comment when asked to sum up the process of bringing children to God: "Remember the order: first the body, then the heart, then the mind."[4] I will unpack this further in a later section of this chapter, but, in a nutshell, it means this: if you want children to learn anything new, the best starting point is to present a concrete object — something that stimulates the senses to "wonder." This wonder sets up a desire to explore further because they have "delighted" in what has been sensed — in this way, the senses give access to the heart. Finally, when the needs of the body and the heart have been met, the experience is encoded into its most abstract form: intellectually in the mind. I speak here of the child, but long experience has revealed something else. It is not just children who work this way — adults do this, too. It seems that all human beings when left free to follow their inclinations prefer to begin with what is most concrete, then move on to delighting in — loving — what they have found and then put it into intellectual form.

Note the simple Trinitarian structure! We can perhaps look at it differently — we are first attracted by beauty, then drawn into goodness, and finally to truth. These classic transcendental properties of being (truth, beauty and goodness) have long been associated with persons of the Trinity…so to put it in yet another way, Christ — the most concrete of the persons of the Trinity — is associated with the attractive power of beauty. By means of the Holy Spirit (Goodness) he leads us to the Father (Truth). It would seem that for human persons, the *abstract* and *spiritual* are accessed by what is concrete and material. The body has an essential role to play in coming to know God — a role that cannot be dispensed with; a role taken on in the Incarnation by the Son of God Himself. We might say, educationally, that this is the key insight of the Theology of the Body, the beauty of the concrete reality evokes "eros" — the desire which draws us into a search for what lies beyond in two further stages before we arrive at the goal.

RELIGIOUS EDUCATION FOR THE BODY

If we accept the view that human development has a Trinitarian structure which gives a place to the body, heart, and mind, then this must have its implication for catechesis. Those who understand human development are in no doubt that the youngest children always begin the process of constructing their own understanding of the world through the senses.

---

4 This comment was made to me during a personal conversation I had with Cavalletti in 2008.

One has only to follow a toddler around to notice what is going on. These children are fascinated by the real objects in their environment—they want to touch, to smell, to hear, to see and (often to the horror of their mothers) *taste* whatever they encounter. It is also obvious that they are gripped with wonder in the presence of every new reality they encounter. This fascination with the concrete, even in the youngest children, begins to take us out of ourselves through the vehicle of wonder, which is evoked by "an attentive gaze at reality."[5] Few would dispute that this is the way young children operate—but we can often forget that older children and even adults never really lose this capacity to be "awed" in the presence of beauty and drawn into a transcendent reality. For human beings, the careful contemplation of concrete objects appears to have a capacity to direct us to a spiritual reality beyond ourselves.

This characteristic indicates the genuinely human starting point for catechesis—attending to the needs of the body through the senses. If we circumvent this step, we are simply not attending to human nature as it is constituted. There is a well-known axiom of good teaching practice, expressed simply as "concrete to abstract." This has also been the understanding of the Church in relation to the sacramental system. In every sacrament, by means of the senses, the human person is drawn into a spiritual reality that is signified by the material element. If religious education is to be successful, it cannot neglect or omit this essential starting point at any stage of development. The senses of the body have a crucial role to play. For example, in presenting the sacraments, it is usually best to begin with a careful, tactile study of the material elements found in the sacramental rites. Each of these, in its own way, draws the participant into a particular reality made present in the sacrament.[6] Any number of instances can be cited in support of this process as the starting point, but there is a particularly poignant story told in *The Religious Potential of the Child* concerning the use of a simple set of materials—cruets for pouring water and wine into a chalice:

> We will never forget seven-year-old Massimo, who continued to
> repeat this exercise for so long a period of time. The catechist,

5 Sofia Cavalletti, *The Religious Potential of the Child* (Chicago: Liturgy Training Publications, 1992), 139.
6 *The Catechism of the Catholic Church* gives quite explicit descriptions of the particular realities that the elements of the sacramental rite stand for in the case of the sacrament of Baptism.

thinking that he was doing it out of laziness, came up to him several times to introduce him to some other work; but Massimo's facial expression was intent and rapt and he was trying to explain the meaning of what he was doing as he repeated the various actions.... Finally—it was almost at the end of the year—he managed to say: "A few drops of water and a lot of wine, because we must lose ourselves in Jesus".... In the end Massimo had known how to express it with words worthy of a mystic.[7]

RELIGIOUS EDUCATION FOR THE HEART: THE ATTRACTION OF THE SCRIPTURES

It is almost a truism in our catechetical practice to observe that the whole project will be futile if we fail to reach the heart—but how? Experienced catechists are well aware that it is impossible to force anyone to make a "heart response"—this is an intensely personal decision. Some may try, using coercive, manipulative techniques to get an *apparent* response, but this will ultimately fail if it is not genuinely personal. In any case, it betrays a lack of respect for the genuine freedom that must lie at the heart of human existence. It is also true in the deepest sense that a human being must have a personal experience of love before becoming capable of entering into a relationship of love with Christ.

The difficulty we may experience in drawing out a "heart response" does not excuse us from making intelligent efforts to facilitate this response. We must be aware that we are leading the child to a place where Christ can be encountered rather than a predetermined educational outcome. Sofia Cavalletti has some extraordinary insights here. She was herself a professional Scripture scholar at La Sapienza University in Rome. When asked to prepare a child for First Communion (she had hitherto no experience with children) she did the only thing she knew—she began to share the scriptures with him. The reaction of the child was something she was not prepared for. Even after two hours, the child was deeply moved and wanting to go deeper. Cavalletti had uncovered one of the key ways in which the heart is won over to God—the scriptures themselves.

A caution must be issued here. This cannot be used as some kind of technique—Cavalletti is not suggesting that if the children are forced to listen to the Bible their hearts will be won over. Quite the contrary: any

---

7 Sofia Cavalletti, *The Religious Potential of the Child*, 92.

force of this kind is more likely to turn the child in the opposite direction. Nevertheless, if the scriptures are offered as the place to go in order to build on and explain the experiences of wonder that have been brought about through the senses, they are invested with an attractive power. The child encounters there a *person* rather than a sequence of words. The Holy Spirit is enabled to complete the task of revealing Jesus. Time and again, this approach has shown its worth. Cavalletti and her collaborators have already spent more than sixty years determining exactly which scriptural passages seem to touch the hearts of children — and, indeed, adults. In order to enhance the natural processes, the initial presentations can be given using wooden models set within simple dioramas to engage the senses and create the scene.

Ultimately, however, it is the actual words of the scriptures themselves that seem to have the effect on their hearts. Like most well-meaning adults, Cavalletti began telling Biblical stories using her own words or those in a children's Bible in order to simplify the message and "get it across." She quickly discovered that this approach did not seem to have the same effect. Eventually, she decided that it was not up to her to simplify the scriptures to instruct their minds — something (or in her words, *someone*) else was at work here. Just as the children had been enchanted by their contemplation of real objects, so too were they enchanted by the "real" words. It was after these experiences Cavalletti articulated the principle of how the scriptures must be presented to those lacking in experience — "rich food, but not too much of it!" Children were to be allowed to read the scriptures for themselves, but given the time to slowly reflect on passages that captured their imaginations.

The use of the scriptures at this level does not usually involve complex intellectual study of the Bible and its principles of interpretation. At this point, we are not trying to create scholars — this is a task for a more advanced stage of development, and too great an emphasis on this intellectual task can actually get in the way of the encounter of the heart. It is a relatively easy matter to correct false impressions that may be picked up when reading and only minimal guidance is necessary at this point. My own teaching of children has verified this approach. When children are allowed to follow the natural processes of human development — starting with the senses — and are then offered the scriptures, they usually seize the opportunity to move in freedom to a deeper relationship with God. The bibles are among the most popular items found among our catechetical tools. Given the freedom to choose, children go to them again and again and spend more and more time reading passages that interest them. They use the scriptures for their intended purpose: to know and love Christ. Indeed, to echo the words of St. Jerome: "Ignorance of scripture is ignorance of Christ."

Some may be concerned that this approach may cause children to misinterpret the scriptures if they read them without proper guidance. Long experience has demonstrated that the opposite is true. Children who begin reading the scriptures in this way — so that they love what they find there — quickly become aware that they are working with a mysterious document and are well prepared to ask questions and seek clarification. In other words, their sense of wonder and mystery about the scriptures has already been stimulated so that they are receptive to further instruction. This has certainly been my experience. It is more likely that if such children are presented with "answers" before they ask questions about the Bible, they will simply not want to read it. An approach which starts with the intellectual understanding first makes them feel incompetent before they have had a chance for themselves to discover the mysterious presence of Christ. Perhaps the best answer to such a challenge is quite simply to try out what happens if the children are given the opportunity to read the scriptures for themselves — then sit back and wait for the myriad of questions that will arise!

RELIGIOUS EDUCATION FOR THE MIND

The current consensus of educational theory shares significant insights with the views of St. Thomas Aquinas, namely, that human beings construct their understanding by moving from concrete realities to abstract concepts, words and propositions. St Thomas, of course, goes further. In his view, the whole material universe has a purpose — to reflect some vestige of its creator. By engaging with it, we are able to build up a basic picture of who God is. Once we have engaged with reality, we form words and propositions that describe the experience. This indicates the proper place for the mind in catechesis — as the synthesis point for describing what the senses and the heart have already discovered. The words then lead us back to the original encounter and to any subsequent reflections we have had about it. The words used to describe objects, events, and reflections are a means of allowing us to participate mentally in those things; they connect us with our own memories and with a cultural tradition that we may not have personally experienced.

Perhaps a common example will illustrate this best. Consider the initial teaching of reading in one of our first grade classrooms. Children arrive at school with a wealth of existing experience in their oral language — drawn from the data of their senses and from things that they have already loved. *Playground*, for example, is a word that is likely to conjure up for them a whole world of happy associations and experiences. *Mum* is much more than a word of three letters! So, even at the age of five, all three components of human learning have begun to operate effectively and are bringing about an integration of body, heart, and mind. Yet, it must be clear that there is also a normal sequence that brings this about — the body-heart-mind sequence.

Often in religious education in the past, we have made the mistake of confusing the final stage (clarifying mental propositions) as the principal task, or even as the necessary starting point, rather than seeing how it should take its proper place into the overall scheme of things. At other times, we have reacted against the sterility of an overly intellectual approach by rejecting it altogether — an outcome that can actually prevent participants from having a proper human mental access to the truth. Undoubtedly, it is essential to connect children with the authentic tradition of their Church and to provide them with clear teaching regarding what the Church holds to be true. But the reality of God is far greater than the propositions written about Him — even though these be true and necessary for us to know. A comment from Pope Benedict XVI (writing as Cardinal Ratzinger) endorses this view:

> Human words, at any rate, the great fundamental words, always carry within them a whole history of human experiences, of human questioning, understanding and suffering of reality. The great theme words of the Bible bring with them into the process of revelation also, in acceptance and contradiction, the fundamental experiences of mankind. So in order to understand the Bible aright, one must always also turn to question the history preserved in its words.[8]

By the same token, it is beyond dispute that appropriate texts must eventually be committed to memory, as noted so forcefully by St John Paul II in *Catechesis Tradendae*:

---

8 Joseph Ratzinger, *Pilgrim Fellowship of Faith* (San Francisco: Ignatius, 2005), 71.

> We must be realists. The blossoms, if we may call them that, of
> faith and piety do not grow in the desert places of a memory-less
> catechesis. What is essential is that the texts that are memorized
> must at the same time be taken in and gradually understood in
> depth, in order to become a source of Christian life on the personal
> level and the community level.[9]

What must be kept always in view, however, is the fact that these texts
cannot stand in isolation from the body or the heart of those they are
meant to serve. Religious education for the mind will always work better
if it is preceded first by suitable sensate experience and then a reflective
engagement of the heart.

THE NATURE OF FAITH: SUPERNATURAL GIFT AND FREE ASSENT

Before leaving this chapter on the fundamental principles of the Trinitarian and Christocentric nature of catechesis, it will be useful to address
the question of how human beings come to faith. This is one of the greatest
challenges currently facing catechesis because of the widespread failure
of many—even many catechists—to recognize the double dimension
of faith itself. G.K. Chesterton has insightfully described a key paradox
in Christian thought and practice: "Paganism declared that virtue was
in a balance; Christianity declared it was in a conflict: the collision of
two passions apparently opposite. Of course they were not really inconsistent; but they were such that it was hard to hold simultaneously."[10]
One manifestation of this conflict is the way in which faith must be held,
since it necessarily involves two apparently contradictory dimensions in
dynamic tension. On the one hand, faith is an undeserved gift of God—a
theological virtue conferred in the Sacrament of Baptism. On the other
hand, it is also involves a genuine human assent, freely given. The insights
of Benedict XVI shed some light on this for us. Pope Benedict points
out that the act of faith comes about in a different way from the act of
knowing: "not through the degree of evidence bringing the process of
thought to its conclusion, but by an act of will, in connection with which
the thought process remains open and still under way. Here, the degree of
evidence does not turn the thought into assent; rather the will commands

---

9 CT, § 55.
10 G.K. Chesterton, *Orthodoxy* (London: Bodley Head, 1909), 99.

assent, even though the thought process is still under way."[11]

Benedict recognizes the difficulties in this approach, and acknowledges the accusations of philosophers such as Karl Jaspers and Martin Heidegger that faith, by pre-supposing the answers, leaves no room for questions.[12] In answer, Benedict cites Pascal's observation: "The heart has its reasons that reason does not know." He notes that we are able to give the assent of faith not because of the depth of our own inquiries or the quality of our evidence, but "because the will—the heart—has been touched by God, affected by him. Through being touched in this way, the will knows that even what is not clear to the reason is true. Assent is produced by the will, not by the understanding's own direct insight: the particular kind of freedom of choice involved in the decision of faith rests on this.... The will (the heart), therefore, lights the way for the understanding and draws it with it into assent."[13]

In other words, a catechetical group must deal with a very different intellectual process than the one used in a science class. In his classic work, *An Essay in Aid of a Grammar of Assent*, Blessed John Henry Newman brought a great deal of clarity to the interface between *faith as a gift* and *faith as an intellectual process of assent* to mysteries beyond human understanding. Newman described three mental acts associated with the holding of propositions of any kind—doubt, inference, and assent. All three, he insisted, were appropriate human behaviors. "We do but fulfil our nature in doubting, inferring and assenting; and our duty is not to abstain from the exercise of any function of our nature, but to do what is in itself right rightly."[14]

Newman draws attention to the fact that, in the case of revealed religion, the holding of certain doctrinal propositions indicates the presence or absence of faith itself. To take up a position of doubt in relation to settled doctrine makes one a sceptic. To give such doctrines a merely conditional acceptance (inference) indicates the position of the philosopher. To offer assent (whether or not one understands it fully, as yet) is to be a believer. Baptized Catholics are believers, having received the gift of faith. To position them in such a way that they are encouraged

---

11   Joseph Ratzinger, *Pilgrim Fellowship of Faith*, 23.

12   Ibid., 20.

13   Ibid.

14   John Henry Newman, *An Essay in Aid of a Grammar of Assent* (London: Longmans, 1889), 7.

to take some other stance (either doubt or inference) is to deliberately undermine their status.

Newman makes a further distinction between "inquiry" and "investigation." He insists that *inquiry* is inconsistent with *assent*, since one who inquires is in doubt about where the truth lies. Hence, a believer cannot at the same time be an inquirer:

> Thus it is sometimes spoken of as a hardship that a Catholic is not allowed to inquire into the truth of his creed;— of course he cannot, if he would retain the name of believer. He cannot be both inside and outside of the Church at once. It is merely common sense to tell him that, if he is seeking, he has not found. If seeking includes doubting, and doubting excludes believing, then the Catholic who sets about inquiring thereby declares that he is not a Catholic. He has already lost faith.[15]

In closing the door to *inquiry* in matters of religious faith, Newman was certainly not advocating *Fideism* or anti-intellectualism of any kind. He simply made the necessary distinction between the way in which believers and non-believers need to engage with the data of revelation and faith. He believed that educated Catholics have an obligation to try to understand what they believe and discern the reasons underpinning this belief. To use Newman's own words:

> inquiry implies doubt and investigation does not imply it; and that those who assent to a doctrine or fact may without inconsistency investigate its credibility, though they cannot literally inquire about its truth...in the case of educated minds, investigations into the argumentative proof of the things to which they have given their assent is an obligation or rather a necessity.[16]

On the other hand, Newman saw the dangers involved in encouraging those who had been poorly instructed or ill-equipped to assess subtle arguments to place themselves in danger through deliberate exposure to such approaches without proper preparation. Perhaps we could include

15 Ibid., 191.
16 Ibid., 192.

in this group those who have not been properly prepared in the body (through the senses) or the heart (by means of a personal relationship with Christ founded in the scriptures and the life of prayer):

> [Some] who, though they be weak in faith...put themselves in the way of losing it by unnecessarily listening to objections. Moreover, there are minds, undoubtedly, with whom at all times to question a truth is to make it questionable, and to investigate is equivalent to inquiring; and again, there may be beliefs so sacred or so delicate that, if I may use the metaphor, they will not wash without shrinking and losing color.[17]

In the current circumstances pertaining in religious education classrooms — particularly in secondary schools — these truths constitute a challenge. Much of the school system encourages a method of inquiry that can best be described as systematic skepticism. If such an approach finds its way into a religious education class, it will effectively undermine and denigrate the dimension of faith as a gift and attempt to evaluate it using inappropriate criteria. Perhaps it is time to subject this kind of critical thinking to a process of critical evaluation to determine whether it is effectively performing a useful role in religious education.

17 Ibid.

2

Catechesis According to Age and Stages of Development

In understanding some of the most elementary truths about catechesis according to stages of development, we owe a great debt to the great Italian educator, Maria Montessori, and those who built upon her legacy in the field of religious education, particularly Sofia Cavalletti and Gianna Gobbi. It was those working with the ideas of Montessori who have provided us with a comprehensive understanding of the typical stages of development from early childhood to adolescence and offered excellent suggestions for the typical kinds of experiences and educational materials that might be offered to children and young people in a way that addresses their needs. The *General Directory for Catechesis* insists that catechesis must be "given by right on the basis of diverse and complementary age groups, on account of the needs and capacity of its recipients...including also up to date scientific data and pedagogical methods prepared for different age groups."[1] Clearly, the presentation offered to a three-year-old must be very different from that offered to an adolescent. There are many psychologists who offer theoretical and scientific perspectives on what they refer to as the "stages of faith," but these, too, must be evaluated in terms of their suitability for expressing a Christian view of the human person. There is a vast body of literature addressing this field, and there are some quite helpful insights to be found among them. Even so, it is only the work of Maria Montessori which has received the explicit endorsement of the popes from Benedict XV to St. John Paul II.

INTRODUCTION: THE PRELIMINARY WORK OF MARIA MONTESSORI

It is now more than a century since the "Montessori Miracle" was first reported from the slums of the San Lorenzo quarter in Rome in 1907. "Here flourished unchecked all the evils of subletting, overcrowding,

---

1   GDC, §171.

promiscuous immorality and other crimes."[2] Working with a group of
children who were considered beyond help by educational authorities of the
time, a young female medical doctor had achieved results that astounded
the world. The application of Montessori's principles had immediate and
dramatic effects, which she described this way:

> I set to work…like a peasant woman who, having set aside a good
> store of seed corn, has found a fertile field in which she may freely
> sow it. But I was wrong. I had hardly turned over the clods of my
> field, when I found gold instead of wheat: the clods concealed
> a precious treasure. I was not the peasant I had thought myself.
> Rather, I was like foolish Aladdin, who, without knowing it, had
> in his hand a key that would open hidden treasures.[3]

In his biography of Montessori, E.M. Standing cites a variety of contemporary sources expressing amazement at the results she achieved. Typical of
these was one provided by a delegate sent to investigate the phenomenon
from the London County Council, Mrs. Hutchison. She returned to report
so enthusiastically that one of the Council, Sir Edward Garnett, remarked:
"Gentlemen, this is not a report, it is a rhapsody!"[4]

SENSITIVE PERIODS

Essentially, Montessori's discovery was based on a careful observation of human development and a serious attempt to match the needs
of children with their particular developmental stages. She describes
these stages as "sensitive periods." Montessori explains this term with
reference to the *prothesia* butterfly, whose egg is laid on the bark where
the branch joins the trunk of a tree. The caterpillar, immediately after it
hatches, is "light sensitive" and this characteristic drives it towards the
soft shoots at the end of the branch; these leaves are the only ones that it
is strong enough to eat at this stage of development. As it grows, the light
sensitivity fades and at the same time, the caterpillar becomes capable
of eating the tougher leaves found anywhere on the tree. Montessori's
observations led her to believe that human development has similar
characteristics. She claimed that there are particular moments in which

---

2 E.M. Standing, *Maria Montessori: Her Life and Work* (New York: Plume Books, 1998), 36.
3 Ibid., 35–53.
4 Quoted in ibid., 54.

some developmental tasks can be undertaken with minimal effort and connect with an underlying drive — *exigencies*. Based on this insight, through long and careful observation, Montessori attempted to identify the sensitive periods for various necessary stages of learning. Once she had arrived at these broadly consistent constructs, her educational method was relatively simple: identify the child's current need and the sensitive period in which they found themselves, and attempt to harness this in the education process. Whatever the child currently needs should be met with suitable materials and practices to enhance their learning. In Montessori's view, once a sensitive period had passed, it would never return and the chance to learn something with ease was gone for good. For example, the sensitive period for the acquisition of languages was said to occur before the age of six. This did not mean that languages could not be learned after this time, but that the task would be difficult and laborious by comparison.

Montessori's views have been largely vindicated by modern scholarship on a number of levels. There would be few neuroscientists today who would dispute Montessori's understanding of *sensitive periods*. The 1999 *Early Years Report* produced by the Canadian province of Ontario brought together all of the known research on early human development, indicating that most of the physical developments in early childhood take place during predictable "windows" after which the moment for "brain wiring" passes. It focused on six key findings from research available from the best of contemporary neuroscience:

1. Early brain development is interactive, rapid and dramatic.
2. During critical periods, particular parts of the brain need positive stimulation to develop properly.
3. The quality of early sensory stimulation influences the brain's ability to think and regulate bodily functions.
4. Negative experiences in the early years have long-lasting effects that can be difficult to overcome later.
5. Good nutrition and nurturing support optimal early brain and physical development and later learning and behavior.
6. There are initiatives that can improve early child development.[5]

---

5 Margaret McCain and Fraser Mustard, *Reversing the Real Brain Drain: The Early Years Study: Final Report* (Toronto: Ontario Children's Secretariat, 1999), 5.

The report uses the words "critical period" interchangeably with "sensitive period." Although not explicitly acknowledged, at every point, Montessori's findings have been vindicated by this carefully documented scientific report. Further collaboration is available from another source as well. In her book *Montessori: The Science behind the Genius*, Stanford University professor of psychology Angeline Lillard conducted an investigation into the key Montessori principles. Lillard found that the key findings had not only stood the test of time, but are now supported by an impressive array of scientific evidence indicating their effectiveness:

> The delegates at Oxford University Press asked that I write a balanced assessment of Montessori, pointing out where the evidence is not supportive as well as where it was. I have done my best to do this, but there is a real problem. Their assumption, like my original one, was that Montessori must have aspects that are supported by research and aspects that are not. Yet her major ideas…are supported by a strong body of evidence in developmental psychology. Some of her main developmental ideas that did not take hold until later and are rarely attributed to her are now mainstream. None of Montessori's ideas that I would consider central have been disproven. Others are not researched.[6]

DEVELOPMENTAL STAGES IN RELIGIOUS EDUCATION

It was Maria Montessori herself who began drawing out the implications of her method for the field of Religious Education, outlined in her 1930 classic text, *The Child in the Church*. At the highest levels, Church authorities have endorsed the soundness of her educational approach; during her lifetime Montessori's work was encouraged by three Popes — Pius X, Benedict XV, and Pius XII — together with the Patriarch of Venice, Angelo Roncalli, who was later to become Pope John XXIII. Pope Paul VI was the first to place this recognition into an official statement in 1970:

> She [Maria Montessori] was convinced that the pedagogy inherent in the liturgy contained the same principles as her own theory of secular education, and she resolutely took the ways towards

---

6 Angeline Lillard, *Montessori: The Science Behind the Genius* (New York: Oxford University Press, 2005), ix–x.

liturgical renewal which were opened by Saint Pius X. Just as the school had to be the children's home, so the church had to be the home of God's children. Maria Montessori's method of religious pedagogy is an extension of her secular pedagogy; it is naturally founded on the latter and forms its crown, by enabling the child to develop its highest potentialities to the full and to bring its whole development to fulfilment in a harmonious way.[7]

In 1995, Pope John Paul II drew attention to the uniquely feminine insights that allowed Montessori to perceive a reality about human nature and human learning that had escaped others. He regretted the fact that many of her insights may have been rejected on this basis: "Unfortunately, looking at the historical reality objectively, it must be noted with regret that, also on this level, women have suffered constant marginalization."[8] The full flowering of Montessori's ideas for religious education, however, has largely been the work of two of her subsequent collaborators, Sofia Cavalletti and Gianna Gobbi. To use Gobbi's words: "The content of the Christian message needs to vary according to the developmental stage of the child…the changing deep needs of the respective developmental period call for a different 'face of God' to be presented."[9]

DEVELOPMENTAL STAGES

Montessori identified four planes of development, each focusing on a different aspect of human learning. Much of her work was delivered in lectures, and it was left to commentators to put this into more systematic form. Perhaps the best of these efforts was by Camillo Grazzini in "The Four Planes of Development."[10] The diagram below very briefly summarizes her views.

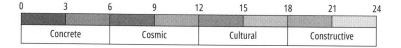

7 Paul VI, "Address to the International Congress of Montessori Educators on the Centenary of the Birth of Maria Montessori" (Vatican City: Libreria Editrice Vaticana, 1970).

8 John Paul II *Angelus Address*: Sunday 6th August, 1995, 1.

9 Gianna Gobbi, *Listening to God with Children* (Loveland, OH: Treehaus Communications, 1998), 89.

10 Camillo Grazzini, "The four planes of development." *The NAMTA Journal* 21, no. 2 (1996): 208–41.

For each of the four planes of development, there are two "sub-planes" of roughly three years each. In the first three-year sub-plane, there is a new intensity, with the person deeply engaged in acquiring new aspects characteristic of the stage. In the second of the three-year sub-planes, the emphasis is more on refining and integrating the data that has been acquired. It is also a time where some awareness of the characteristics of the next plane of development begin to dawn. It is noteworthy that Montessori insisted that the basic educational process is not achieved until about the age of twenty-four years.

Those who have been involved in education will find themselves in ready agreement with Montessori's observations about the dramatic changes that seem to accompany the movement to a new sub-plane of development every three years or so. Obviously, there is no "set date" on which these changes occur; they are gradual, but there is a predictable sequence. Each new stage is characterized by a growing independence and typical set of interests. A quick survey of these "switch-points" will illustrate this. Human beings become more "difficult" to deal with at these ages: two–three years of age; six years; nine years; twelve years; fourteen–fifteen years; eighteen years; twenty-one years; twenty-four years. At these ages, they become less predictable as they move to a new stage of development and those dealing with them have to work out different ways of approaching them.

For those who are used to seeing these changes, it does not come as a surprise; teachers working at a particular level for an extended period or parents who have dealt with a number of children come to see them as a normal part of human development. It is clearly more difficult for parents, however, since they are generally very emotionally invested in their own children and can often be too close to a situation to look at it objectively. It can be perplexing and challenging because they are called on to have to change their way of relating to a child who has suddenly become unresponsive in terms of strategies that worked with them before. In some ways, parents almost need to go through a process whereby they grieve the loss of the person their child used to be and come to terms with a new one. If parents do not accept these natural developments, they can set up conflicts with the child in order to preserve the status quo. There are two possible outcomes to this. In the first case, the parent may succeed in frightening the child back into former patterns of "acceptable" but childish behavior and in this way damage the child by causing developmental delay. Alternatively, the unbending parent can provoke such a strong reaction that the only way for the child to grow is to defy and confront the parents in an exaggerated and unhealthy way simply in order to attain the normal developmental level. It is therefore essential for those who want to encourage the healthy development of children (both parents and teachers) to recognize what is likely to be happening at each stage of development and adjust their approach accordingly.

3
The Data Gatherer

*Developmental and Religious Characteristics
of the Three-to-Six-Year-Old Child*

THE ABSORBENT MIND

Montessori used the term *absorbent mind* to describe the first plane of development from birth to six years of age. In keeping with her general theory, children working on this plane go through two sub-planes. The first one, ending at about the age of three years, is simply based on experiencing physical reality and classifying these experiences with basic labels. Anyone who has paid attention to a very young child will be aware of this — what they most want to do is to explore their immediate environment. This involves using their all of their senses, but particularly touch. Objects which can be held are of particular interest to the youngest children. They will also try to taste most things as well, including flowers and beetles from the garden and dirt from the sandpit — or anything else that those responsible for looking after them are not attentive enough to notice before the deed is done. These grosser manifestations of the absorbent mind are usually over by the age of three years. What they do indicate, however, is that in this very early stage, the human brain seems to be naturally disposed to gather a great deal of information without wasting time trying to relate the components to each other or to seek out complex meaning. It can best be described as a *data gathering* stage. The richer these experiences are at this point, the more material will be available for making "big picture" links later on. It can be amusing to watch inexperienced parents trying to give explanations to their two-year-old children: it may be a valuable experience of relating to one another, but it is doubtful whether the toddler is actually learning any enduring principles for action from the experience.

The next sub-plane, roughly three to six years of age, is the period during which most children enter the formal education system, and the point at which explicit religious education begins. These children are still in a

27

stage where the absorbent mind is operating, but they have passed onto a more refined capacity for complex labelling of objects and experience. Some elements of the next plane are also becoming evident. In terms of the way in which the absorbent mind operates at this level, it is still the case that they will learn best by encountering specific objects which allow them to be absorbed in what is real. This goes hand in hand with another characteristic of this age: a sense of wonder. Cavalletti noted that wonder is actually brought about by "an attentive gaze at reality."[1] Even at this age, children remain fascinated with every new reality they encounter and are drawn into it. This is a profoundly human quality which affects us to some degree for the whole of our lives. Older children and even adults never really lose this capacity to be "awed" in the presence of beauty of any kind and drawn into a transcendent reality. We experience this as a simple and inexplicable sense of joy — not for any reason, just "because." For human beings, the careful contemplation of concrete objects appears to direct us to a spiritual reality beyond ourselves. This characteristic surely points us to the genuinely human starting point of religious education: attending to the needs of the body through the senses. If we circumvent this step, we are simply not attending to human nature as it is constituted. There is a well-known axiom of good teaching practice, expressed simply as "concrete to abstract."

This is an age where the child's focus is on "what" something is called. Children at this level are not yet interested in "why" things are the way they are, although some more advanced children show signs of this interest later in the sub-plane. I have often invited parents of children at this age to let me know whether this reflects their experience and I am usually overwhelmed with multiple instances. Children will be captivated with simple but real things, especially in the natural world. They will stop and stare for a long time at a spider spinning its web, a snail leaving a trail on a path, or a bird feeding its young in the nest. One family told me a story of a very special trip they had made to Disneyland, to the delight of their older children. The youngest child — three years old — also had a wonderful time, but not for the usual reason. While inside, she noticed a mother duck with newly hatched ducklings swimming and moving about. This was her highlight of the trip — and completely understandable for a child of this age.

---

1   Sofia Cavalletti, *The Religious Potential of the Child*, 192.

This is entirely in keeping with the Church's understanding of human nature: we are composite beings who have both bodily and spiritual abilities that are thoroughly integrated. Indeed this is the basis of the whole sacramental system: through what we can see, hear, touch, smell, and even taste, we are drawn into a spiritual reality beyond ourselves. If religious education is to be successful at any level, but particularly in the ages of three to six years, it cannot neglect or omit this essential concrete starting point. The bodily senses have a crucial role to play.

Religious Education Activities for the Absorbent Mind. In offering religious education for the youngest children, certain key points must be kept in mind. Education must focus on what is real, and children should be encouraged to experience these realities without the teacher attempting to explain how they fit into an overall picture. Children at this age will often ask the question "why." Don't be misled: they are not asking for an explanation; they just want the conversation with you to continue. Despite your best efforts, they are not likely to remember what you told them the next day. This is a time when children have an enormous capacity to absorb data: they are interested in having many names and images of important religious realities in their head without having any need to know how they fit together. This is the task of the next stage of development. If they are pushed too soon to begin this "linking together" phase, the breadth and depth of their images will not be as rich as it might have been. They will learn best if they are allowed to be children and follow what their sensitive period naturally disposes them towards.

Practical Life Activities. Montessori and her later collaborators in the Catechesis of the Good Shepherd propose as the starting point something that does not seem to be particularly religious, but which is entirely in keeping with the child's capacities and natural interests. It goes by the name of "practical life activities." It consists of training the children to take on a variety of chores within their classroom. There are four key components: controlled movement, care of the person, care of the environment, and practices of grace and courtesy. The immediate focus of these activities lies in performing very simple tasks such as: dusting; dry pouring of lentils; polishing; flower arranging; leaf washing; and keeping their immediate environment tidy. This has the effect of causing the children to "slow down" and take the time to really look at concrete objects. The sense of wonder is thus evoked by an "attentive gaze at reality." Visitors to Montessori-style classrooms are often captivated by the slow and deliberate movement and rapt attention of the faces of children washing leaves or dusting a very small statue with a paint brush. In training children to do this, it is not usually enough to tell them about it: the process must be carefully modelled by the teacher.

Some years ago when I first began working in this kind of environment, one of my co-workers expressed disappointment. She recalled that we had gone to a lot of trouble to put together many of the beautiful biblical dioramas, but all that the children seemed to want to do was work on their practical life activities—to water plants, wash leaves, and arrange flowers in vases. In fact, the children we doing exactly what came naturally to them and, in so doing, they were laying the best possible foundation for their religious development. They were learning the lesson that the ordinary is holy, that all life is permeated by the divine. They were making this space of theirs special by acts of routine care. The reverence they were showing towards the ordinary things from God's creation was a beginning for the recognition they would move on to offer to the Creator himself, as is so eloquently put in the *Compendium of the Catechism of the Catholic Church*: "Respecting the laws inscribed in creation and the relations which derive from the nature of things is therefore, a principle of wisdom and a foundation for morality."[2] They were creating a disposition of calm, of focus and the kind of listening that serves as an aid to prayer. Montessori (and St. Thomas Aquinas before her) recognized that such work aids in the construction of the person through the work of the hand. Moreover, carefully modelled lessons about how to act graciously and courteously are to be the basis for learning how to live and work in a community. In this way, children are allowed to contribute to the care of their own environment with a degree of independence and ordered calm.

Basic Content of the Christian Message. It took Sofia Cavalletti and Gianna Gobbi over fifty years of careful observation to identify the aspects of the scriptural stories that appeal to this age group of children. The process involved presenting an enormous variety of these narratives, and then observing the children to see which ones they were attracted to and returned to often. Their results have been confirmed repeatedly in thirty-eight countries around the world. Remarkably, what the children seem to find attractive focus directly on the key aspects of the two great

---

2 *Compendium of the Catechism of the Catholic Church* (Strathfield, NSW: St. Pauls, 2006), § 64.

mysteries of the Christian Faith: the Incarnation and the Paschal Mystery. Specifically, these include: the Annunciation; the Visitation; the Birth of Jesus; the Presentation in the Temple; the Last Supper; and a brief mention of the Death of Jesus followed immediately by the Resurrection. In accordance with their preferred method of learning, these stories are not just related in words. The children are offered small and simple wooden models within dioramas in order to let them touch and attentively gaze at the realities embodied there. The teacher presents the story from the scriptures, and then steps back to allow the children to use the materials and continue to reflect on them in their own way.

There are two further aspects of the scriptures which appeal to this age group — the Parable of the Good Shepherd and the Kingdom Parables — but these will be examined as components of different categories. Those who are familiar with the traditional devotion of the Rosary will be struck by the place held by the Joyful Mysteries in this listing — indeed there is only one missing, the Finding of Jesus in the Temple. (This should be obvious: young children do not want to think too much about someone being lost!) The capacity of young children to recognize what is truly important should not surprise us; it points to a spiritual reality — that God is already in a relationship with young children and they are open to being guided towards a relationship to Him. These important elements form the essential core of the Christian message which children approach with joy.

THE NEED FOR LOVE, CARE, AND PROTECTION

Of all the needs and desires felt by the youngest children, one of these is absolutely foundational: the need for love, care, and protection. Before all else, human beings need to *experience* genuine love from someone in their lives if they are to understand what it is to love. Without this, no human being can thrive or feel comfortable. Typically, this need is met, in the first instance, by the child's parents. The theologian Hans Urs von Balthasar has developed an insightful theological reflection of the place of the mother's smile in drawing forth comfort and joy in the infant. This need is so fundamental that those who do not have it met will continue to seek it all through their lives. St. Teresa of Calcutta well understood the importance of this foundational experience, and she made it an important part of her work to seek out those who had been deprived of this love and to make up for what was lacking. It seemed useless to many who watched her that she would "waste her time" lovingly caring for outcasts who were at the point of death. She was not deterred, and did all that she could to give these people at least one experience of love in their lives. Perhaps this does not need to be stated — but no religious education is possible if there is a complete absence of this kind of love. It is something that teachers continually report in their classrooms, too. There are now more and more students who do not appear to have experienced natural parental affection and care in the early stages of life; even though they have access to many of the material goods that our society has to offer, they can seem desperate for personal attention. Such children will go to greater and greater lengths to have this need met — even to the extent of serious misbehavior which will at least give them access to "one to one" experiences with an adult who tries to work with them and solve their problems. The need for this love does not abate even in adulthood, where the primary need remains. Human beings cannot become properly human unless there is someone to love them.

Religious Education Activities Emphasizing Love, Care, and Protection. Although it may seem too obvious to need stating here, one of the best things a religious educator can do is to encourage parents to be affectionately involved with their children. Taking the time to explain these simple things to parents can have more effect on the relationship than anything else. Pope John Paul II in his encyclical *Catechesi Tradendae* made this pertinent observation:

> The fact that these truths about the main questions of faith and Christian living are thus repeated within a family setting impregnated with love and respect will often make it possible to influence the children in a decisive way for life. The parents themselves profit from the effort that this demands of them, for in a catechetical dialogue of this sort each individual both receives and gives.[3]

While recognizing this essential dimension of religious education, Cavalletti and Gobbi searched for scriptural images that might begin to support this need in other ways as well. They found it in the Parable of the Good Shepherd. It is clear that teachers and catechists cannot properly make up for inadequacies in parental love, but they can introduce children to the love, care and protection offered to them by their loving God. The

---

3 CT, 68.

Parable of the Good Shepherd contains all of the elements that children are seeking. He knows them by name; he loves and cares for them, feeding them with good pasture and refreshing them at cooling streams. If they are lost, he will not stop until he has found them and brought them home. If a wolf comes, the shepherd will put himself at risk in order to protect the sheep. To help children become aware of this parable, Cavalletti created a simple set of materials — small wooden models of a shepherd and some sheep — and allowed them to spend time looking, touching, and reflecting on the meaning in the typical way in which an absorbent mind is nourished.

This method has been used throughout the world, and, time after time, those involved with young children have reported the same thing — that children seem to be drawn to this set of materials more than any other. There seems to be some mystical force at work, drawing them into this particular image of God. I have experienced it myself often. As a Catholic primary school principal, I would often take prospective parents and their children on a tour of our school facilities. The young children would normally stay very close to their parents, feeling quite naturally hesitant in an unfamiliar environment. Almost without exception, as soon as we entered the place where the catechetical materials were kept, the young children would suddenly lose their inhibitions and go straight to the Good Shepherd materials and begin using them. I would never stop them from touching and moving these models — it was exactly what I wanted to see. Perhaps the most dramatic episode on this subject, however, took place during a religious education conference. Some parents who attended had brought their young children, who had remained very well behaved at the back of the conference venue. As part of a conference presentation, I brought out the Good Shepherd materials and began to refer to the impact that they seemed to have on young children. As I was speaking, the children at the back of the hall began moving together to the materials and used them as if there were no other people present in the room. It was such a poignant moment that I stopped speaking and the seventy or so adults in the room simply sat in silence for five full minutes to watch this extraordinary illustration of the impact of the Good Shepherd on his children.

THE NEED FOR MOVEMENT AND TOUCH

Children of this age have a deep need for movement that goes hand in hand with their need for tactile stimulation. There is a drive towards what is concrete and sensorial. Aristotle first articulated what has become known as the peripatetic axiom: there is nothing in the mind that is not first in the senses. Most human beings (apart from the very small percentage of the population that is quite at home with "abstractions") need concrete realities—or at least examples—in order to understand more abstract principles. For the youngest of children there are no exceptions; they cannot learn unless they engage with concrete objects. Moreover, gross motor and, more particularly, fine motor movement appear to be indispensable in the formation of a healthy human personality. A great deal of research has been conducted in this field and has been referred to elsewhere in this book.[4] Suffice it to say that a child of this age whose movement is needlessly restricted will experience a diminished capacity to learn. If given concrete starting points, even young children can attain surprising levels of abstract understanding.

Incorporating Movement and Touch into Religious Education Activities. The most obvious application of this principle to religious education is in the provision of concrete materials to facilitate learning. We have already referred to the wooden models and dioramas used to reflect on scriptural stories. There are many other materials that children of this age group find useful. A well-equipped miniature church, for example, would include a scaled down version of an altar, an altar cloth, lectern, tabernacle, and credence table. Miniature replicas of the chalice, water and wine cruets, ciborium, candles, and altar crucifix, together with the basic linens—corporal, purificator, and finger towel—should also be available. At this level, it will be sufficient just to have handled each of these items and know the names—this is what a child of this age is equipped to do very well. They will become curious about their purpose at the next level of development, so they need not be rushed into trying to understand complex explanations about the purpose of each item and the symbolic links with the life of Christ.[5]

The use of concrete materials taps into the principle of sacramentality: the notion that the spiritual is accessed by the concrete. If children at this age become accustomed to delighting in concrete objects and spend time allowing the sense of wonder to flower into the experience of joy, they are laying a foundation which will help them to appreciate the purpose

---

4 In particular, the work of Angeline Lillard in describing the importance of movement for cognition is relevant.

5 A more complete outline for a developmental continuum of the basic religious experiences can be found in the Appendices.

of sacraments in their lives. Ultimately, the goal of the senses is Christ himself: God made visible in concrete form.

THE NEED FOR ORDER, ROUTINE AND REPETITION

Of all the characteristics of three-to-six-year-old children, the one that is most evident to the adults who spend time with them — parents, teachers, or others — is their need for order, routine, and repetition. Children of this age need this external order in their physical world in order to feel safe and secure. Changes and novelties are not particularly attractive to children of this age. I well recall giving delivering a lecture on this subject to a group of teachers on Saturday morning, when one of the participants took what seemed to be an urgent phone call. When she returned, she let us know what the problem had been. Her husband was looking after the children while she attended the class, and her three-year-old son had become inconsolable. She asked to speak to the child, and he told her through deep sobs what was wrong: "Daddy put my cereal in the green bowl instead of the blue one!" There would be very few parents who would not be able to supply a similar story. Substitute teachers who are brave enough to stand in for a regular teacher of this age group know exactly what is waiting for them. No matter how well briefed, the substitute teacher will be "found wanting" by the class because there will be some very minor detail of the routine that has not been followed exactly, and causes them some concern. "We don't take the roll until after we have handed in our reading books. Don't you know that?"

A disordered classroom — one in which "the rules" are not carefully followed — will cause stress and discomfort to children of this age. Their behavior will reflect the chaotic nature of the classroom organization. What is more, there is a very brief window during which the children can be formed in these routines. As a rule of thumb, the behavior you expect of them on their first day of school is the behavior you will get from them for the rest of the year. Wise teachers will spend their first week with the children running through all of the necessary rules of grace and courtesy, procedures and routines for the year in intimate detail. It continually astonishes adults to witness the way in which children are capable of absorbing so much information on the day of their initial encounter. Months later, all of the children in the class will be able to quote back the exact details that they were trained in and expect to be implemented with precision and order. The kind of training where the children are actually "stepped through" the procedures and have a memory of the physical movements that accompanied the training will be the most effective. This kind of explicit modelling, whereby the children are given things that they can do, easily gives them the confidence to believe that they will be able to face all of the other challenges of the year as well. In no way do they find this kind of repetition and routine to be boring, nor do they see it as a tedious chore. It is their way of gaining mastery of their environment, establishing their sense of belonging and growing in confidence.

INCORPORATING ORDER AND ROUTINE INTO RELIGIOUS EDUCATION ACTIVITIES

Religious education activities for children of this age need to follow a predictable format. The precise way in which these routines are set up is not as important as the fact that the same procedure will be followed each time. At every point where something new is offered to the children, it needs to be presented by means of careful and explicit modelling. These need to be thought through very carefully by the teacher and, if necessary, written down. If they are done well in the first instance, a great deal of time will be saved. The teacher's job at this age is not to see that the children "understand" everything from the beginning. Rather, the children need to know the procedure for using the learning material, and will then be able to absorb the necessary content by being allowed to return to it through repeated use.

It is, of course, impossible to present every detail of what the children need to learn on the first week, but the basic procedures need to be in place. In organizing a work session, a small amount of time is expended in preparing or presenting new material. The majority is used in allowing the children to work with their materials in the ways that they have been shown. Little instructional procedures accompanying each set will serve to remind them how it is to be used. In addition, a material can be used in a number of different ways which allow the children time to continue to reflect on them. As new materials are presented, they become part of the extended repertoire. Children will naturally be drawn to the materials that they have not yet mastered. Once they have done so, they will not need to use them again. This modus operandi was one of Montessori's key insights, and can be seen working very effectively in Montessori schools. It is essentially a kind of "self-selection" of materials which saves a great deal of time. It is not the teacher who is responsible for "thinking for everyone." Rather, the children themselves are aware of the gaps in their own learning and can select educational materials that will help them to address these needs. All that is necessary for the teacher is to note what materials the children are using and then make adjustments with individuals if they do not seem to have spent sufficient time with any particular work. The seasons of the Church's year provide an ideal framework for structuring the religious education program. The appropriate presentation will follow the liturgical season.[6]

IMITATION LEADING TO INDEPENDENCE

Research into effective learning is quite clear about the way in which inexperienced learners begin the process. They need to imitate those who are able to perform the task competently. For the three-to-six-year-old child, as already noted, this requires very explicit modelling. The required task must be reduced to very clear steps, and each stage should not be too complicated: it must be simple enough for the children to succeed at it. Ultimately, by joining the stages together, the children will be capable of quite complex tasks, but they must rise up to the occasion by slow steps. At first, children will want to imitate exactly what the "expert model" is doing. Many older siblings will be able to recall the experience of a younger brother or sister annoying them by copying their every word and action. Many teachers have had the experience of walking back into a classroom after having been briefly called away and found one of the children continuing the session with the same words and mannerisms that they would have used themselves.

There can be a tendency for very creative teachers or parents to be alarmed by this — to see in it a crushing of the child's creativity by forcing them to conform to exact patterns of behavior and procedure. If this attempt to copy the behavior of the competent teacher or peer continues much into the next stage of development, it would certainly be a cause for concern. At this point, however, it is necessary if the child is to learn. Montessori described it as the child's plea "help me to do it by myself." The careful imitation is a necessary stage on the way to independence. Once children are comfortable being able do it someone else's way, they will soon move on to putting their own personal stamp on it. It might be noted that even adults proceed in this way when they are learning a new skill. The first thing they want to do is to copy an expert exactly; they will

6 A possible structure for this has been offered in the Appendices.

innovate later. This had been well documented in the celebrated paper by Kirchner, Seller and Clark.[7]

Incorporating "Imitation Leading to Independence" into Religious Education Activities. Some of the religious education activities appropriate for children of this age group can look very uncreative. Young children respond well to very specific instructions and want to follow these exactly. One activity particularly suited to their needs is "tracing" from simple line drawings. Very few children are competent to draw at this stage of their development, and yet they want to produce a product that closely resembles the original. Paradoxically, the practice effect of this imitation contributes to their creativity at a later stage; the confidence they gain gives them the willingness to try things for themselves. Usually, by the time they are approaching six years of age, many of them put the tracing paper aside and try to produce the line drawings of themselves, and then add little variations and features of their own.

One of the most useful ways in which to teach children of this age to work towards independent reflections of their own is to teach them a wide variety of art responses that they can make to the stories and other materials that they are using. These activities can include using simple water color paints, colored pencils, collage, play dough, sand tray modelling, and letter illumination. The effort that goes into teaching the children how to use these simple techniques effectively allows them the freedom to choose which medium they will use for responding to the presentations that are made to them. It no longer falls to the teacher to tell children what they must do; they are given a degree of freedom of choice that every human being craves, but remain focused on one of the necessary tasks.

It must never be forgotten that the ultimate aim of religious education for the child, even at this very early stage, is to draw them into their own relationship with Christ[8] — one in which they continue to ask their own questions based on their own experiences of wonder and joy. The role of the teacher is the same as that of John the Baptist: "He must increase, I must decrease."[9] As the children grow in competence, they will develop their confidence and seek more and more of their own independence.

---

7 See P.A. Kirschner, J. Sweller, and R.E. Clark, "Why Minimal Guidance during Instruction Does Not Work: An Analysis of the Failure of Constructivist, Discovery, Problem-based, Experiential and Inquiry-based Teaching," *Educational Psychologist* 41 (2), (2006): 75–86.

8 See CT, § 5.

9 John 4:30.

4

The "Big Picture" Seeker

*Developmental and Religious Characteristics
of the Six-to-Nine-Year-Old Child*

THE REASONING MIND

There is dramatic contrast between the typical child of five years and one who is seven years of age. The key differences cluster around one central characteristic — the absorbent mind gives way to a reasoning mind. Whereas the three-to-six-year-old was basically concerned with absorbing information and appeared to be naturally disposed toward this purpose, the six-to-nine-year-old child no longer has the same capability for absorbing new information: the focus has shifted to understanding how the pieces fit together. Children are no longer satisfied with asking the *what* questions; they want to know *why* things are the way they are and *where* they come from. This is not to say that children are no longer capable of absorbing information; it just means that the sensitive period — the moment when this was natural and easy — has now passed, the absorption of new information is something that must be worked at. This is readily evident in a task such as learning a new language. Children prior to the age of six years have no difficulty in learning the complex structures and vocabulary of a language, and in the case of bi-lingual children, more than one language. The sensitive period of the absorbent mind allowed them to effortlessly and naturally succeed at this task. It will never be the same again. Those who try to learn a language after this critical sensitive period has gone will need to put in serious effort over a number of years if they are to succeed. If the earlier stage of their development has been rich and varied, children will be already equipped with a huge store of data. These discrete pieces of information now become the material they want to work with and link together. They will continue to encounter new things and learn their names, but their real interest is in the explanations: why are things the way they are, and where do they come from?

Incorporating the Needs of a Reasoning Mind into Religious Education Activities. Six-to-nine-year-old children need more that what was offered to them in the previous stage, when they were simply acquainted with models of people and places, stories from the Bible, and objects from the liturgy and sacraments. While these things remain mildly attractive (if they are new), they will no longer hold the attention of the child; something more is needed. They need to "synthesize" — to put things together in such a way that they can begin to see the relationships between them. It is a mistake to "tell them the answers" to such questions. They are actually capable of working out for themselves how these things might fit together, so long as they are not asked to incorporate too many things at once. The beginning stage for these children is to put together certain items with which they are already familiar and allow their minds to work on them. They are in a "sensitive period" for this activity, and their learning will be much "deeper" if they are given sufficient support to be able to see obvious connections, but allowed to discover these connections for themselves.

Typical activities at this level would consist of offering children sets of material and cards that are naturally linked together. Depending on their competence, the teacher may show how the material fits together—once. If they are more advanced, it is possible to simply ask the children to fit the pieces together for themselves without significant input from the teacher. This works better if a completed picture of the way the set is supposed to look is made available for the child. They prefer to be self-correcting. If they are allowed to check for themselves and discover their own minor errors, they are likely to learn further valuable lessons. The teacher can then be brought in to celebrate the child's competence rather than identify potentially embarrassing errors. As with other materials, the children should be allowed to work on this a number of times at their own discretion in order to gain mastery.

THE ROLE OF IMAGINATION AND CREATIVITY

A child prior to the age of six years is focused on what is real: that is fascinating enough. This can be confusing for adults, who can misread this focus on the real for an imaginative mind. A three-year-old child who is told about Santa Claus or the Tooth Fairy will invest these characters with a "real" existence; that is all they know. Adults can then mistake this for a rich and varied imaginative life. On the contrary, it is when children cease to invest fictional characters with a real existence (at around about six years of age) that they become genuinely capable of imaginative activity.

They reach a stage of being able to distinguish between what is real and what is merely a mental construct. Imagination is an important element of a human reasoning mind and it serves a vital purpose. It has already been noted that children at this level begin to make links between the data that they have acquired. The faculty they need to do this is none other than imagination. It is their capacity for making links between the real things that they know. Indeed, it goes even further than this, since they also try to make links between what they know and what they don't yet know, filling in the gaps with their own imaginative speculations. Their imagination will never be more powerful than it is during this stage of their development, and it needs to be indulged if human development is to proceed normally. I recall one particularly creative teacher at this level who was well aware of her need to encourage this. Every day she set up the classroom with some unexpected set of items and asked the children to suggest what might have happened. On one occasion, in the center of the classroom, she set up a stand with a silk cloth and left on a silver high-heeled shoe on it, surrounded by empty chocolate boxes. The wild and imaginative scenarios that emerged from this stimulus bore only one thing in common: they were completely internally consistent even if they were wildly imaginative and differed from child to child.

There can be little doubt that children who are allowed to develop their imagination in this way will be the innovators of the future. On the other hand, I have also witnessed some school systems which frown on such imaginative activity and insist on narrowly focused exercises which can result in only one possible answer. Such systems are capable of producing technically excellent results, but at the cost of resulting in "wooden personalities" and adults who are incapable of thinking "outside the square." Imagination allows the child to look beyond what is available immediately to their senses. It nourishes their interest in the universe and allows them to put the pieces together in their own way.

Incorporating Imagination and Creativity into Religious Education Activities. In 1940, the insightful French theologian Cardinal Henri de Lubac drew attention to what he perceived to be a loss of the sense of the sacred in religious education. He claimed that the reliance on a program that relied heavily on catechism questions and answers had the potential to undermine the reality that God is far beyond any proposition that we can have of him. He did not doubt that these propositions had their place for clarifying matters and ensuring that the picture we have of God did not fly off into mere wild imaginings. Yet they had a tendency to narrow the vision of God into manageable, predictable, and "safe" categories. God had been tamed and placed in a box. Perhaps an example will illustrate what he meant. For human beings, there have always been two principal ways of presenting the truth: scientifically and poetically. For example, if we are describing a cold morning, we might say that it was zero degrees. This is accurate and leaves nothing more to be said. If we were presenting it poetically, however, we might use this image from John Keats:

> St Agnes' Eve — Ah, bitter chill it was!
> The owl, for all his feathers was a-cold;
> The hare limp'd trembling through the frozen grass
> And silent was the flock in woolly fold:
> Numb were the beadsmen's fingers while he told
> His rosary, and while his frosted breath,
> Like pious incense from a censer old,
> Seemed taking flight from heaven, without a death...[1]

Here, a series of concrete images invites us to enter personally into the picture and to keep reflecting on the meaning...much like the parables in the scriptures and the seasonal celebrations presented through the liturgy. Each time we return to these images and stories, they are likely to evoke different insights and emotions within us. In this way, children can be invited to enter personally into the mystery. In this the faculty of imagination is indispensable. Rather than offer the children a compressed conclusion in the form of a pre-digested answer, we should allow them to work through to their own.

In contrast, the scientific explanations of the world always suffer from the same limitations: they are "time bound." Our human understanding of scientific realities is always expanding; the images and words used to express the current understanding in one generation will come across as limited and even primitive to subsequent generations. For example, the Ptolemaic explanation of the movement of stars and planets — with the earth at the center of the universe — was "cutting edge science" in its time, but is looked on as quaint and amusing today. Current scientific knowledge looks with wry amusement at the ideas of even fifty years ago.

---

1 John Keats, "The Eve of St Agnes."

Science does not have a good record of providing timeless understandings of reality as it is because it is inflexible in its expression: everything must be couched in precise and limited language. During the sixteenth century, the Church made the mistake of attempting to link the poetic biblical account of creation with the existing scientific understanding in the Galileo case. We now understand that the Bible uses evocative, poetic language in stories of God's dealing with people in order to convey the truth, not scientific language. This approach releases us from the doubtful certainty of scientific facts and allows us to look beyond this into timeless truths and mysteries without ever believing that we know all there is to know about an infinite God. The *Catechism of the Catholic Church* has put this beautifully in its entry on the account of the Fall of Adam and Eve:

> The account of the fall in Genesis 3 uses figurative language, but affirms a primeval event, a deed that took place at the beginning of the history of man. Revelation gives us the certainty of faith that the whole of human history is marked by the original fault freely committed by our first parents.[2]

There is no insistence here that we are being given exact details; only an acknowledgement that something of great importance and significance is being conveyed in a story which we are meant to reflect upon imaginatively and throughout our lives. The whole Bible must be seen in this light. If vital religious truths had been conveyed in the scientific language of the Biblical times, they would be considered worthless today; but this was not so.[3] They were recorded in poetic language which invites further reflection on God's dealings with us.

Music, art, and literature can be very useful in stimulating the imagination, and children are usually interested in making their own contributions to at least one of these fields. High quality religious art can play a very important role in helping them to do this. There are very few aspects of the Catholic faith that have not, in some way, been represented artistically through over

2 *Catechism of the Catholic Church* (Vatican City: Libreria Editrice Vaticana, 1997), § 390. [Afterwards CCC]

3 Some contemporary scientific writers who try to denigrate the Bible because it does not accurately convey current scientific understandings entirely miss the point. They fail to understand that they are reading the poetry and stories through which God has chosen to make himself know to the people of every time, not the science of today which may well find itself superseded among educated people in the future.

twenty centuries of reflection, now made available very quickly by means of computer image searches. By offering children an artistic representation, we can be confident that a number of essential elements will be present, but will not impose themselves all at once on the mind's eye. The meaning will unfold gradually and even when the child has seen all that there is to be seen, another art work can be provided to open the same question from a different perspective. It has been found that this use of art works best when the image is transferred to a simple wooden board so that it can be held and carefully examined individually. In terms of literature, there is an enormous corpus of material to draw from. Most people will be aware, for example, of the astonishing impact that a first reading of C.S. Lewis's *The Lion, the Witch and the Wardrobe* can have on a child's understanding of the self-sacrifice and the resurrection of Christ, represented in the figure of Aslan.

It needs to be stated, however, that within this context, summary propositions which can be learned by heart still retain a role. Even the great gift of a creative imagination needs to be fitted into an overall picture. In particular, the words of scripture, the creeds, parts of the Mass, the words from some of the sacramental rites, traditional prayers, and some significant summary statements will allow the child to retain an accurate summary of certain key points — but these come at the end, not at the beginning of the process, and the children need to be made aware that there is much more to know and love about God that what can be compressed into a few pertinent phrases.

FOCUS ON THE BIG PICTURE

Having spent the first six years or so of their lives focusing on the detail of individual objects, this stage takes them to a totally different place: to a focus on the "big picture." This new-found interest complements their need to make links. One indicator of this change in perspective is the child's capacity to deal with the notion of time. Up to this point, young children tend to deal with the succession of events by relating it only to themselves: for example, when parents might tell them that it is "five more sleeps" until their birthday. Children of this age now begin looking for some grand integrating strategies in order to make things fit into their developing worldview. This need was so evident to Montessori that she developed a series of five lessons that would offer children of this age a suitable framework to facilitate their development; big picture lessons offer the child the context they seek at this age. Every work that they undertake then becomes a springboard for something else. These have continued to develop and are known as "Great Lessons." Each of the five touches on a different area of reality which is of interest to the six-to-nine-year-old child.

The first Great Lesson, *The Story of the Universe,* uses storytelling, photographs, and simple but beautiful diagrams and charts to stimulate the imagination of the child in relation to the origin of the universe. Like all the Great Lessons, it does not provide detailed information, only sufficient detail to make the child curious and make further inquiries into everything involved in God's creation: astronomy, geology, meteorology, and geography. It also sets the scene for future studies in chemistry and physics. The second of these lessons is called *The Coming of Life.* It is essentially a long ribbon which is unrolled as a timeline detailing the amazing diversity of life forms developing over time. In Montessori's view, this was meant to do more than acquaint children with these forms of life. It was meant to communicate the "cosmic task" of every living thing, from the smallest microorganism to the human person. Further studies in ecology, biology, and the life sciences can be indicated from this "big picture" framework.

The third of the great lessons shifts focus away from the cosmos to one unique species: it is called *The Coming of Humans.* It is also based on a timeline of human life with a particular focus on the development of tools. This lesson encourages the children to look at the basic needs of human beings and the way in which different civilizations have met these and how they have contributed to the world as we know it today. This is a framework for the study of history and anthropology. This lesson is followed by *The Story of Writing,* sometimes known as *The Story of Communicating in Signs,* which allows the children to see the great human advance that was made which allowed people to express themselves in written form. No other species known on the earth is capable of this intensely human activity. The ability to write allows us to recall and make present things that are past so that we are no longer entirely dependent on our personal memory. In this great lesson, the timeline is accompanied by pictures and alphabets and other codes. They can also see how various words came into the English language. Finally, *The Story of Numbers* is offered to help children understand the way in which human beings communicate in concepts that refer to quantities: mathematics.

Incorporating "Big Picture" Thinking into Religious Education Activities. Maria Montessori understood, along with Thomas Aquinas and the whole Catholic Tradition, the interconnections between all of creation. Every aspect bears the mark of its creator—the transcendental properties of truth, beauty, and goodness. There is not one truth for science and another for religion: the truth itself is *one* and it has its origin in God. Cavalletti and Gobbi were well aware of the need for "big picture" contexts for the children of this age group and offered this through works incorporating elements of the Great Lessons applied to religious concepts. These activities include *The Fettucia* — a long ribbon timeline which seems to draw its inspiration from the second Great Lesson, *The Coming of Humans.* The difference is that where Montessori's works make the presence of God in history implicit, Cavalletti offers elements which allow children of this age to make this presence explicit.

By this stage, religious education needs to offer children "context" in the same way that Montessori's Great Lessons do. The simplest way of doing this is to provide them with timelines in which they can fit God's activity in the world into the stages of actual history. Children at this age need a "big picture" first before they can be satisfied with details. In religious education activities, it is no longer enough to offer them unrelated activities; they need to know how it fits into a larger context and why they are doing it. Without this, they will only engage on a surface level and offer only the minimal compliance necessary to satisfy the demands of the teacher. A little bit of extra effort is required to ensure that their enormous capacity for making connections is given scope; teachers need to be able to offer them big picture contexts. If the children have not been exposed to the Montessori Great Lessons in other parts of the curriculum, it is a relatively simple matter to present them, and then add aspects of creation and salvation history as part of the overall context. In working at this level, children often discover areas they would like to explore. This means that teachers need to offer them more generous time limits to complete their projects. They should also be allowed to negotiate more time if it is clear that they are learning. It is perhaps difficult for teachers of this age group to accept that a "finished product" does not necessarily indicate high quality learning. The creativity of making connections and getting a clear idea of the "big picture" is necessarily messy.

MENTAL ORDER REPLACES PHYSICAL ORDER

There is a very clear — often very unwelcome — indication that a child has moved into this plane of development. They become quite messy. In the previous stage, order in the physical environment was necessary for them to feel safe and comfortable. This can be a very attractive feature of this age group in terms of the way adults relate to them. While I was a school principal, I would visit classrooms on a regular basis, generally once a week. I took this opportunity to encourage the children to keep the classroom ordered and tidy and I would select one class each week for the "tidy award." It was always a delight to see the seriousness with which the youngest children took this task — it was one that put them in a very competitive position in relation to the other classes. It is not easy for teachers and even less comfortable for parents to see their once fanatically tidy children lose this endearing characteristic. Nevertheless, if six-to-nine-year-old children are developing normally, they will reach a point where they are capable of mentally organizing their world and of moving beyond their reliance on the merely physical. Tidiness will no longer be crucial to their sense of security.

Accounting for the Change from Physical to Mental Order in Religious Education Classes. This can be a difficult moment in the six-to-nine-year-old child's development if they are not treated sympathetically. Some parents and teachers may not recognize what is happening and insist that on exactly the same standards of neatness that was the hallmark of the younger child. This is likely to have long-term consequences — either the child will become chronically messy, often for a lifetime, in reaction to this attempt to interfere in natural development. Alternatively, they might remain in a state where they become compulsive "neat freaks" more or less permanently.

Every aspect of a religious education class teaches something. The way in which children are treated as human beings will tell them a great deal about how their faith teaches them to treat others. What is needed in response to this new characteristic is both understanding and continued guidance. The wise parent or teacher will accept a degree of messiness and will not turn it into a source of tension in the relationship. Nor will they permit the classroom (or, in the case of the parents, the bedroom) to be turned into a chaotic mess. The simplest way of dealing with this matter in a healthy way is to allow children to work with some degree of mess, but build in times when they must tidy up. These "tidying moments" should be routine and conducted without rancor. Indeed, this was one of the reasons why I would visit classes. It would give the teacher a reason to have the children attend to this need for maintaining some order in the environment at least once a week. Most teachers of this level take the opportunity of a general tidy-up once each day. If a session has been particularly messy, it may be necessary to incorporate tidying sessions immediately afterwards. In any case, the children of this age group should not be prevailed upon with guilt and shame or even worse punishments for their natural messiness. They need help to be tidy, and if this is given in a calm and pleasant way, they will eventually move to a point where they will take responsibility for it themselves.

THE DAWN OF MORAL AGENCY

The moral development and formation of children is dealt with in a separate section of this book. Even so, it is important to note the dawn of moral agency which is a feature of this age group. There can be no fixed rule about when children become aware of the moral principles which should undergird their actions. Some particularly advanced children can develop this moral sense as early as four or five years of age. It is important to be clear about what is meant by moral agency in this context. Even young children will be aware that some things are "right" and others "wrong"; parents usually begin to instill this notion in them from the time they can communicate. What is lacking for the youngest children, however, is a real understanding of *why* these things are right and wrong. The dawn of the reasoning mind brings with it this other capacity which matches their development in other areas. Children of this age can begin to discern the presence of rules and regulations which govern their lives and the whole universe: this is what the six-to-nine-year-old sensitive period prepares them to do.

In the previous section, the change from *physical* to *mental* order that begins to affect the six-to-nine-year-old was outlined. One very significant aspect of this mental order consists of a series of very clear rules which these children want applied rigidly. It is similar to the way in which children at the previous stage required very rigid physical order in order to feel safe. Teachers who are involved in playground duty will be very familiar with the regular complaints of seven- and eight-year-old children who want to report other children who have failed to obey even one of the many rules that they deem essential for the good ordering of the social group. Often these rules will be self-inflicted. I well remember one group of children who played in a particular corner of the playground and had invented an elaborate set of protocols to determine which sticks and rocks could be used as part of their game. An indignant group of them came to report that their sticks had been "stolen" and they suspected that an older child had come into the school grounds the night before to perform this frightful crime. Parents of children at this age will also be familiar with their elaborate rules of fairness.

What must be understood is that this stage of development is normal. The rigidity can be somewhat unnerving for parents and teachers alike, but it allows children to set up the moral framework that they will be able to apply with more subtle understanding about the principles of justice. This generally comes to them at around the ages of eleven or twelve. Until then, unbending fairness derived from black and white rules constitutes the moral world in which the six-to-nine-year-old child lives.

Accounting for the Dawn of Moral Agency in Religious Education Classes. Children of this age crave moral guidance, and on this matter a note of caution must be sounded. If they are offered a very lengthy set of rules which they must adhere to, there will be a risk of making them stressed and needlessly anxious. They will take these rules so seriously that every time they break one of them, they will feel excessively guilty. There is no need for this: they will make up enough rules of their own without having the burden added to. For Christianity, morality is more than a set of rules; it is a relationship of love which leads to action: "If you love me, you will keep my commandments."[4] Only deep and genuine love is capable of bringing out the best in human beings; we are capable of making great sacrifices for someone we love, and these must be given freely. If the same sacrifices are demanded or exacted, the motive is inadequate and it will be almost impossible to fulfil these requirements. A mother can love and respond to a crying baby: a stranger finds this much more difficult.

Even at this level, children need to encounter morality in these terms or they may develop in unhealthy ways. They will either tie themselves up in joyless legalistic prescriptions or they may ultimately abandon the guidance of the Christian moral code altogether, mistaking it for a set of impossible demands from a judgmental God. There are two very effective ways of bringing out both dimensions of morality: the motive of love, and the wise rules that will make us happy. Both require a connection with the life of Christ, with whom they already acquainted as the Good Shepherd who loves them. The first strategy is to introduce them to the moral maxims of Jesus, drawn from the Gospels. It is recommended that these be pasted, carved or written onto little wooden boards so that the children can hold them and reflect on them. They can be kept in a suitable

4 John 14:15.

box near the prayer table, and the children can take up any one of these at a time they choose. Sometimes, they like to choose them at random, without looking at which one they are selecting. The maxims are best introduced briefly and simply as part of a morning prayer session, and then placed in the container to be used later. Once all of them have been introduced, children can be asked to come and select one to be read as part of each prayer session. In this way, they will become very familiar. These twelve are recommended by Cavalletti:

1. "Love your enemies." (Matthew 5:44)
2. "I give you a new commandment: Love one another as I have loved you." (John 13:34)
3. "Do good to those who hate you." (Luke 6:27)
4. "When you pray, go into a room by yourself, shut the door and pray to your Father in private." (Matthew 6:6)
5. "Ask and you will receive. Seek and you will find. Knock and the door will be opened." (Matthew 7:7)
6. "Your body is a temple of the Holy Spirit." (1 Corinthians 6:19)
7. "You must be perfect, just as your heavenly Father is perfect." (Matthew 5:48)
8. "Say *yes* when you mean *yes* and *no* when you mean *no*." (Matthew 5:37)
9. "I do not say forgive seven times, but seventy times seven." (Matthew 7:22)
10. "Always treat others the way you would have them treat you." (Matthew 7:12)
11. "Give when you are asked to give and do not turn your back on someone who wants to borrow." (Matthew 5:42)
12. "Pray for those who persecute you." (Matthew 5:44)

The second strategy for encouraging the children to engage in moral reflection is the use of the parables: stories Jesus told which should guide the way we act and treat others. These are likewise best introduced at a morning prayer session. It is useful to leave them written out on little cards so that these two can be left in a container near the prayer table for repeated use. There are two categories of parables that have been found useful: Parables of Mercy and Moral Parables. The best starting point is the story of the Centurion's servant (Matthew 8:5–10, 13), and the two parables of Mercy: the Forgiving Father (15:11–24) and the Lost Coin (Luke 15:8–9). This focus on the mercy of God underlines the relationship of love as the foundation of moral behavior and reflection. Once this has been reinforced, it will be possible to begin looking at the stories Jesus told to guide our behavior towards others: the moral parables. These include:

1. *The Good Samaritan* (Luke 10:30–37)
2. *The Pharisee and the Tax Collector* (Luke 18:9–14)
3. *The Insistent Friend* (Luke 11:5–8)
4. *The Debtors* (Matthew 18:23–34)
5. *The Sower* (Matthew 13:3–8)

In the next stage of development, this focus on moral parables can continue with some more demanding requirements:

1. *The Wedding Feast* (Matthew 22:1–14)
2. *The Ten Bridesmaids* (Matthew 25:1–12)
3. *The Workers in the Vineyard* (Matthew 20:1–15)
4. *The Talents* (Matthew 25:14–30)
5. *The Pearl of Great Price* (Matthew 13:45–46)

It is at this point, the six-to-nine-year-old sensitive period, that children become aware of their personal need for the mercy of God and of God's desire to offer forgiveness. This is the ideal moment for introducing children to the Sacrament of Reconciliation. Generally speaking, this should take place somewhere after the age of seven and before the age of nine. The maxims, the parables of mercy, and the most basic moral parables can form the basis of their "examination of conscience" for this stage of their life. If the Sacrament of Reconciliation is left to a time beyond this, the children may have a greater understanding of moral principles, but they will have passed beyond the easy familiarity of the affective relationship with Christ which finds little difficulty in approaching the one they love to receive forgiveness.

This list is not exhaustive: as the children become more familiar with the Gospel, they will be able to continue to draw lessons for themselves about the way in which they might act. The Ten Commandments also have a role to play in moral formation, but this will be dealt with under the next stage of development, the nine-to-twelve-year-old, at which point the child is more capable of integrating these more abstract principles. The formal study of the rules and principles of ethical behavior is a valuable and necessary study for a later stage of development — but, even then, if it does not proceed from the foundation of God's love and mercy, it will not be Christian morality. At best, it will be an elevated form of ethics which emphasizes duty and mutual obligation, but lacks the motive power of the loving relationship.

There is another strategy which is currently found in the practices of good schools which can be very valuable in supporting moral development: the regular class meeting in which children discuss the problems they are facing in relationships and seek solutions. The wise teacher will offer the children good strategies for solving these difficulties, but will also know how to integrate the spiritual resources referred to above into this program if it is taking place within a Catholic school. Sometimes, the reading of a parable that offers insights into Jesus's way of acting will be very valuable and will allow the children to apply solutions for themselves without needing the teacher to give them the answer. This will always be a more effective learning experience, encouraging the children to see things for themselves, and to discern the power of the scriptures in reinforcing the relationship with Christ and applying it to their own actions.

JUSTICE VS. EQUAL TREATMENT

Very closely related to the development of morality at this age is the desire of children to ensure that rules are applied fairly. In the earlier stages of this development, this takes a very basic form: everyone must be treated exactly the same way, and there can be no exceptions. It is not difficult for an adult to see that this approach does not always result in true justice. Once, when teaching a group of seven-year-old children, I took a phone call in the morning from a distressed family: the family pet had been run over and killed in front of their house while the whole family watched. Their child would be late for school that day. When the girl entered the classroom, I simply nodded sympathetically at her. One of the other children drew my attention to the fact that this child was late, and I had made no attempt to correct her because she had broken the rule. I explained why I had done this, but it was not good enough for many of the children in the class. This girl had broken the rule and needed to face some consequence in their view! Obviously, there are occasions such as this one where the usual rules governing our behavior are set aside in the interests of justice and compassion. These are the kinds of subtleties that children need to be exposed to during this stage of their lives in order to move from the simple demands of an over-arching rule of equal treatment to a more realistic understanding of what just treatment really is. Teachers should not be surprised by the way children are thinking at this stage; they need to preserve the basic understanding of fair and equal treatment of all, tempered with appropriate shades of grey that can only come from sharing human experiences of compassion as well as justice. They will find it difficult to learn if they are not shown.

A NEED FOR REPETITION / A DISLIKE OF REPETITION

There is an important change that takes place in the six-to-nine-year-old child. Whereas a three-to-six-year-old child loves the feeling of competence that comes from repeating the same task competently, the six-to-nine-year-old dislikes repetition. Even so, as with human beings of any age, repetition is necessary if they are to learn; this is required if the formation of a neural pathway in the human brain is to be successful. The research available on this subject is consistent, and has already been presented. Repetition is indispensable.

Incorporating Repetition in the Religious Education Program. Montessori educators have long recognized the need for dealing with the repetition conundrum among six-to-nine-year-old children, and Cavalletti has adapted this for use in religious education. Essentially, there are two elements to this. The first consists of offering a variety of activities based on the same essential need. This can be achieved by providing different materials, or by giving children a variety of different ways of using the same materials, identified by different task cards of varying complexity. In both cases, the usual Montessori technique is used. Children are not required to follow a strict schedule in terms of what activity must be covered at a particular time. A degree of freedom allows them to "space out" their practice rather than be forced into a strategy of "massed practice." Teachers still need to ensure that the children return to a basic content repeatedly, but the children are not made to do this in exactly the same way each time.

The second element which enables a program to structure in the necessary repetition goes by the name of "spiral curriculum." This means that certain concepts are arranged in such a way that children are able to return to the same content at deeper and deeper levels over time. They may encounter the same basic content at every level of their stages of development. There will even be different aspects of the same content covered according to the needs of the sensitive period. (For specific details of how this works out in a religious education program, refer to Appendices A and B.) This approach is well known in educational theory, but there is an additional framework available in the field of religious education: namely, the cycle of liturgical seasons and feast days. The Catholic Church has been using a spiral curriculum for two millennia. As an educational process, it simply means that the same basic realities are celebrated each year, but each time one returns to these foundational ideas and events, there are new reflections and insights available to perceive "something more." The *Catechism of the Catholic Church* describes this in terms not just of whole lifetimes, but of centuries over which this process develops: "Yet even if Revelation is already complete, it is not completely explicit; it remains for Christian faith gradually to grasp its full significance over the course of the Centuries."[5]

DEVELOPMENT OF SOCIAL RELATIONSHIPS

It is noteworthy among three-to-six-year-old children that they tend to be happy as individuals; when they do play with others, it is often "in parallel" — they play side by side rather than together. Their interest in others is usually in terms of having the other child fulfil their own needs rather than any genuine sharing. The closer the child comes to six years of age, the more this begins to change, until finally they reach a point where other children become very important in their lives. As three-to-six-year-olds, children were generally willing to work or play by themselves so long as what they had before them was interesting and engaging. The six-to-nine-year-old needs to begin exploring social relationships, and this need expresses itself in their desire to be in groups and work together. When left to themselves, children of this age group in a school playground will rarely be found alone. They will often form clubs and societies with elaborate rules; they will even make up their own language and passwords to identify themselves as members of a group. Some will make their own special badges and mark out their "territory" in the school playground. They like to ensure that they wear clothing that is very similar to that of their friends; they will want to speak and act like them as well.

5 CCC, § 66.

In the classroom, the desire to be in regular communication continues. Children of this age tend to prefer to work together most of the time. As a well-meaning young teacher, I well remember my attempts to impose a "work silence" on this age group to make sure that they achieved their goals instead of "wasting time" talking. Try as I might, they kept coming up with new and original ways of communicating: notes written on paper planes; signals with flashing mirrors; a basic form of Morse code tapped out on the desk; furtive eye movements; synchronizing "needs" to go to the bathroom; even carefully timed and sequenced flatulent noises! There will be no stopping the creativity of children who need to be in contact with one another. Montessori described this need for being together as a "herding instinct" and wisely counselled educators to work with this characteristic rather than against it. In her view, this social communication served a vital need in their human development: children of this age need to be with others in order to discover who they are themselves. This is more important, more foundational than almost anything else that we might think it is necessary for them to learn. They understand this intuitively, and move in this direction until the need is met.

Accounting for the Dawn of Social Relationships in Religious Education Classes. How, then, does one deal with this characteristic, which can lead to so much disruption within the classroom? The teacher's response must begin with acknowledging that these children need to talk and to work together. These things need to be managed, not denied. It is entirely possible to give the children strategies for meeting these needs, and even of harnessing them to assist in the whole learning process. One strategy is to have a "supply center" where children need to come in order to get the things that they need to do their work. It serves the same basic need as the water cooler in an office; its other purpose is to allow for the quick exchange of news and pleasantries that breaks up the day, providing mental and emotional refreshment in order to continue working. Children of this age should be discouraged from having too much of their own equipment, as it can serve as a "currency" to bribe other children ("you can use my sparkle highlighters if you..."). The supply center teaches many other lessons, too. It teaches children to wait courteously for others; it points out that resources are not inexhaustible and that they cannot ask their parents to cover their own carelessness by demanding materials that they have not taken care of themselves; and it provides the opportunity to work with others to keep shared resources in good order.

It must be acknowledged that children of this age learn best (most of the time) when they work together. Teachers must be attentive that this characteristic does not result in a small group of children doing all of the work. This will not support learning very well. Every task that children work on together needs to be divided into discrete parts. While a large group can work together, each child needs to be responsible for a particular aspect of the work. Teachers also need to be attentive to which parts children are typically working on and ensure that these are shared around so that all gain some competence in a variety of tasks. This group activity presumes that the arrangement of classroom furniture is flexible enough to allow groups to work together when necessary, and perhaps shifted back into other configurations for those occasions where individual work is required. Finally, the children need to be trained to work with one another in a way that does not create loud distracting noise. A low working "buzz" takes time to create, and a great deal of effort needs to go into this at the beginning of the school year. Children need to be trained to speak in quiet voices, and teachers need to model this. It takes about six to ten weeks of repeated insistence (pleasantly and calmly!) before it becomes a habit. This cannot normally be achieved in a single day.

THE GOAL OF INDEPENDENCE

The three-to-six-year-old seeks independence that can be expressed as "help me to do it for myself"; by contrast, the six-to-nine-year-old child expresses the need for independence more in keeping with a reasoning mind: "help me to think for myself." This manifests itself in a variety of ways. Six-to-nine-year-olds come into a new need for mental, rather than physical, independence; they want to be in charge of themselves and may be stubborn, refusing to do things. By the same token, they become more mentally tough and can handle just criticism. If they are told that they have fallen short of expectations and they know that this is true, they are usually willing to accept this from those in authority who draw their attention to it. No longer is it sufficient to tell children that you want them to do something: they want to know the reason behind it; they want to know why. Montessori also described this as the "age of rudeness" in which children seem to lose their good manners. If they have developed normally, six-to-nine-year-olds are no longer desperately seeking to please the adults in their lives; they are already confident of being loved and start to take more emotional risks in this regard. This often comes across as rude and "bratty."

Accounting for the Goal of Independence in Religious Education Classes. There are some simple strategies for ensuring that children of this age have the opportunity for developing their mental capacities. One of these is a change of stance in relation to the child's questions. Since they have now grown in competence, six-to-nine-year-olds should be capable of finding their own answers. An appropriate answer to most of their questions might be something like: "I'm not sure; what do you think?" This shifts responsibility for their learning back on themselves. There can be no doubt that children of this age do not like hearing this from adults; they prefer learning to be easy, but this is not helpful to them. When they do find answers for themselves, their confidence grows and they begin to understand why you might be acting in this way.

The adult should not at first take away all support from the developing child. It is useful to give them sufficient background so that they can find their own way to satisfactory answers. This may be as simple as saying: "I think you will find out how to spell that word in the dictionary, it starts with p-h…" It is also useful to ask a series of questions which allow them to find the answer for themselves. Such an approach allows them begin using their developing mental capacities and even to begin seeking help from their peers. A learning journal, detailing things they have learned during the day, can help them to be responsible for themselves and for their work.

Religious education materials that are presented to this age group should leave space for children to work some things out for themselves. Instead of presenting the whole material from beginning to end, it is often sufficient to group the components into related categories and then have the children put these together in the proper sequence for themselves. All of the necessary elements will be present, but the links between them will be something that the six-to-nine-year-old must work out. Eventually, it may be possible to simply present the learning materials and tell the children to see what they can make of it for themselves. Once they have mastered the basics, they may wish to propose further projects for investigation.

5
Testing and Analyzing
the Big Picture

Developmental and Religious Characteristics
of the Nine-to-Twelve-Year-Old Child

The nine-to-twelve-year-old child works within, essentially, the same plane of development as the six-to-nine-year-old, although there are some significant refinements of these characteristics that can be expected.

REFINEMENTS OF EXISTING CAPACITIES

Imagination. The most obvious of these refinements can be found in the tempering of the imagination. This still remains present, but it is less extravagant in its application. The links that it makes among existing items of data become more and more constrained by the child's actual experience of reality, and this begins to take on its adult form. The nine-to-twelve-year-old is far less likely to seek solutions in "magical" possibilities and begins to distinguish more clearly between facts and fantasy. While they continue to enjoy creative and fanciful possibilities, they are more likely to seek "scientific" explanations that explain their actual experiences. Nine-to-twelve-year-olds remain capable of looking "outside the square" in their search for solutions, and can readily imagine things that have not been set before them, but this capacity is waning. If their imaginative and artistic endeavors have not been encouraged in the earlier period, it will be fading quickly during this stage.

Big Picture and the Concept of Time. One of the significant developments of the six-to-nine-year-old stage is a basic orientation to time as a way of providing a "big picture" framework for their thoughts. In contrast with the fading of the imaginative sense, this capacity for understanding the abstract notion of time strengthens considerably. They develop a great interest in and ability to explore time—especially history as basic chronology of events. Not only will they seek more details by way of historical

59

events, but they will also enjoy focusing on particular aspects, events, or historical figures within these events and will continue to investigate them until they are satisfied.

Repetition. As with six-to-nine-year-olds, the nine-to-twelve-year-olds continue to need repetition, but they are even less content about repeating things in the same way. They need more than just different approaches to the same content; they need to understand why they are being asked to look at this again, and they need to have greater challenges associated with it. This can be achieved partly by offering greater responsibility for the organization of their time and the sequencing of their activities, coupled with requirements for the number of times they must focus on the same material.

Social Dimension. The nine-to-twelve-year-old child continues to be focused on the social dimension of relationships, but this narrows down to a smaller number of very close friends rather than a very large "herd-like" structure. This allows them to focus even more deeply on the lessons that must be learned about social relationships and it carries with it the attendant difficulties that must be faced. There is a growing self-consciousness and a concern about what their peers think of them. More than ever before, they begin to care about what their peers think about them, and they do not want to stand out for any reason. They are beginning to anticipate the primary focus of their next level of development when the peer group becomes central to their thinking.

Moral Development. The nine-to-twelve-year-old child still tends to make the world "safe" by means of mental rules, but these children begin to see more of the nuances that must be taken into account. Their earlier focus on rigid and exact standards of fairness and equal treatment gives way to a concern for social justice. They have begun to make the transition from a preoccupation with their own safety and fair treatment to a more altruistic concern for others as well.

Accounting for the Nine-to-Twelve-Year-Old Refinements in Religious Education Classes. Cavalletti believed after long observation that there were three mysteries that pre-occupy the nine-to-twelve-year-old child: life and death; relationships; and time. The mystery of life and death is one that every human being must come to grips with, but children of this age become capable of grasping its full impact and understanding its place. A Christian understanding of this mystery is capable of giving hope and purpose to their whole lives; it should not be passed over or ignored. If it becomes particularly personal through the death of someone who has been close to them, this should be dealt with quite specifically. There are now many excellent materials for dealing with the stages of grief and children should have their grief acknowledged in healthy ways such as these. They should also be encouraged to pray for the repose of their souls. Some understanding of the theology of the Last Things, the Sacrament of the Anointing of the Sick, and the consoling doctrine of Purgatory find their most appropriate point of introduction within this age group. Cavalletti has assembled some particularly fruitful materials for helping children of this age to ponder these mysteries. One is called *The Holy Bible and the Parousia*. On one set of cards, there is a brief phrase describing attributes that the Bible and Catholic Tradition apply to our ultimate eternal happiness in Heaven. The other set of cards, which need to be matched with these, consists of scriptural verses that describe these attributes.

CHARACTERISTICS: RELATIONSHIPS

Relationships will always be of critical concern to children of this age group, and this concern will intensify as the child approaches the stage of adolescence, where it will become the primary focus. More and more, these children will need to be with their peers to continue to discover who they are. They will need increasing levels of independence which should reflect the Church's key principle of social teaching: subsidiarity. From this point, difficult though it may be, parents and teachers need to begin actively promoting independence. In a nutshell, the principle of subsidiarity in relation to these children means that adults should not do things for them that they should be capable of doing for themselves. This includes allowing them to make their own decisions on simple matters where they no longer need direct adult guidance. Unless this begins as a slow process at this time, adult caregivers (parents and teachers) are likely to miss the natural window of development and the children will ultimately need to insist on their legitimate freedom during a needlessly turbulent and angry adolescence. Teachers must learn to stand back even more and make sure that the children are not given quick answers, but must work towards finding these for themselves.

SEXUALITY

Another vital aspect of relationships at this time is concerned with sexuality education. There can be no doubt that the child's parents are best placed to take on this responsibility.[1] One of the most effective ways of meeting the child's needs at this age is for parents to make a regular time — as little as half an hour a week — with each child individually. If the child can rely on their parent's undivided attention, they will be able to learn many of the necessary relationship skills which will fit them for adulthood. The Pontifical Council for the Family's document "The Truth and Meaning of Human Sexuality" advises that it is the father who is best equipped to build this relationship with boys, and the mother with girls.

THE MYSTERY OF TIME

The mystery of time is the nine-to-twelve-year-old child's window on eternity. Their simple grasp in concrete objects and their attempts to link these things together have already been part of their development and this has prepared them for the notion of mystery. They will normally have a willingness to accept that there are sometimes aspects of reality beyond their present grasp. What they already have is real, but there will always be more truth, more beauty and more goodness to ponder in the infinite riches of the Trinity. They will be ready to discover that the God who called them into life is also the God of history, who has what the *Catechism of the Catholic Church* calls "a plan of loving goodness."[2] Cavalletti describes two ways in which this developing capacity of the nine-to-twelve-year-old can be developed.

Salvation History: The Plan of God. The first is a study of the Plan of God, both as a big picture and in detail. They are meant to discover the cosmic unity which is found not just in the world of the present, but goes back to the beginning of time and leads to the Parousia: the final fulfilment of the Kingdom of God. Biblical history reveals three key moments in time: Creation; Redemption; and Parousia. The Creation is the marker for the beginning of history; Redemption, the saving death and resurrection of Christ, indicates the center point of history; the Parousia points to the fulfilment of history. This framework allows the children to structure their thoughts and sequence the events and personalities involved in the history of Salvation. This is the "big picture" which allows a proper sequencing of events: before, during, and after each one of these. As the children become more competent, more markers will be able to appear

---

1 The parent training resource "As I Have Loved You" is one of many ways in which parents can be given the confidence not only to undertake this task but to enjoy it as well.
2 CCC, § 50–51.

on the time line, each of them standing in relation to all of the others. Cavalletti also insisted on a particular phrase to emphasize the child's role: "the blank page." This stands for the history that has not yet been written, because that is what we are called to do: contribute to God's ongoing "plan of loving goodness." Cavalletti does not distinguish on her timelines any separation of sacred and secular history. God is part of all history, whether people acknowledge it or not. If we are attentive, we will find God's action worked out in every age; we will be able to discover what St. Augustine called "history's golden thread."

Biblical Typology. The second study Cavalletti recommended for this age group in relation to the mystery of time is the study of typology. Typology is a traditional Catholic way of reading the Bible. It comes from the Greek word, "typos," the hollowed out imprint of a mold. When applied to the Bible, we begin from a belief that God already knows the whole of history from beginning to end. Consequently, when the events of the Old Testament are taking place, God already knows their significance and places into the writing of the Bible some events that give a faint indication of what is to come. The people living at this time would not be able to recognize what the events and signs were pointing to in the future; they could only be read once the fulfilment had taken place. St. Ambrose described this very well by saying that God's revelation of his plan took place in three stages: first the *shadow*, then the *image*, and finally the *reality*. For example, at the time of the Exodus of the Jews from Egypt, Moses received the instruction to sacrifice the Passover lamb and sprinkle its blood on the doorposts so that the angel of death would pass over their houses. Although the people could not have understood the way this event would be interpreted in the future, from the perspective of our time, it is quite a simple matter to see in it a foreshadowing of the sacrifice of Jesus and of the subsequent tradition of the Catholic Liturgy, which addresses Christ as the "lamb of God who takes away the sins of the world." The Bible abounds in these typological images, but Cavalletti specifies five key studies to help children of this age with their understanding of the scope of salvation history. They are: Creation, The Origin of Sin and the Fall; Noah and the Flood; The Story of Abraham; and Moses and the Exodus.

These studies also serve as a stimulus for the children to begin reading the Bible for themselves. Experience has demonstrated again and again that this kind of activity nourishes their relationship with Christ on the level of the heart; it allows them to get to know their God better and piques their curiosity to undertake more serious study about what they discover. To use the words of St. Jerome: "ignorance of Scripture is ignorance of Christ." Many teachers have reported that when children are offered the opportunity of reading the Bible for themselves, it frequently becomes the activity they enjoy the most, and will occupy their attention for lengthy periods of time. Sofia Cavalletti, as she spent time observing children, became ever more convinced that the Scriptures had a mysterious power to touch their hearts, and she lamented that the opportunity was offered to them so infrequently. They would either be given paraphrases of the Biblical text (because it was deemed to be too difficult for them) or they were offered lengthy studies about how to approach the scriptures, without spending a great deal of time actually reading them. Cavalletti re-discovered the reality that the Holy Spirit is entirely capable of drawing young children to Christ through the inspired Word. There is a relevant caveat that must be offered here. Once children have begun to read the scriptures and are given the opportunity to do so on a regular basis, there is also a need to begin offering them the skills they need to understand it in a more scholarly way, though suited to their age and stage of development. Nevertheless, nothing can replace the reading of the actual text.

Prudent Integration of Technology. Towards the end of her life, Cavalletti became aware of what she described as cultural threats to the religious development of nine-to-twelve-year-old children. While not rejecting technology as a useful tool, she was also firm in describing it as a bad master. Now more than ever before, children are offered opportunities of avoiding genuine concrete engagement with the real world — the world for which they were created, the world for which their senses were designed — and replacing this with a virtual and unreal world artificially created for their entertainment. If pursued to excess, this will actually slow down their development, and prevent them from facing the real challenges of life: the challenges of relationships, of facing up to the necessary monotony of repeated effort, and the like. The focus on their own entertainment and the insistence that they should never have to feel bored keeps children in a state of immaturity and selfishness. Only genuine acts of self-giving and self-sacrifice can make them truly happy as human beings, and these necessary lessons are being delayed by the unhealthy focus on self-gratification.

The real religious work of the nine-to-twelve-year-old child is to find their place in the real world by pondering the theological implications of time and history; and they must discover this for themselves as far as possible. To do so, they need to work in collaboration with their peers and with adults on appropriately demanding tasks. In a similar way, the use of excessive "hand-outs" in a classroom will not be helpful. This will be especially so if these are filled with pre-digested information: answers to questions which the children ought to find for themselves. This gives completely the wrong message; it seems to indicate that they are not competent to work their own way towards the answers for themselves and need someone else to do it for them. On the contrary, if nine-to-twelve-year-old children are not challenged intellectually, morally and emotionally, they will be ill-equipped to deal with the profound human challenges they must face in their coming adolescence.

6

Personalizing and Reconstructing

The Developmental and Religious Characteristics of the Adolescent

Most of Montessori's key ideas in this field can be found in her book *From Childhood to Adolescence*.[1] As with other age groups, adolescence constitutes a *sensitive period* for specific types of learning and development. She believed that adolescence is an age of great social development, an age of critical thinking and re-evaluation, and a period of self-concern and self-assessment. It is a transition from childhood to adulthood with the corresponding physical, mental, and sexual maturation. Above all, adolescence is like an odyssey—an arduous yet exciting adventure—where the adolescent tries to find his or her place in the world.

There are five key themes running through adolescence and although it may be necessary to consider them separately, they cannot ever be compartmentalized. Each one of them is linked, sometimes in unexpected ways. The mixture is never tidy or predictable and is always unique to the individual. There is no replacement for actually getting to know an individual in a direct, one-to-one relationship.

ADOLESCENCE IS A SOCIAL AGE

The need for social relationships with peers begins to be noticeable at around the age of six, but in the adolescent this is more than an important aspect of their development. Rather, it is the primary focus and, indeed, the lens through which almost everything else is filtered. Adolescents are overwhelmingly influenced by what their peers say and think. To discover who they are in themselves, they need friends or at least close companions so that they can discern the similarities and differences in their developing personalities. This is a time when friendship is often at its most intense, and it is to their friends that adolescents turn to share their secrets, their

---

1 See Maria Montessori, *From Childhood to Adolescence: Including "Erdkinder" and the Functions of the University* (New York: Schocken, 1987).

problems and their aspirations for the future. To be without a friend is extremely damaging; the adolescent "loner" is something that should sound warning bells to those who look after their needs.

It is at this time of their lives that healthy human development causes adolescents to begin looking beyond their own families and to build their own sense of community. This is an essential task of this age: to learn how to live and work with others, those they like and those they dislike. They also need to begin relating to adults.

Strategies for Meeting the Adolescent Need for Social Relationship. Given the need to see themselves in relation to others, it is helpful to have adolescents engage in shared projects in which contrasting skills are necessary and everyone in the group is able to contribute in a constructive way. It will be particularly helpful if such projects are directed at producing something tangible or doing a recognizable service for others. It is more useful if these activities or products can be valued for what they are and not "assessed" competitively for credit. If such a focus on assessment is absolutely necessary, care should be taken to ensure that each student's individual contribution can be credited separately. Otherwise, those who are more competent will feel pressured to "carry the load" for those not as competent. This has the potential for causing resentment and can actually result in undermining the sense of community that is supposed to be the goal.

If the focus is on social relationships, there will be a need for some basic input on the different levels of friendship that can be met in normal human relationships. At least three levels need to be made familiar to them so that they can discern what is happening in their groups. The Aristotelian divisions into utility friendship, pleasure friendship, and virtue friendship can serve as an illustration of the basic outline that needs to be covered.

Utility Friendship. Someone is your friend because they want something from you. They will offer just sufficient input for them to get what they want from you. A utility friendship may involve two or more people, but the focus is selfish. One person wants something from the other, and if this is not forthcoming, the friendship will end. It takes many forms, depending on what the initiator wants. Most business promotions are based on this kind of perceived friendship: "True Bargain Industries" wants you to have this special gift of a carry bag because we care about our customers! Utility friendship can also be quite manipulative and difficult for adolescents to deal with as in this scenario: "If you really loved me, you would sleep with me."

Pleasure Friendship. In utility friendships, there is a focus on the initiator getting what they want. In a pleasure friendship, another level is reached. In this case, there is mutual benefit to being friends. Both enjoy the same thing — football, music, ballet, or something else. Even though the benefits are mutual, the pleasure friendship is still essentially selfish. If the mutual enjoyment of something passes, then the friendship ends. It was never about the other person; it was only about an individual's own enjoyment.

Virtue Friendship. It is only at this level that friendship crosses a bridge, so to speak. The virtue friend is the one whose purpose is to do good things for the other person, irrespective of whether there is a return. The hallmark of virtue friendship is that the other person in the relationship can be "annoying" and yet the friendship remains. A virtue friendship will stand the test of time because it is no longer selfish, and it is only this kind of friendship that can serve as the basis of a happy, sacramental marriage.

Adolescents need to be able to perceive their various friendships for what they are or they will find themselves deeply disappointed — and even suicidally depressed — if they fail to "read" what is happening in their friendships. The model of the true friend is Christ himself: the one who calls out the best in us, forgives us, and is always there for us. This model of relationship is the essence of Catholic Christianity and the only one in which adolescents can comfortably work. It is possible to proceed from sound, loving relationships to the next level of idealistic giving of the self to worthy causes and high principles that have always been characteristic of this age group. However, if the demands are made without presenting them as the expression of a deeply felt loving relationship with God, it has little chance of success.

In supporting adolescents in their search for genuine community, teachers and parents need to be careful that they are not seen to be imposing their own detailed agenda. Adolescents need to be given serious input about matters that concern them and they need to find their own friends. Schools have become quite good at making it possible for students of this age to do this. A wide variety of activities, chess clubs, drama societies, sporting teams, and the like have become a normal part of school experience. These serve the purpose of allowing the adolescent to mix in circles that have broadly the same interests and therefore find potential friends. It also allows them to work together on projects in which they are likely to share the same interests. It may seem to some adults that this approach shifts the focus away from serious study, but it must be remembered that an unhappy student is unlikely to do well at school. Adolescents need to find their own identity, and they will tend to react against anything that is imposed on them; they are human, and one of the most fundamental characteristics of the human person is the desire for freedom to make decisions of their own.

ADOLESCENCE IS A TIME FOR CRITICAL THINKING

The Christian tradition is almost unanimous in its affirmation concerning a key human characteristic: freedom of the will. Ultimately, we are rational creatures who are meant to think our own thoughts and make our own decisions. Young children need a long apprenticeship before they become capable of exercising this freedom in appropriate ways; they need the opportunity to integrate the necessary component faculties and clear perceptions. They must be shown, for example, how to eat and drink in a healthy way, to respect the rights of others and of the society in which they live, to give due consideration to spiritual and human values which make them happy. Parents and others who care for the needs of children need to understand that this guidance must be progressively wound back as the child matures. During adolescence, this "stepping back" from imposed guidance gathers pace until, at the age of eighteen in most Western countries, parental legal authority ceases altogether, and the influence takes the form of advice and persuasion. This is a difficult time for those who have exercised a caring role. Even the force of habit makes it difficult to allow children to begin making some of their own decisions, but, at all times during their development, children need to be prepared for the time when they are completely independent. In this regard, the principle of subsidiarity has already been referred to as foundational and indispensable.

In the stage that precedes adolescence, children have a powerful mind turned towards discovering the secrets of the universe and the world in which they live. Adolescents also have powerful minds, but they are usually more focused on relationships — on *who they are* and their place in the world rather than the world itself. For this reason, adolescents must come to their own conclusions about the world. Their capacity for imagination diminishes — they are no longer so concerned with creating mental constructs for explaining the world to themselves. Their purpose is "de-construction" — critical evaluation of the explanations they have received and of those they have made themselves. One of the most salient characteristics of adolescents is this critical faculty. They apply it to the world in general, to each other, to adults — but mostly, they are critical of themselves, although this tends to be disguised by external bravado and the appearance of self-confidence. They can appear quite negative and are inclined to take a contrary position when those who have hitherto guided them (parents or teachers) make any kind of assertion. This must be handled sensitively, and not treated as a personal attack. It is normal; it is to be expected from this age group, and it serves a vital function in their development. If parents or teachers attempt to "impose" their worldview, even if it is superior and full of well-grounded arguments, it is still entirely possible that it will be rejected. It is also helpful to keep in mind that this criticism is frequently associated with emotions: how they are feeling today. It can be quite unpredictable and inconsistent. Perhaps the best advice for adults is to "fall back" into a respectful silence and to acknowledge that the adolescent is making interesting points that should be considered.

Whatever conclusions adolescents eventually come to, they must arrive at these by themselves and any insistence that they must adopt a particular conclusion will generally only paint them into a corner from which they will stubbornly refuse to move. This is the time for them to object, to analyze, and to argue; adolescents see the persuasiveness of opposing reasons and want the opportunity to weigh these for themselves. It does not mean that they are ultimately going to turn against all that they have learned; they just want to make sure that things have been subjected to proper scrutiny. Adolescents engaging in this kind of critical thinking are actually subjecting themselves to challenges. They are "pushing themselves" in order to find their own authentic personal limits. In this process, they will learn more about themselves. Critical thinking is their way of posing intellectual challenges — to themselves as well as to others.

Strategies for Meeting the Adolescent Need for Critical Evaluation. There is a significant danger to adolescent faith if the need to acknowledge their critical thinking stage is not handled well. Two extremes need to be avoided: at one end, allowing everything about the gift of faith to be reduced to mere personal preference, capable of being created in one's own image; at the other extreme, insisting that there is no room for any process of investigation whatsoever.

The Relationship of Faith and Reason. The adolescent's critical thinking adventure is rational, but it is neither extreme nor foolish. Not everything in the universe is subject to critical re-appraisal. For example, adolescents do not normally want to change the names of the color spectrum:

black remains black, white is white, and blue is blue. They spend no time re-evaluating this. Furthermore, they are quite willing to accept that fire burns, water is wet, and that they need air to breathe. The basic data of existence remain stable for them and it is simply absurd to subject these things to critical thinking. Blessed John Henry Newman, in his celebrated work *An Essay in Aid of a Grammar of Assent*, insisted there are some things that we simply have to accept on faith if we are not to make our existence impossible and invite madness. To paraphrase the words of Newman: I live in Great Britain, which is an island, and my sovereign is Queen Victoria; of these things I am certain. Yet, I have never sailed all the way around Great Britain to prove it is an island, and I have never seen Queen Victoria in person. There are also some basic data of revealed faith that must simply be "received" as the truth. If they have been baptized, adolescents will have received the virtue of faith which enables them to accept these things at a spiritual level that is beyond intellectual rationality. This needs to be explained to them, while at the same time giving them opportunities for exploring religious truths and what these might mean for them. In his Apostolic Exhortation, *Evangelii Gaudium,* Pope Francis made it quite clear that critical thinking is a necessary part of education, but it is not to be applied to the data of faith itself. While it is entirely legitimate for adolescents to ask how the Christian life might be lived better, they cannot, from the perspective of Christianity, ask whether or not the revealed doctrines of faith are true or not, which would be similar to asking whether the color green is really green and might not be red.

Relating Content to Critical Thinking. In terms of content, it is difficult to get the best out of adolescents by tying them down to a specific content pursued in terms of a course in religious education. Younger children are able to rise to advanced and rigorous understanding of appropriate content so long as it proceeded in a natural order of body, heart, and mind. It is the same for adolescents. The critical thinking faculty can be harnessed very effectively if the starting point is some concrete experience: of relationships (including the relationship with Christ through prayer and the sacraments), of human dignity and what it means to *be* human, of social justice and moral behavior, of significant issues which have captured their imagination and the like. These starting points create the context for learning about relevant content. As much effort needs to go into thinking about how these contexts might be created as into the course content itself.

Care must be taken to ensure that it is the adolescent who is doing the thinking when engaged in intellectual content. Pre-digested notes giving the answers may be effective in helping the students to pass their examinations, but such an approach betrays the very nature of the educational enterprise: instead of helping students to form their own independent stance through a legitimate process of critical thinking, it substitutes it for the short-term goal of attaining a passing grade. Relevant articles or chapters written in simple, direct language and coming from some respected external authority will give the adolescent a sense of achievement and intellectual freedom. They can then make decisions based on their own reading rather than the imposed directions of the teacher or parent. This is always a risk: freedom is like that. God's plan for humanity means that they must ultimately come to him because they have been given the *freedom* to love Him sincerely and without coercion.

The Value of Apologetics. Apologetics is the branch of theology which offers explanations for the difficulties raised in relation to a particular doctrine or practice. Adolescents often pose complex questions from the point of view of a "devil's advocate," trying to get at the truth by raising difficulties. For this reason, apologetics can be very useful for adolescents under certain conditions. In particular, such study should follow the interests of the students. For this age group, apologetics should not normally be pursued as a systematic study; adolescents are intolerant of being forced to listen to answers to questions that they have not asked. Nor would it be wise for the answers to be mediated via the teacher or parent. Adolescents will respond better if they are given access to the material for themselves. The arrival of the internet has made apologetics much easier, since it is now possible to have access to a wide variety of excellent written material as well as professionally produced online videos which can respond to difficult questions.

The Value of Committed Witnesses. As already noted, critical thinking in an adolescent is not a purely rational exercise; it is usually connected with how they are feeling. The affective dimension should not be excluded from the religious education of an adolescent. For every human being, the heart is as important as the mind. To this end, critical thinking in the religious education program should include access to inspiring witnesses. Adolescent decisions are almost never made solely on the basis of rational argument; they need to be convinced by seeing it lived out in practice. Visiting speakers whose life and work is an inspiration for others have a special importance at this stage of development. In addition, inspirational movies and biographies of the saints can have a very powerful impact on them.

The Relationship of Adolescent to Teacher. The adolescent values a close relationship with respected adults, but not one that is imposed. Nothing will shut down such a relationship faster than the adult who tries too hard to be like the students. The closeness of any such relationship needs to be in the hands of the adolescent. Teachers and adults who work with them need to begin by keeping a respectful distance and act in a warm and friendly manner when approached. A great deal of effort needs to be made on the part of the adult to affirm the good things that they see in the adolescent; but these must be real things and sincerely expressed, or this will be perceived as manipulative. In trying to work through some issues brought on by their critical nature, adolescents may seek a mentor relationship with particular teachers or other adults whom they respect and whose opinions they value. If an adolescent seeks out a kind of mentoring relationship with a chosen adult, this is a privilege, but it is one that calls for prudent reserve — friendliness side by side with a little bit of distance. Under no circumstances would it be acceptable for a teacher to be alone with a student in a completely private place. One-to-one meetings can take place, and sometimes this is necessary, but such meetings should not be "out of sight": a glass panel in the door or some other such strategy will be necessary.

ADOLESCENTS MUST CONFRONT THE DILEMMAS OF LIFE

To the extent that it is possible, children are protected from the more difficult dilemmas of human existence. They are kept in relatively safe environments and are only slowly introduced to the responsibilities they will be expected to bear as adults. In adolescence, the tempo changes and they must begin to face the dilemmas and contradictions of life. Not everything is fair, not every relationship is benign, pain and suffering will come to everyone, and yet, from these difficulties, the mature human being is expected to emerge with a positive attitude, believing, despite all of these contradictions, that life is beautiful. Adults who have made this journey and have made their own peace with the world can forget how difficult this time is as well as the degree to which anxiety and insecurity can cloud one's vision. Many apparently prosaic questions can be very important. Will I pass my test? Will I be selected in the sports team? All of these appear to have the same urgency as the genuinely important issues. What am I meant to be doing in this world? Will I ever find someone whom I can share my life in marriage? How can I deal with my failings, faults, weaknesses and sins? To use Montessori's words, this is an intensely human age. It is a time when all of the human questions must be faced seriously for the first time. For this reason, the adolescent can seem completely self-absorbed. But this must be so. The task of this age is for children to find their place in the world, and this can only be done by viewing everything in terms of how it affects them personally. The onset of puberty brings with it a heightened sense of self-awareness and brings with it the added challenge of properly integrating their sexuality into a mature and healthy personality.

Montessori drew attention to *The Canterbury Tales* as a good metaphor for adolescence. The travelers are on a journey together, and as they make their way along the road, they share their stories. In doing this, they learn about others, but the sharing together with their peers actually helps them to understand themselves by way of contrast and similarities. They discover at the same time the essence of their shared humanity and the uniqueness of the individual characteristics that make up their personalities. The description of adolescence as an odyssey or a pilgrimage during which there is a sharing of very human stories has much to recommend it. This is the time when they must accept their weaknesses along with their strengths, and in this sharing lies the seed that will eventually take them out of themselves again as they develop empathy and understanding of their companions. Not only will they begin to see their own potential and their limitations, but they will start to recognize and celebrate the same characteristics in others. And, finally, they must lay to rest the unrealistic expectations they have had as children. They may never become the world's greatest sports star or a famous musician, perhaps they will never be anything so great as an astronaut or a train driver; but they do have a place in the world, and they must find what it is. Compromises will have to be made along with decisions about what they must let go and what they must hold onto with all of the strength and determination they can muster.

Strategies for Supporting Adolescents through the Dilemmas of Life. Until adolescence arrives, teachers and parents tend to keep a close watch over the "decisions" made by those in whom they have an interest. In general, children are not allowed to make decisions that could make a serious difference to their circumstances. Adolescence is a time for this to begin changing, and the transition can be quite difficult for the parents and other adults who have had responsibility for an extended period. If children are to grow up, however, it is essential that they begin to take genuine responsibility for their choices. They need to have the freedom to plan some of their own activities and even to make mistakes. This freedom is not absolute. Some degree of vigilance from parents and teachers is justified, but the process must begin. The adolescent must begin to exercise some degree of the freedom of will that is the hallmark of being human, but must also experience the accountability required of adults to ensure reasonable safety. There can be no genuine freedom without responsibilities.

Sharing Their Stories with Each Other. Adolescents need opportunities to share their stories with others with whom they feel comfortable, usually their peers. This is one of the ways in which they can begin working out who they are. It is unwise to force this kind of activity. Often, this kind of sharing arises spontaneously while they are hiking or involved on a long walk or pilgrimage. It can be useful to offer the opportunity on a school camp or retreat, but only if they feel comfortable in doing this and are not pressured to "share" afterwards. Their personal dignity must be respected and the mystery of the human person should never be violated by any kind of demand that one should reveal oneself prematurely. The unfolding of a relationship requires a slow peeling back of the layers to reveal who they are at deeper and deeper levels to chosen friends. Sometimes, they will choose to share their stories with trusted adults, but this is something that must be entirely up to them. It is in this area that a priest who acts as the school chaplain, one who is connected with a Catholic school but not part of its authority structure, can be particularly helpful by offering spiritual direction.

Other Modes of Discovery. There are two further modes of discovery about the world and themselves that can be useful for the adolescent. Once they become aware of the moral dilemmas they face in the course of life, it will be useful to offer them a background in the principles of moral decision-making. Much of contemporary culture is infused with relativist and utilitarian views, and adolescence is the best moment to illustrate the weaknesses of these positions. Ultimately, these views can be shown to denigrate the value of the person, and a human being at this stage of development is disposed to perceive the value of every human person individually. For example, in the *Star Trek* movie series, the "logical" character, Spock, is fond of reciting the utilitarian moral principle: "The needs of the many outweigh the needs of the few." Yet in the film in which Spock himself is at risk ("The Search for Spock"), his friends completely depart from this approach and risk all to save him, at great cost. This romantic quest to save a friend is much closer to what human beings know to be true: morality flows from a relationship with God; it can never be just a simple articulation of detached principles. Because this can be articulated in terms of a personal story, such authentic moral principles are likely to be very appealing to adolescents.

Another highly suitable means of reaching the adolescent on this level is literature, and for the same reason. Good literature is capable of creating authentic human characters who must face the dilemmas of life that the adolescent must confront. For this reason, care must be taken to present them with what is both challenging and inspiring. The offering of "dark themes" at this point of their development is counter-productive. What adolescents find most appealing are stories that illustrate the capacity of human beings to triumph over danger and adversity. Literature must offer them what is beautiful and hopeful; themes of hopelessness, despair, and ugliness will not be helpful to their formation as human beings.

ADOLESCENTS NEED TO DEVELOP A PERSONAL VISION FOR THEIR LIVES

It will be evident from what has already been written that earlier stages of development are concerned with allowing the human person to perceive the world as it is. Once that task is completed, it is time for the adolescent to come to terms with his or her place in the world. At some time during this stage of development, normal human beings will need to give some thought to a personal vision which will serve to guide and sustain them through their lives. An integrated vision which incorporates a supernatural perspective can be encouraged at this point. While it is not helpful to the adolescent for adults to offer to do this task for them (they must do it for themselves), it can be very encouraging to provide them with models from others who have undertaken it. The following example written by Blessed John Henry Newman in 1848 has been found to appeal strongly to this age group:

> God has created me to do Him some definite service;
> He has committed some work to me
>   which He has not committed to another.
> I have my mission — I never may know it in this life,
>   but I shall be told it in the next.

Somehow I am necessary for His purposes....
   I have a part in this great work;
I am a link in a chain, a bond of connection
   between persons.
He has not created me for naught. I shall do good,
   I shall do His work;
I shall be an angel of peace, a preacher of truth
   in my own place, while not intending it,
   if I do but keep His commandments
   and serve Him in my calling.

   Therefore I will trust Him.
   Whatever, wherever I am,
   I can never be thrown away.
If I am in sickness, my sickness may serve Him;
In perplexity, my perplexity may serve Him;
If I am in sorrow, my sorrow may serve Him.
My sickness, or perplexity, or sorrow may be
   necessary causes of some great end,
   which is quite beyond us.
He does nothing in vain; He may prolong my life,
   He may shorten it;
   He knows what He is about.
   He may take away my friends,
   He may throw me among strangers,
   He may make me feel desolate,
   make my spirits sink, hide the future from me —
   still He knows what He is about....
Let me be Thy blind instrument. I ask not to see —
   I ask not to know — I ask simply to be used.[2]

ADOLESCENCE IS AN AGE OF BOUNDLESS ENERGY

The healthy adolescent can be described as having enormous physical energy. They are constantly moving, acting, playing, working, talking, planning, and the like. This energy can be harnessed for good or can do a great deal of damage if it is not. Maria Montessori held that this energy

---

2 From "Hope in God — Creator."

is there for a purpose: to sustain a spirit of adventure. She claimed that every adolescent is a young Odysseus, each on a personal journey; adventure brings challenge and the purpose of this challenge is self-discovery.

Strategies for Channeling the Boundless Energy of Adolescents. If they are to discover *who* they are and *what* they can do, adolescents need to be given challenging and ennobling work and they must be "admired" by adults for what they have achieved. Many Catholic high schools have begun to understand the importance of this need and have accordingly made available opportunities for their students to serve in disadvantaged missions in needy countries or places closer to home. This works best when the adolescents are asked to do things with their hands — to build and create, for example, perhaps under the supervision of experienced artisans. This gives an intense feeling of satisfaction and achievement; it covers all of the necessary ground. They have done something they consider useful to others; they leave behind a concrete reality that they have created; they receive the gratitude and admiration of the people they have helped.

Another example of the way in which this need can be met is World Youth Day. Pope John Paul II seemed to deeply understand the needs of young people in putting this together. Participants are required to go on a challenging journey: not with their parents, but with their friends. They must gather beforehand to do some service or activity in a nearby diocese. Camaraderie with their peers is built up around their Catholic identity, and in general, they are admired in the places they go for their youthful enthusiasm and good-natured humor. Moreover, something extraordinary always seems to accompany these events wherever they go; namely, something seems to go seriously wrong with the planning so that the event is far more challenging than was expected. For example, in Rome 2000 temperatures exceeded forty degrees centigrade as the pilgrims were walking to the venue. In Toronto 2002 a thunder storm broke over the pilgrims who were camped out overnight without shelter. In Cologne 2005 the unthinkable happened and German efficiency failed: the public transport system that was designed to bring pilgrims back from the event shut down and they needed to walk all the way back after midnight. One might expect that such problems might dampen the spirits of the young people involved — yet the opposite is the case! Almost invariably, these difficulties are the very aspects of their journey that the pilgrims remember with the greatest affection: they were on a difficult journey with friends and companions, pushing their limits, and not finding themselves wanting. This is exactly what adolescents need but are generally protected from by well-meaning adults. In sharing this insight in a number of secondary schools, without exception, teachers of this age group have utterly concurred with this insight, and usually have examples of their own to share.

Much of the failure experienced in contemporary society in dealing with adolescence can be traced back to a failure to challenge them in meaningful ways and to give them a real part to play in society. This does not need to be so.

7

Faith and Reason in Religious Education

The Contemporary Problem of Religious Education in Catholic Schools[1]

Human beings must address some serious dilemmas brought about by their anthropological constitution as both spiritual and physical beings. The relationship between the natural and the supernatural is "simple" in its reality yet complex when we must explain it. The relationship between faith and reason, in particular, is something we must grasp and fully understand if we are not to do violence to either. In 1847, the American Protestant theologian Horace Bushnell published his classic work, *Christian Nurture*, wherein he alluded with good-natured envy to the success of the catechetical work of the Catholic Church.[2] Indeed, Catholic educational practices have had a long history of effectiveness. At the outset of the twenty-first century, however, it seems that Catholic schools in the western world are substantially failing in their mission to hand on the faith to a new generation. In Australia, research has chronicled this problem for over twenty years. A 2006 investigation into the attitudes of *Generation Y* found that less than 3% of recent graduates from Catholic schools participated regularly in the Sunday Eucharist while relativism was identified as their predominant philosophy:

> ✓ Generation Y are what their parents and Australian culture have made them. They have taken strongly to two "late modern" principles: that an individual's views and preferences, provided they harm no-one else, should not be questioned or constrained, and

---

1 Much of the content of this chapter appeared first in Gerard O'Shea, "Restoring the Foundations of Faith and Reason in Religious Education," *Studia Elckie* 14 (2012): 41–56.

2 See Horace Bushnell, *Christian Nurture* (New Haven: Yale University Press, 1847), 25.

that spiritual/religious beliefs and practices are purely personal
lifestyle choices — in no way necessary.[3] ⌉

In 2010 Pope Benedict XVI acknowledged this problem to journalist Peter
Seewald who asked him how it was possible that, despite spending years in
Catholic schools, students in the Western world seem to end up knowing
more about Buddhism than their own faith. The Pope replied: "That is a
question I also ask myself. Every child in Germany has nine to thirteen
years of religion in school. Why, in spite of that, so very little sticks, if I
may put it like that, is incomprehensible."[4]

This chapter will explore the relationship between faith and reason in
terms of its impact on the effectiveness of religious education in Catholic
schools and suggest possible solutions by applying the insights of John
Henry Newman. It will outline some current challenges for religious
education, including the anti-realist educational philosophy of Radical
Constructivism. It will then take up the request of Benedict XVI to explore
relevant aspects of the work of John Henry Newman with a particular
focus on his clarification of the relationship between religious faith and
theology. Finally, it will apply some of Newman's insights directly to the
field of religious education and argue for the importance of certitude in
this context.

SOME CURRENT CHALLENGES FOR RELIGIOUS EDUCATION

Radical Constructivism: A Relativist Theory of Knowledge. Since the mid-
1980s, Constructivism has held an unassailable place in the educational
establishment of the western world. A definition of Constructivism in its
radical form will typically contrast the active role of learners in constructing
knowledge for themselves with a so-called passive alternative, whereby
truth is held to exist independently and is presented to the learner and
confirmed by the authority of some external source. In the words of its chief
theorist, Ernst von Glasersfeld: "knowledge is the result of an individual
subject's constructive activity, not a commodity that somehow resides outside the knower and can be conveyed or instilled by diligent perception or

---

3 P. Hughes, M. Mason, A. Singleton, and R. Webber, *The Spirit of Generation Y.* 2006.
http://library.bsl.org.au/jspui/bitstream/1/764/1/Spirit_of_Gen_Y_Summary_Report_2006.pdf
4 Benedict XVI, *Light of the World: The Pope, the Church, and the Signs of the Times: A
Conversation with Peter Seewald.* Trans. Michael J. Miller and Adrian J. Walker (San Francisco:
Ignatius Press, 2010), 140.

linguistic communication."[5] Essentially, this is the position of the German Enlightenment philosopher, Immanuel Kant: human knowledge cannot be identified with external reality, but refers only to our own experience. Other philosophers, including Richard Rorty, go further and insist that truth does not exist and our perceptions must be continually re-negotiated in a social context. In his own words: "we understand knowledge when we understand the social justification of belief, and thus have no need to view it as accuracy of representation."[6] These ideas constitute a challenge for religious education, as they directly undermine the Catholic Church's claim that human beings live in an intelligible universe created by God.

Nevertheless, Constructivism is a term with many meanings. Its claims are so broad that there are some aspects of the theory on which almost any educationalist can agree. Radical Constructivists acknowledge this difficulty with definitions as evidenced by von Glasersfeld:

> A few years ago when the term Constructivism became fashionable and was adopted by people who had no intention of changing their epistemological orientation, I introduced the term trivial constructivism. My intent was to distinguish this fashion from the "radical" movement that broke with the tradition of cognitive representation.[7]

The tradition to which Glasersfeld is referring is the philosophy of realism: the view that reality exists beyond the individual. The epistemology of St. Thomas Aquinas and the educational theory of Maria Montessori take this view, which puts them in a perplexing position for many Constructivists. Both agree that the human being actively constructs knowledge, but each one does so using the kind of real external data whose validity the radical Constructivists reject. While the philosophical origins of Constructivism can be found in the likes of Kant and Rorty, its educational pedigree includes the names of Piaget, Vygotsky, and Dewey, all of whom rejected an objectivist view of knowledge and the possibility of attaining truth as it actually exists.

5 E. von Glasersfeld, "Environment and Education," in L.P. Steffe and T. Wood (eds.), *Transforming Children's Mathematics Education: International Perspectives* (Hillsdale, NJ: Lawrence Erlbaum, 1990), 37.

6 Richard Rorty, *Philosophy and the Mirror of Nature* (Princeton: Princeton University Press, 1979), 170.

7 E. von Glasersfeld, "Environment and Education," 37.

It is not just traditional Catholicism which has difficulties with radical Constructivism. Challenges from other educational researchers have grown significantly in recent years. Kirschner, Sweller, and Clark (2006) demonstrated the ineffectiveness of the typical Constructivist teaching — inquiry or problem-based learning strategies — when used for students working with new or complex material.[8] Clark (1989) noted that even when students express preference for Constructivist methods, they do not learn as effectively as they would from direct instruction.[9] Lundeberg (1987) as well as Pressley and Afflerbach (1995) indicated that mastery of a variety of learning strategies — not just Constructivist ones — was necessary for developing expertise across different domains.[10] Samuelstuen and Braten (2007) confirmed that students benefit more from using a variety of learning approaches.[11] Small (2003) identified the fallacy of Constructivist epistemology and pointed to the unhelpful confusion between the legitimate and well established learning process (by which human beings construct knowledge by relating component parts) and the teaching strategy of Constructivism.[12] Phillips (1995) concluded that the issue should be considered from the learner's perspective. The construction of knowledge by an individual benefits more from direct instruction and does not need inquiry methods to achieve the best result.[13] John Hattie, the world's most-cited educational researcher, expresses the frustration of those who have pointed out the shortcomings of radical Constructivism:

> Every year I present lectures to teacher education students and find
> that they are already indoctrinated with the mantra "constructivism

---

8 See P.A. Kirschner, J. Sweller, and R.E. Clark, "Why Minimal Guidance during Instruction Does Not Work: An Analysis of the Failure of Constructivist, Discovery, Problem-based, Experiential and Inquiry-based Teaching," *Educational Psychologist* 41 (2), (2006): 75–86.

9 See R.E. Clark, "When Teaching Kills Learning: Research on Mathematics," in H.M. Mandl, N. Bennett, E. de Corte and H.F Friedrich (eds.), *Learning and Instruction: European Research in an International. Vol. 2* (London: Pergamon, 1989), 1–22.

10 See M.A. Lundeberg, "Metacognitive Aspects of Reading Comprehension: Studying Understanding in Legal Case Analysis," *Reading Research Quarterly*, 61 (1): 94–106.

11 See M.S. Samuelstuen and I. Braten, "Examining the Validity of Self-reports on Scales Measuring Students' Strategic Processing," *British Journal of Educational Psychology,* 77 (2), (2007): 351–78.

12 See R. Small, "A Fallacy in Constructivist Epistemology," *Journal of Philosophy of Education*, 37 (3), (2003): 483–502.

13 N.B. Phillips, C.L. Hamlett, L.S. Fuchs, and D. Fuchs, "Combining Class-wide Curriculum-based Measurement and Peer Tutoring to Help General Educators Provide Adaptive Education," *Learning Disabilities Research and Practice,* 8 (3), (1995): 148–56.

good, direct instruction bad." When I show them the results of these meta-analyses, they are stunned, and they often become angry at having been given an agreed set of truths and commandments against direct instruction.[14]

A SYNTHESIS OF FAITH AND REASON: THINKING WITH ASSENT

From a Catholic standpoint, it is untenable to suggest that current difficulties in religious education can be solved by abandoning essential Catholic claims. Yet the challenge remains: how can the dimension of faith be integrated into the learning process without violating the integrity of reason itself? For a Catholic, *believing* is essentially *thinking with assent*.[15] The act of faith comes about in a different way from the act of knowing:

> not through the degree of evidence bringing the process of thought to its conclusion, but by an act of will, in connection with which the thought process remains open and still under way. Here, the degree of evidence does not turn the thought into assent; rather the will commands assent, even though the thought process is still under way.[16]

> John Henry Newman foresaw many of the problems of modern rationalism and proposed perceptive solutions, and St. John Paul II expressed considerable admiration for the way in which Newman confronted the issues of Rationalism and Fideism — challenges with pertinent similarities to those of our own time:

> > Rationalism brought with it a rejection of both authority and transcendence, while Fideism turned from the challenges of history and the tasks of this world to a distorted dependence upon authority and the supernatural. In such a world, Newman came to a remarkable synthesis of faith and reason.[17]

Indeed, Newman's own century had seen traditional religious belief attacked by subjectivist philosophers like Kant, Feuerbach, and Schleiermacher. These

---

14 John Hattie, *Visible Learning: A Synthesis of Over 800 Meta-analyses Relating to Achievement* (New York: Routledge, 2009), 204.

15 Joseph Ratzinger, *Pilgrim Fellowship of Faith* (San Francisco: Ignatius, 2005), 21.

16 Ibid., 23.

17 John Paul II, *Letter to Archbishop Vincent Nichols on the Occasion of the Second Centenary of the Birth of Newman, 22 January, 2001*. Cf. also John Paul II, *Fides et Ratio* (Vatican City: Libreria Editrice Vaticana, 1998), § 74. Afterwards FR.

speculations attempted to undermine the possibility of any philosophical support for revealed truth. It was against this background that the First Vatican Council (1870) taught that human beings are capable of knowing God by the light of reason alone.[18] This teaching is upheld in the 1993 *Catechism* which offers the added insight that "without this capacity, man would not be able to welcome God's revelation."[19] The position is further clarified thus:

> In the historical conditions in which he finds himself, however, man experiences many difficulties in coming to know God by the light of reason alone....So it happens that men in such matters easily persuade themselves that what they would not like to be true is false or at least doubtful.[20]

The Catholic Church also teaches that the supernatural virtue of faith creates a capacity for belief that is otherwise inaccessible. In *Fides et Ratio*, Pope John Paul II reiterated this claim:

> Based upon God's testimony and enjoying the supernatural assistance of grace, faith is of an order other than philosophical knowledge which depends upon sense perception and experience and which advances by the light of the intellect alone....
>
> Philosophy and the sciences function within the order of natural reason; while faith, enlightened and guided by the Spirit, recognizes in the message of salvation the "fullness of grace and truth" (cf. Jn 1:14) which God has willed to reveal in history and definitively through his Son, Jesus Christ.[21]

In other words, human beings arrive at the truth about God using the supernatural gift of faith together with their natural capacity for reason — not *either*, but *both*.

NEWMAN'S CATEGORIES OF ASSENT

Newman's writings touching on these issues can be found in his classic work *An Essay in Aid of a Grammar of Assent*, in which he offers a

18 See Vatican Council I, *Dei Filius* 2: DS 3004.
19 CCC, § 36.
20 Ibid., § 37.
21 FR, 9.

sophisticated investigation of the process of assent, describing three mental acts associated with the holding of propositions of any kind: doubt, inference, and assent. All three, he insisted, are appropriate human behavior:

> We do but fulfil our nature in doubting, inferring and assenting;
> and our duty is not to abstain from the exercise of any function
> of our nature, but to do what is in itself right rightly.[22]

Newman identified six different kinds of "assent" which can be helpful in clarifying the relationship between faith and reason in religious education. His primary distinction is between *notional assent* (given to abstract propositions) and *real* assent (given to concrete objects of direct experience).

Notional Assent. Newman describes five kinds of notional assent: *profession, credence, opinion, presumption,* and *speculation. Profession* is an assent so feeble that it barely rises above the level of assertion. It involves little thought or reflection — such as a decision to follow a fashion or to accept information from an advertisement.[23] *Credence* is a step beyond this, and expresses the fact that a person has no doubt about a proposition. It is readily given to information taken in by our senses or from books and results in spontaneous assent.[24] In describing *credence,* Newman notes that theology is essentially notional, whereas religion should be real.[25]

Newman then describes *opinion.* Whereas credence is held to be true, opinion is *probably* true. An opinion is held independent of premises, because human beings claim the right to think whatever they wish, whether or not they have good reasons.[26] *Presumption* is the kind of assent given to first principles: those propositions with which reasoning starts. While not as strong as real assent, presumption is a very strong kind of notional assent, drawn from our consciousness of self. Finally, there is *speculation,* a mental awareness of the reasoning process itself. This is attained by contemplating *mental* reasonings and their results as distinct from the assent derived from experience or the senses.[27] An awareness of the legitimate role of speculation has implications for religious education.

---

22 J.H. Newman, *An Essay in Aid of a Grammar of Assent* (1870; reprt. Westminster, Maryland: Christian Classics, 1973), 7.
23 See ibid., 42.
24 Ibid., 55.
25 Ibid., 57.
26 Ibid., 58.
27 See ibid., 74.

Real Assent. Real assent occurs when the mind is directed towards *things*, represented by the impressions they have left on the imagination.[28] Newman noted that the Catholic practice of meditation on the scriptures permits the believer to encounter a God who speaks of things, not notions: "the facts which they relate stand out before our minds as objects such as may be appropriated by a faith as living as the imagination which apprehends them."[29] In company with Thomas Aquinas and Maria Montessori, Newman affirms that "the concrete" is more likely to affect human nature than the abstract.[30] The implications for religious education and catechesis are obvious. If students are to commit to the Faith as their own, they must be offered the *real* and the *concrete* prior to abstract propositions. Instruction in the Catholic faith which confines itself to intellectual dimensions will have very limited appeal. Moreover, Newman claimed that real assents are what make individual human beings unique, for these have a personal character. The particular experiences that each one has are what constitutes every human being's unique condition in history and form the data of an unrepeatable personality.[31]

APPLYING NEWMAN'S INSIGHTS TO RELIGIOUS EDUCATION

The Stance of the Religious Education Class. According to Newman, in the case of revealed religion, the way in which one holds certain propositions distinguishes the presence or absence of faith itself. To take up a position of doubt makes one a sceptic. To hold propositions as conditional (inference) indicates the position of the philosopher. To offer unconditional acceptance (assent) is to be a believer. What are the implications of these positions for religious education? Obviously, different strategies are required depending on the status of the students. Some will be baptized believers who, according to the *Catechism,* have received the theological virtue of faith in Baptism.[32] There may be others in the class who have not received this gift and are therefore in the position of "philosophers" needing convincing reasons for belief while awaiting the conferral of the gift of faith. To paraphrase St. Augustine, before receiving the gift of faith, one must understand in order to believe; after receiving faith, one must

---

28 See ibid., 75.
29 Ibid., 79.
30 See ibid., 37.
31 See ibid., 86.
32 See CCC, § 1266.

believe in order to understand.[33] The third stance, skepticism, would be a logical absurdity in a Catholic religious education class, since it would be a deliberate undermining of its purpose.

Inquiry or Investigation? Newman makes a comment of particular relevance to the *inquiry approach* favored by radical Constructivism. He distinguishes between *inquiry* and *investigation*, insisting that inquiry into revealed truth is inconsistent with faith. One who inquires is in doubt about where the truth lies; hence a believer cannot, at the same time, be an inquirer:

> Thus it is sometimes spoken of as a hardship that a Catholic is not allowed to inquire into the truth of his creed; — of course he cannot, if he would retain the name of believer. He cannot be both inside and outside of the Church at once. It is merely common sense to tell him that, if he is seeking, he has not found. If seeking includes doubting, and doubting excludes believing, then the Catholic who sets about inquiring thereby declares that he is not a Catholic. He has already lost faith.[34]

While closing the door of believers to inquiry in matters of faith, Newman was no advocate of *Fideism* or anti-intellectualism. He simply made a distinction between the way in which believers and non-believers engage with the data of revelation:

> inquiry implies doubt and investigation does not imply it; and that those who assent to a doctrine or fact may without inconsistency investigate its credibility, though they cannot literally inquire about its truth...in the case of educated minds, investigations into the argumentative proof of the things to which they have given their assent is an obligation or rather a necessity.[35]

The Real and the Notional in the Religious Education Class. As noted already in his description of credence, Newman claimed that religion must be based on real assent, while theology is essentially notional; theology builds on the foundation of an existing faith. Both aspects should receive attention in the religious education class, with the balance of this emphasis depending on

33 *Ten Homilies on the First Epistle of John*, Tractate XXIX on John 7:14–18, § 6.
34 J.H. Newman, *An Essay in Aid of a Grammar of Assent*, 191.
35 Ibid., 192.

the needs of individual students. Those with little knowledge or experience of Catholic faith should be offered more concrete experiences to which they can offer *real assent*. Some contemporary programs have made the mistake of attempting to meet the needs of older students by confining their religious education presentation to the notional sphere without regard to the students' individual situations. To put it in Newman's terms: in cases where the students lack a sufficient religious foundation, theology has *replaced* religion rather than *supporting* it. Those more firmly established in their faith could be offered a developmentally appropriate level of theological investigation, although a degree of caution needs to be exercised here too.

Speculative Theology in the Religious Education Class. It is possible and indeed helpful to engage in speculation based on a foundation of faith in real things; this is merely an application of St. Anselm's definition of theology: *faith seeking understanding.* Yet speculation cannot *cause* faith; this is a gift. Moreover, there exists the possibility that speculation may overwhelm and destroy faith if one choses to give more credence to one's own reasoning than to the gift of God. There are numerous examples of theologians who have in this way abandoned faith. If inexperienced students are exposed too soon to speculative theology which does not rest on a foundation of real faith, there is a risk that they will mistake speculation for faith and claim the right to be arbiters of revealed truth. Their training in Constructivist methodology and scientific method will certainly pressure them to act in this way. Newman discouraged those who were intellectually ill-equipped for assessing subtle arguments from placing themselves in danger by deliberate exposure to them:

> [Some] who, though they be weak in faith...put themselves in the way of losing it by unnecessarily listening to objections. Moreover, there are minds, undoubtedly, with whom at all times to question a truth is to make it questionable, and to investigate is equivalent to inquiring; and again, there may be beliefs so sacred or so delicate that, if I may use the metaphor, they will not wash without shrinking and losing color.[36]

Religion as a Cultural Study. In many "post-Christian" jurisdictions, the Church has been conceded the opportunity of presenting its teachings as

---

36 Ibid.

a body of cultural knowledge, isolated from the actual sacramental, and affective devotions that contribute to its life and power. On one level, this seems attractive: an opportunity for Evangelization. In practice, the results have not been encouraging. Students are positioned to take the stance of philosopher, subjecting the Faith to the processes of Constructivist inquiry. As Newman demonstrated, this undermines rather than enhances faith. Students have the impression that they understand what Christianity has to offer without experiencing its affective power; the mind is informed but the heart is left untouched. The aspect of "wonder" is neutralized and students are "inoculated" against future interest in Christianity.

The Role of the Church in Relation to Belief. Newman's view on role of the Church regarding the content of faith is also relevant for religious educators. He would not have conceded legitimacy to *negotiating believers* who make their own selection of the aspects of Catholic teaching that they find acceptable, while rejecting those elements that are found to be inconvenient. Newman insisted that part of the Church's role was to identify opinions that are incompatible with the truth received from God.[37] Catholics need to trust the Church in its doctrinal and moral teaching, even if one does not comprehend the reasons: "Even what he cannot understand he can believe to be true; and he believes it to be true because he believes in the Church."[38] Furthermore, he insists that one does not immediately need to know or understand the meaning of every doctrinal proposition the Church teaches. Catholics believe *on the authority of* the Church, which is deemed to be the authority of Christ himself:

> every Catholic, according to his intellectual capacity, supplements the shortcomings of his knowledge without blunting his real assent to what is elementary, and takes upon himself from the first the whole truth of revelation, progressing from one apprehension of it to another according to his opportunities of doing so.[39]

The Place and Value of Certitude in Religious Education. It is beyond dispute that relativism has had a powerful effect on modern culture. The influence of Radical Constructivism in reinforcing this mental habit has already been noted. Another tendency, perhaps more general, is the application of the

37 See ibid., 149.
38 Ibid., 150.
39 Ibid., 153.

scientific method to religion. The scientific method proceeds by way of hypothesis and empirical experimentation, an entirely appropriate means for establishing material facts. By definition, however, such an approach excludes the spiritual dimension. Will a prayer for rain always produce the same results? Can the transformation of bread and wine into the body and blood of Christ be tested? Some realities are known only by faith. This leads to a legitimate question: is human access to the truth or to any kind of certitude possible at all? In science, the answer is no — a hypothesis is always held to be conditional, dependent on further experimental data.

With religious faith, however, certitude is indispensable and Newman has provided a suite of persuasive arguments. He defined certitude as: "the perception *of* a truth with the perception that it *is* a truth... as expressed in the phrase *I know that I know*."[40] Newman acknowledged that human perceptions change, but that it does not follow that access to unchangeable truth is impossible: "What is true is always true and cannot fail whereas what is once known need not always be known and is capable of failing."[41] For Newman, religion requires more than assent to truth, since it is more than an intellectual acceptance of an argument. Religious faith requires certitude and this must include a principle of persistence: "Without certitude in religious faith... there can be no habit of prayer, no directness of devotion, no intercourse with the unseen, no generosity of self-sacrifice."[42] Newman acknowledged that some of his remarks seemed to go against the proper functioning of the human mind which acquires understanding largely through sense experience and by relating these experiences to one another.[43] Yet he insists that relentless introspection using our intellectual processes actually tends to weaken them. Should this become a habit, it will cause the mind to abandon even the most rudimentary assents in favor of a paralyzing uncertainty. "And thus, even those things which it may be absurd to doubt, we may, in consequence of some past suggestion of the possibility of error... [be] hampered with involuntary questionings, as if we were *not* certain when we *are*."[44]

A process whereby every religious belief is subjected to "critical" thinking — perhaps more accurately described as systematic doubting — and

---

40   Ibid., 197.
41   Ibid.
42   Ibid., 220.
43   Ibid., 216.
44   Ibid., 217.

a demand for empirical proof will undermine religious education just as surely as it will undermine any other intellectual discipline. If the same process were applied to science, the scientific method itself would be undermined by endless questioning. For example, how do we know that the published results in scientific journals are not fraudulent? How can we be certain that the results from an experiment have been accurately reported? If in the field of science we must trust in some basic certitudes, why is this unacceptable for religious faith? Newman acknowledged that a host of imponderable questions which challenge the doctrines of faith must arise in every thoughtful mind. If, however, reason is unable to resolve the dilemma created, then such questions

> must be deliberately put aside, as beyond reason, as no-thorough-fares, which, having no outlet themselves, have no legitimate power to divert us from the King's highway....A serious obstruction they will be now and then to particular minds, enfeebling the faith which they cannot destroy.[45]

Newman accepted the possibility that certitudes in any individual may turn out to be mistaken. Yet, if one were to refuse to act unless *absolutely* certain, the result would be paralysis. The human mind is incapable of infallibly perceiving the difference between real certitudes and apparent ones. It is the Church, under divine guidance, which is charged with this task, not individuals. In his *Essay on the Development of Doctrine*, Newman laid down conditions for what would constitute due consideration and these have found their way into settled Catholic teaching.[46] There may be times when the Church seeks to weigh arguments for and against particular doctrines. Once the matter has been settled, the faithful are called on to simply accept the conclusion as a certitude:

> It is our duty deliberately to take things for granted which our forefathers had a duty to doubt about; and unless we summarily put down disputation on points which have been already proved and ruled, we shall waste our time and make no advances.[47]

45 Ibid., 218.
46 See John Henry Newman, *An Essay on the Development of Christian Doctrine*, 171–203.
47 Ibid., 229.

The case for resting in such certitudes must be put clearly to students and argued in the face of its Constructivist alternatives which are far from incontestable. As demonstrated by Newman and confirmed by a weight of evidence, human beings relate better to concrete forms than abstract ones; and, so as far as possible, encounters with concrete realities should precede propositional formulations and any kind of speculative theology. Both real and notional assents (faith and reason) are necessary for sustaining Catholic faith, but the starting point must always heavily favor the *real*. Sacraments, liturgy, and the concrete approaches to religious education pioneered by Maria Montessori, Sofia Cavalletti, and their collaborators give the best hope for the practical and educationally sound renewal of religious education and catechesis in our times.

8
Moral Formation and Moral Reasoning
Integrating Mind and Will

MORAL FORMATION OF THE WILL

Closely related to the relationship of nature and grace is the task of moral formation. Much contemporary reflection on this errs on the side of rationalism, insisting that human beings can intellectually determine their own moral principles. This view was held to be deficient as early as the time of Aristotle's *Eudemian Ethics*. Moral formation can sometimes be seen, mistakenly, as a branch of the philosophical study of ethics: that it is merely *knowing* the correct principles to apply in order to live a moral life. To see it in this way is to take the necessary dimension of "mind" and make it the only relevant consideration. As in all other aspects of catechesis, moral formation requires the usual interplay of body, heart, and mind.

MORAL FORMATION OF THE BODY

Perhaps the most obvious way to make this point about moral formation is to view it from the perspective of the youngest children who are not yet capable of living their lives in accordance with self-chosen moral principles. It can be quite amusing to see young parents in a shopping center trying to reason with a two-year-old in terms of the moral principles they should observe. This is simply not the way children of that age think. Although it may sound surprising, the starting point for moral formation is the body. From the time children can walk, wise parents will be ensuring that they acquire good habits and that their actions will be limited by moderation in every area of their existence. Their parents will ensure that they eat properly, speak courteously, move safely, tell the truth, treat others fairly, and so on. Only in the rarest of circumstances are these children actually capable of acting out of intellectually-derived moral principles. Mostly, they are simply trained to respond in the appropriate way. Parents may even "walk them through" the steps that they are meant to follow. Maria Montessori developed a wide variety of teaching tools to assist in this basic moral formation of the body. She referred to it as "practical life" activities, and "training in grace and courtesy." Montessori observed that these basic tasks involving the body were found to be the basis of future moral action.

A note of caution must be sounded here: the development of children does not follow an exact timetable; it is more like a continuum in which they acquire growing degrees of competence in a completely individual way. Even young children will be aware that some things are "right" and others "wrong," and parents usually begin to instill this notion in them from the time they can communicate. There are often occasions where children as young as three or four years of age, in particular circumstances, appear to be applying principles of moral behavior. What is lacking for the youngest children, however, is a real understanding of *why* these things are right and wrong. This is typical behavior; children do not suddenly arrive at a capacity for moral agency on their sixth birthday. There will be incremental steps along the way leading to an ever more stable pattern of action. Nor should we neglect the capacity of children at this age to act out of a motive of love in producing specific moral behaviors.

Montessori and her collaborators rightly perceived that it is overwhelmingly difficult for the mind to direct a body which has not been physically habituated in this way to carry out virtuous acts. This remains true at every age: human beings must make choices about doing the right thing, even if they would prefer not to. Self-discipline often requires the capacity to overcome the insistent demands of the body. While this is the foundational task of moral action, it remains necessary at every stage of human existence. While it does not constitute moral agency, it is an indispensable support. Self-discipline, or, to use its traditional name, self-denial, is indispensable at every age. Sports psychologists also have a simple phrase for it: "no pain, no gain." Failure to gain proper control over the body in the early stages of childhood can lead to self-indulgent behaviors of many different kinds, behavioral habits that can be very difficult to change if they have established an early habitual pattern. Regular acts of self-denial play a vital role in supporting the moral task of the body.

The problem of the child who has not been properly trained from infancy in the exercise of restraint is becoming more common. What can be done for the child who lacks self-discipline? Fortunately, there is another traditional plank that has been employed in this task and is still quite popular in normal child-rearing practices: the use of team sports. In this area, it is quite appropriate to demand rigorous physical training in order to achieve appropriate sporting goals. This practice can be used to make a sound case for more rigorous moral discipline. If we can be careful about what we eat because we need to be fit, surely we can engage in some level of fasting and abstinence for spiritual purposes. Team sports, however, may come with attendant moral challenges in our contemporary society. Some sporting teams are composed of members who may be capable of great efforts on the sporting field, but do not have any intention of following through with strong moral behavior. Care must be taken to ensure that the sporting teams chosen are not contaminated with strong physical discipline on the field and weak moral behavior off the field. Nevertheless, the value of team sports is so great that it is worth the effort of parents, coaches, and teachers banding together to form teams where suitable physical discipline is connected with strong moral behavior.

MORAL FORMATION OF THE HEART

Once this task of the body has laid the appropriate foundation, it is time to unfold the Christian motive which, alone, can sustain moral activity—namely love. This, obviously, takes us into the realm of the heart. Only those who love deeply are genuinely capable of sustained moral effort. At around the age of six years, children become capable of understanding that there can be necessary rules that underpin the way they should act. At this point, they will become focused on rules and regulations about how to behave, about what is fair. This is a natural development and should be allowed to run its course in a way that allows them to work through to a more mature approach that allows them to resolve the tension between justice and compassion in appropriate ways.

Parallel with this development, however, is another deep need. Those who would acquire moral virtue need to be given the opportunity to fall in love with God—without coercion or manipulation. The moment when this mysterious personal development takes place is not in the hands of the teacher, or even the parent. It can be said from the experience of many who work with children, however, that there will be a myriad of opportunities for it at this time. Often it is associated with the child's preparation for First Communion. While this development cannot be forced, it appears that it can be aided by offering inspiring, beautiful stories about what human beings can achieve at their best when they act from a motive of love. Once again, the scriptures offer many expressions of this as do the lives of the saints or other literature. Most of all, however, it must be stated that those who are most likely to be capable of love resulting in action are those who have been loved themselves. This kind of love is the second (and perhaps the most important) foundation of genuine moral agency. "If you love me, you will keep my commandments."[1]

St. Teresa of Calcutta made this task the basis of her life's work. She understood that people who felt abandoned, uncared for, and unloved were not likely to be open to the message of Christ. It was for this reason that she and her sisters engaged in the ministry of love. The idea of picking up a dying man from the streets and preparing them for death seemed, to many, to be a waste of time and resources, but she insisted that everyone deserved at least one experience of love before they died. Only this could win over their hearts and open them to the love of God.

There are many children today who seem to be lacking this experience of love. They may have many "things" from their parents, but can be lacking the one thing necessary: the certainty that they are loved and cared for. The behaviors that flow out of this lack of love are clear enough. Some children will try desperately to be "worthy" of love by doing anything they can to make themselves "loveable": over-attention to helping out, buying special treats for others so that they will be their friends, or even enlisting the support of teachers to "make those children play with me." On the other side of the spectrum, there are children who will engage in appalling behaviors in order to gain attention, crying out for someone to show enough love to impose limitations on them. What all of these children are really seeking is the expression of genuine love from another. No human being can ever be truly happy without this. We can describe this kind of love, then, as the foundation of genuine moral agency.

The literature of the Christian world returns again and again to this very theme, but perhaps the most evocative example in English is this sonnet by the seventeenth-century poet, John Donne:

> Batter my heart, three person'd God; for you
> As yet but knocke, breathe, shine and seeke to mend;
> That I may rise and stand, o'erthrow mee, and bend
> Your force, to breake, blowe, burn and make me new.

1 John 14:15.

I, like a usurped towne, to'another due,

Labour to'admit you, but Oh, to no end,

Reason your viceroy in mee, mee should defend,

But is captiv'd, and proves weake or untrue,

Yet dearly'I love you, and would by love'd fain,

But am betroth'd unto your enemie,

Divorce mee, 'untie, or breake that knot againe,

Take mee to you, imprison mee, for I

Except you'enthrall mee, never shall be free,

Nor ever chaste, except you ravish mee.[2]

MORAL FORMATION OF THE MIND

The Dawn of Moral Reflection and Agency. As already noted, at around about the age of six-to-seven-years, there is a dawning of the child's reasoning faculty. Children of this age crave moral guidance, but this must be handled sensitively. If children are offered a very lengthy set of rules which they must adhere to, there will be a risk of making them stressed and needlessly anxious and in some cases, even scrupulous. They will take these rules so seriously that every time they break one of them, they will feel excessively guilty. There is no need for this: they will make up enough rules of their own without having the burden increased. Children of this age begin to discern the presence of rules and regulations which govern their lives and the whole universe. It is similar to the way in which children at the previous stage required very rigid physical order in order to feel safe. Often the rules they create for themselves are self-inflicted. Teachers who are involved in playground duty will be very familiar with the regular complaints of seven- and eight-year-old children who want to report other children who have failed to obey one of the many rules that they deem essential for the good ordering of their social group. Such rigidity can be somewhat unnerving for parents and teachers alike, but it allows children to explore and then establish the moral framework that they will be able to apply with more subtle understanding about the principles of justice.

This process indicates that a moral reasoning process has begun to develop. The fact that it is "rule based" and derived from models they have drawn from elsewhere should not be a cause of undue concern. It should be seen as a way in which children of this age begin to understand the

2 *Holy Sonnets*, 14, 1633.

distinction between unfailing standards of justice and minor regulations which can be set up for the smooth running of some local situation. The process of discernment is underway and they are seeking to make moral sense of the universe: this will be all the more effective if they already know themselves to be loved. If this is not firmly established in their lives, they run two risks at opposite ends of the spectrum. On the one hand, they may try to work out the rules and procedures by which they will make themselves lovable to God and others. On the other hand, they may reject all rules and guidance in order to test out whether or not they are loved for their own sake, without conditions. It must be stressed again and again: Christian morality is a response to love. Unless they know themselves to be loved, moral reasoning will descend into a cold and unworkable variant of Kantian ethics or its flip side, moral chaos.

By the time the child is about ten years old (earlier for some, later for others) a change normally becomes obvious: a further refinement of the moral sense. The previous adherence to even the most inconsequential regulations begins to be replaced with a kind of empathy for others that draws its strength from their realization that they are not always able to follow all of the rules themselves. This process is meant to develop further until it reaches the point where the adult can hold in creative tension the competing demands of justice and love. It is most important to stress here that both of these apparently opposite virtues *need* one another. Love is *not love* without justice; and justice is *not justice* without love. Children need to be acquainted, at a moment when they are able to understand it, the traditional Christian approach. Namely, the sin must be separated from the sinner. The sin needs to be dealt with in a way that justice is properly served; the sinner needs to be forgiven.

Supporting the Moral Development of the Mind. Once children have had an ongoing experience of love, the time comes when they must be offered Christian insights into how they can respond to this love. If all has gone well in their development, this moment arrives around about the age of six-or seven-years-old, although there can be signs of it earlier. Cavalletti has identified a particularly effective way of making the link between the love of Christ and the appropriate moral responses. Her suggestion is that we make use of the moral maxims of Jesus himself. These are gospel texts in which Jesus gives direct moral advice. Cavalletti recommend that these be pasted, carved, or written onto little wooden boards so that the children can hold them and reflect on them. Those who have used this method report that it is surprisingly effective, and it seems to make a significant difference if the maxims are held in the hand rather than simply viewed on a screen. The maxims can be kept in a suitable box near the prayer table, and the children can take up any one of these at a time they choose. Sometimes, children like to choose these maxims at random, without looking at which one they are selecting. They are best introduced briefly and simply as part of a "morning prayer" session and then placed in the container to be used later. Once all of them have been introduced, children can be asked to come and select one to be read as part of each prayer session. In this way, the children will become very familiar with them. These twelve are recommended by Cavalletti:

- "Love your enemies." (Matthew 5:44)
- "I give you a new commandment: Love one another as I have loved you." (John 13:34)
- "Do good to those who hate you." (Luke 6:27)
- "When you pray, go into a room by yourself, shut the door and pray to your Father in private." (Matthew 6:6)
- "Ask and you will receive. Speak and you will find. Knock and the door will be opened." (Matthew 7:7)
- "Your body is a temple of the Holy Spirit." (1 Corinthians 6:19)
- "You must be perfect, just as your heavenly Father is perfect." (Matthew 5:48)
- "Say *yes* when you mean *yes* and *no* when you mean *no*." (Matthew 5:37)
- "I do not say forgive seven times, but seventy times seven." (Matthew 7:22)
- "Always treat others the way you would have them treat you." (Matthew 7:12)
- "Give when you are asked to give and do not turn your back on someone who wants to borrow." (Matthew 5:42)
- "Pray for those who persecute you." (Matthew 5:44)

Parables of Mercy / Moral Parables. Another resource for encouraging moral refection is the use of the parables: the stories Jesus told which should guide the way we act and treat others. There are three Gospel accounts point is the parables of mercy seems to be the story of the Centurion's servant (Matthew 8:5–10, 13), and the two parables of Mercy: the Forgiving Father (Luke

15:11–24) and the Lost Coin (Luke 15:8–9). Once this has been reinforced, it will be possible to begin looking at the stories Jesus told to guide our behavior towards others: the moral parables. These include: The Good Samaritan (Luke 10:30–37); The Pharisee and the Tax Collector (Luke 18:9–14); The Insistent Friend (Luke 11:5–8); The Debtors (Matthew 18:23–34); and The Sower (Matthew 13:3–8). In the next stage of development, this focus on moral parables can continue with some more demanding requirements: The Wedding Feast (Matthew 22:1–14); The Ten Bridesmaids (Matthew 25:1–12); The Workers in the Vineyard (Matthew 20:1–15); The Talents (Matthew 25:14–30); and The Pearl of Great Price (Matthew 13:45–26).

Link with Sacrament of Reconciliation. The dawn of moral agency is an ideal moment to introduce children to the Sacrament of Reconciliation. Generally speaking, this should take place somewhere after the age of seven years and before nine years. In most cases, earlier is better; the children are less self-conscious and have a deep desire for forgiveness. There are many rules that they are likely to have broken and feel uneasy about. In these circumstances, the chance to be forgiven is a very welcome development for them. The maxims, the parables of mercy, and the most basic moral parables can form the basis of their examination of conscience for this stage of their life. If their introduction to the Sacrament of Reconciliation is left to a time beyond this, the children may have a greater understanding of moral principles, but they will have passed beyond the easy familiarity of the affective relationship with Christ which finds little difficulty in approaching the one they love to receive forgiveness.

"Class Meeting" Strategy. There is another strategy which is currently found in the practices of good schools which can be very valuable in supporting moral development: the regular class meeting in which children discuss the problems they are facing in relationships and then seek solutions. The wise teacher will offer the children good strategies for solving these difficulties, but will also know how to integrate the spiritual resources referred to above into this program if it is taking place within a Catholic school. Sometimes, the reading of a parable that offers insights into Jesus's way of acting will be very valuable and will allow the children to apply solutions for themselves without needing the teacher to give them the answer. This will always be a more effective learning experience, encouraging the children to see things for themselves and to discern the power of the scriptures in reinforcing the relationship with Christ and applying it to their own actions.

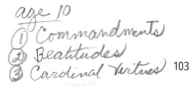
Introducing Commandments, Beatitudes, and Virtues. The Commandments are complex and difficult to introduce to younger children. This is best left until about ten years of age. These are best introduced in the context of appropriate rules for relating with other people in a fair and just way. Beatitudes can follow on from the Commandments, together with a more focused study on the meaning of the Cardinal (Moral) Virtues.

CHRISTIAN MORALITY: INTELLECT OR WILL? MIND OR HEART?

The relationship of intellect and will in the field of moral action has been widely explored and is well summarized by St. Thomas Aquinas in the *Summa Theologica*.[3] St. Thomas makes the point that we cannot love what we do not know, and so it is the *mind* which moves us to act. But it is not as simple as this. St. Thomas also recalls the view of St. John Damascene: that if we do not love something, we will not be interested in knowing it better. St. Thomas concludes that there is an interplay of knowing and loving: each one playing a different role, mutually intensifying the experience. In other words, *the more you know, the more you love; the more you love, the more you will want to know.* This is easy to recognize if we look at the example of a young couple moving towards marriage. First, they must become aware of one another, usually through the senses at a very basic level; the other is seen and heard. This is a preliminary kind of knowing in which one or both of them is attracted by some good that they see in the other. As the relationship develops, each of them wants to know more about the other, and this knowledge is used to express love with more and more intensity.

MORAL REASONING AND ETHICS

The process of moral reasoning, when detached from its Christian roots, usually goes under the name of "ethics." The philosopher, Immanuel Kant, articulated such a system, based on what he called the *categorical imperative.* This is essentially a notion of *duty* which comes from simply being human: "I can, therefore I must." There are two other twentieth century theorists whose work is better known in schools, namely, Jean Piaget and Lawrence Kohlberg. The use of either of these theorists in a Christian context can be confusing. Their systems make no provision for

---

3 Thomas Aquinas, *Summa Theologica* (New York: Benziger Brothers, 1948), II-I, q.82, a.4. [Afterwards ST]

moral formation outside the intellectual dimension of the human person, and neither system acknowledges the role of divinely revealed truth in moral reasoning.

The notion that a moral system can exist outside of God is unacceptable in a Christian context, but it is also problematic philosophically. It was Aristotle in his *Eudemian Ethics* who first identified the difficulties associated with locating a moral or ethical code entirely within the realm of individual intellectual choice. Basically, what it comes down to is that if rational deliberation is the wellspring of ethical behavior, you eventually commit yourself to a fallacy known as infinite regression in a series of steps like these:

- How do you know that your belief about what is the right way to act is true?
- *Because I worked it out for myself…*
- How do you know that what you worked out doesn't have any fallacies?
- *If it did, I'd change my opinion…*
- If you change your opinion once, you may need to do it again…

This means that, ultimately, everyone is his or her own "god," determining what good and evil are. A myriad of possible ethical interpretations then becomes possible; for example, in one chilling example from the times of Nazi Germany, some people may assert that it is morally acceptable to determine that Jews are expendable, and then act on this belief. Faced with the instability in ethical principles, Aristotle advised people that the only way to solve this problem is to follow a higher law beyond ourselves — God.

St. Thomas Aquinas. For St. Thomas Aquinas, rational deliberation about morality must itself be excited and drawn by an exterior principle. Human beings require special providence because of our perfection as free agents endowed with a unique end: our divinization through Christ in the life of God. St. Thomas advised (as did Aristotle) that we must therefore reach out for a morality which is essentially beyond our human capacities. To achieve true happiness, humans need help and they must arrive at this by moral actions that are performed with divine assistance through grace. For St. Thomas, Christian morality is beyond natural human capacities. It is not inhuman; it is a human morality perfected and made perfect by the grace of God. The necessity of seeking for divine grace that is beyond our natural capacities can be misrepresented as depending on someone else to tell us what to do in our moral decision-making, but the alternative is demonstrably flawed in far more serious ways.

The Catechism of the Catholic Church. The *Catechism of the Catholic Church* offers excellent guidance regarding the essential principles of moral reasoning. It states that: "A morally good act requires the goodness of its object, of its end, and of its circumstances together."[4] This language is elaborated in paragraphs 1751–1753. When the *Catechism* uses the term "object" in this context, it is drawing attention to the "objective" — what good thing are we seeking to achieve.

The *object* is a *good* thing that we are trying to achieve. This is a key principle of Catholic moral thinking: it is never morally right to do something evil so that some good might come from it. Some acts are always evil. To break a commandment, for example, can never be justified. Others are possibly good if they are pursued with the right intention. For example, Jesus drew attention to two people offering money in the temple treasury, one a poor widow and one a rich man who had his gift marked by trumpeters. The widow's offering was a good act, made so by her intention; not so the rich man's offering.

The *end* means the *intention* that lies behind the act; our motivation for acting in the way we do. The proverb "the end does not justify the means" is an excellent piece of moral advice. If our intention is good, but what we do is evil, this is not a morally sound way of thinking. For example, condemning an innocent person in order to save others can never be justified, unless the person freely offers his or her life as a sacrifice to save another, as in the case of St. Maximilian Kolbe.

The circumstances in which a moral act takes place can be thought of, perhaps, as "extenuating circumstances." These would include the consequences of the moral act. The circumstances can never change a bad act into a good one. Circumstances only refer to the moral agent's personal responsibility for the act. Consequentialism, a modern tendency to judge an action by its consequences, is a completely inadequate moral tool. It is sometimes necessary to separate in our minds the person who has done something evil from that evil act itself. The person may have been insane, and therefore not responsible; but this in no way changes the fact that some evil act has taken place.

---

4 CCC, §1760.

To put it briefly, then, for an act to be morally sound, it must involve a choice of something that is good in itself and this must be done for the right reason. The circumstances in which the decision is made may increase or diminish the guilt or innocence of the person making it, but the circumstances do not change whether the decision in right or wrong. The study of Christian moral reasoning must stand on these foundations. It must begin from an understanding that our moral agency is a means of exercising free will so that our love can be genuine and sincere.

MORAL PERSONS ACT MORALLY

There is a great deal of research evidence available on moral agency, but perhaps none is more compelling than that of Samuel and Pearl Oliner, who investigated a number of people who had put themselves at grave personal risk to rescue Jews in Nazi Europe.[5] While there was a small minority of rescuers who attributed their actions to self-chosen ethical principles, perhaps disturbingly, many who went through the intellectual process of moral reasoning ended by rationalizing and defending their decision not to help. Those who did end up being rescuers most frequently cited their family values. They acted out of the "totality" of who they were as human beings, formed in families whose values were deep and lasting. Moreover, it is compelling to notice in the research, again and again, how quickly the rescuers came to their decision. There was no lengthy Hamlet-like weighing up of consequences: "to be or not to be." This research indicates what Christian moral teaching has continually asserted: morality is primarily a spontaneous activity that arises from a love of Christ and an entrenched habit of virtue. Moral reasoning is possible in a detached way; but in the heat of the moment when a decision must be made, that decision needs to be made instantaneously and this is frequently based on having observed how the members of one's own family have behaved. Trying to reason it out will often result in a rationalization of the most comfortable behavior. Moreover, the Christian moral subject who listens to the Church as mother and teacher is "reconstituted in the lived experience of this maternity which the family also needs in order to carry out its function as 'domestic Church.'"[6]

5 See Samuel Oliner and Pearl M. Oliner, *The Altruistic Personality: Rescuers of Jews in Nazi Europe* (Chicago: University of Chicago Press, 1990).

6 Vatican Council II, *Lumen Gentium* (Vatican City: Libreria Vaticana Editrice, 1964), §1.

9
Mystagogy:
Reaching Spiritual Realities through the Liturgy
Drawing the Pieces Together[1]

Faced with the myriad tasks necessary to raise a child, parents can feel overwhelmed by the responsibility that faces them. How are they to do this? What if they leave out something really important and fail their children in the one thing that really matters? These are not inconsequential questions; many new parents have felt like this. Perhaps a good way of responding to this can come from contemporary research into human learning. Some of the most useful ideas in this area cluster around concepts about human learning that are quite easy to understand: the notions of short-term memory, long-term memory, and "chunking." Human beings appear to have a short-term "working memory" which can hold about seven discrete items of information without exceeding their capacity. For example, most adults would be about to retain seven unrelated numbers after hearing them once, so long as they concentrate on what they are being told. (The capacity is less for young children; the average five-year-old can retain four items in the short-term memory.) Each discrete piece of information is referred to as a "chunk." If we want to extend our capacity, we need to undertake a process referred to as "chunking," by which individual pieces of information are related to one another in a way that transforms them from multiple chunks into a single one. For example, if you were given these chunks of information: blue, lady, dress, you are holding three discrete items in your mind. If you relate them in this way: "a lady in a blue dress," you have "chunked" them into a single piece of information, which can then be stored as one chunk in the long-term memory.

---

1 The content in this chapter has been redeveloped from an article I first published in *Catechetical Review* 1, 4, (2015), 10–13. It is used here with permission.

There are many different "chunking" strategies that help us to relate these items together. It seems that one of the best ways of doing this is to link things into a story, where one item leads you to the next one in the sequence, and the whole range of information is held as one. We can also repeat things in the same sequence until it is recalled by the mind in this way: music and songs are good examples of this. For centuries, the Church has had access to a complex and comprehensive "chunking strategy" like this: the sacraments, particularly the Eucharist. Of course, the Eucharist is far more than a chunking strategy, but it certainly includes this function in terms of religious education. Everything of importance that God has ever done, everything that He is doing now, and everything that He will do in our future is symbolized in some way in the sacred liturgy. The Eucharist makes present the whole mystery of God. To be absent from the Eucharist will have many consequences, but one of these is that children (and indeed adults) will not be able to make the necessary links between the different elements in the mysteries that we must live. Indeed, prolonged absence from the Eucharist as an adult can also result in the kind of forgetfulness causes someone to lose touch with important realities that they had once understood. In *Lumen Fidei*, Pope Francis made this point quite clearly: "There is a special means for passing down this fullness, a means capable of engaging the entire person, body and spirit, interior life and relationships with others. It is the sacraments, celebrated in the Church's liturgy."[2] For a Catholic, there can be no effective religious education without participation in the Sacraments, especially the Eucharist.

THE REVIVAL OF MYSTAGOGY

In his Apostolic Exhortation, *Sacramentum Caritatis*, Pope Benedict XVI reiterated the Church's central teaching about the Eucharist, which, he wrote, "is constitutive of the Church's being and activity. This is why Christian antiquity used the same words *Corpus Christi*, to designate Christ's body, born of the Virgin Mary, his Eucharistic body, and his ecclesial body."[3] If catechesis is about "intimacy with Jesus Christ"[4] then it is little wonder that the primary context in which this intimacy is enacted and made present, the Eucharist, must lie at the heart of the whole catechetical project. Perhaps for this reason, Pope Benedict, with

2 Pope Francis, *Lumen Fidei* (2014), §40. [Afterwards LF]
3 Benedict XVI, *Sacramentum Caritatis* (2007), §15. [Afterwards SC]
4 CT, §5.

the unanimous approval of all the bishops meeting in the 2007 synod, nominated mystagogy as the preferred method for catechesis. *Sacramentum Caritatis* went on to articulate the three essential components of a mystagogical approach:

1. it must interpret each element of the rite in terms of the events of salvation history and the Church's living tradition;
2. it must present the *meaning* of the signs contained in the rites;
3. it must link the rites with every aspect of the Christian life and must ultimately lead to an awareness among participants that they are being *transformed* by the mysteries they are celebrating.[5]

In *Evangelii Gaudium,* Pope Francis again drew attention to this preferred catechetical approach and summarized it in more compressed language. He noted that mystagogy consists of "a progressive experience of formation involving the entire community" and "a renewed appreciation of the liturgical signs of Christian initiation."[6] In other words, catechesis works best when we are incorporated into a sacramental community where we can encounter the real presence of Christ, the *Corpus Christi*, in the Eucharist and in the Church. Once in this place, we are thereby linked to the Church's living tradition, going right back to the dawn of salvation history. Moreover, we are enabled with much greater clarity to perceive the meaning of the signs that we are encountering on a regular basis through the sacraments. Finally, we will slowly, perhaps imperceptibly at first, become aware of the transformation taking place within us through which we enter, ever more deeply, into the realities being signified.

THROUGH CONCRETE SIGNS

Sometimes we can miss the most obvious point about why this approach might be so effective. It is, quite simply, this: liturgical signs are concrete. Through our own senses, we have physical access to the sacred mysteries revealed in the scriptures and made present in the sacraments. Moreover, these liturgical signs do not just *remind* us of the action of God in history; they make His mysteries *present*. As the *Catechism* puts it:

5 See SC, §64.
6 EG, §166.

> Christian liturgy not only recalls the events that saved us but actualizes them, makes them present. The Paschal mystery of Christ is celebrated, not repeated. It is the celebrations that are repeated, and in each celebration there is an outpouring of the Holy Spirit that makes the unique mystery present.[7]

Our senses can use these divinely-designated visible signs to recognize the invisible yet still genuinely *present* spiritual realities that connect us with Christ. So it is actually the liturgy which plays the major role in helping us to "stay connected" to the mystical life of Christ and to experience the ongoing support of the grace of the Holy Spirit through the life of the Church.

Catechesis is first and foremost a relationship with Christ, mediated to us through the Church. The signs and symbols of the Liturgy that are central to a mystagogical approach will be incomprehensible outside this context; one must be a participant in order to understand what is going on. The detached observer or the one who is seeking merely a body of knowledge may be able to report on the observable mechanics, but will not properly experience the "life" that animates the believer. The story of the true vine offers us a rich image of how the Church needs to work.[8] Christ is the vine, we are the branches. Cut off from him, we can do nothing. When we are grafted into the vine through our baptism, we begin to experience a new, divine life empowering us to grow into the likeness of Christ. This is not an inconsequential occurrence: it is significant enough for all three persons of the Blessed Trinity to be involved.

THE TRUE VINE

Clearly, this gospel passage has much to teach us about the importance of the Church's role in passing on the faith. Yet, there is another aspect that I would like to highlight here. It is the way in which a profound concept which is difficult to explain is made accessible through a simple concrete image. I have always loved teaching about the True Vine to children, but, for many years, they did not seem to share my enthusiasm. Eventually, I stumbled upon a strategy that captured their attention. There was a plant sitting on the prayer table in the classroom, and, as I read the passage aloud, I pointed to the plant and tore off one of the little branches. Immediately,

7 CCC, §1104.
8 See John 15:1–11.

a gasp of horror wafted through the room. "Oh no, now it's going to die!" protested one of the forthright eight-year-olds. It was one of those moments when the scales fell from my eyes and I realized that the best access to the scriptures was through the same "sacramentality principle" that suffuses all of human existence and by which spiritual realities are made present through concrete signs. The catechetical approach of mystagogy is so effective because it taps into this essential human reality mysteries need to be pondered using concrete signs

The Catechism of the Catholic Church provides us with an excellent example of how we might begin by offering mystagogy for the Sacrament of Baptism.[9] It goes through each of the nine stages of the rite of Baptism, and indicates which aspect of the mystery is being signified.[10] The following table provides a brief summary:

RITE	SIGNIFYING / BRINGING ABOUT
Making the Sign of the Cross on the forehead	*The redeeming grace of Christ, won by his death on the cross and claiming the candidate for Christ.*
Proclaiming the Word of God	*Enlightening with revealed truth and eliciting the response of faith.*
Anointing on the chest with the oil of catechumens	*Liberating from sin and from the devil and enabling the candidate to confess the faith of the Church.*
Consecrating the baptismal water (Epiclesis)	*Asking Christ to send the Holy Spirit upon the water to enable the candidate to be born of water and the Spirit.*
Pouring/immersing in the water; baptizing in the name of the Holy Trinity	*Dying to sin and immersion into the life of the Trinity.*
Anointing with sacred chrism	*Anointing by the Holy Spirit and incorporating the candidate into Christ, who is priest, prophet, and king.*
Clothing in the white garment and giving the gift of the Baptismal candle, lit from the Paschal candle	*That the neophyte has "put on Christ" and has been enlightened by him.*
Reciting the Lord's Prayer	*Newly incorporated into the Church, the neophyte is truly invoking God as Father.*
Solemn Blessing	*Offering the candidate (and parents) a blessing for the journey that must now be undertaken.*

LINKING THE LITURGY AND THE SCRIPTURES

There is another significant element in the mystagogical process: the connection between the Liturgy and the scriptures. Many books have been

---

9 See CCC, §1234–1245.
10 This is the only sacrament for which the *Catechism* offers such explicit details.

written on this connection in which a very strong case has been made for
seeing the Liturgy as the authentic context for interpreting the scriptures.[11]
I will confine myself here to three observations from *Verbum Domini*. First,
"a faith-filled understanding of sacred Scripture must always refer back
to the liturgy....In the liturgy the Church faithfully adheres to the way
Christ himself read and explained the sacred scriptures."[12] Second, "the
Church has always realized that in the liturgical action the word of God
is accompanied by the interior working of the Holy Spirit who makes it
effective in the hearts of the faithful."[13] Third, "Word and Eucharist are so
deeply bound together that we cannot understand one without the other:
the word of God sacramentally takes flesh in the event of the Eucharist."[14]
If we pursue the strategy of mystagogy, we will discover that the Liturgy
not only links us to the presence of Christ in the sacraments, but also to
the mysteries revealed in the scriptures. The link is unbreakable.

When I first attempted to make these ideas accessible to children (ages
ten–twelve years), I expected them to struggle with such apparently abstract
concepts, but the very opposite turned out to be true. I had set out a simple
table on a poster that listed the stages of the rite of Baptism and asked them
to find pictures of these stages from Google Images. This exercise proved
very easy for them. Then I asked them to go back to Google Images and
find pictures based on the scriptures which seemed to link in with each
of these stages. What they managed to do with this assignment surprised
me. For example, the sign of the cross on the forehead of the candidate at
the door of the Church was matched with a picture of Jesus dying on the
cross; the sign of epiclesis over the baptismal water was matched with a
picture of the Holy Spirit descending on Jesus as a dove at the Baptism
in the Jordan, and so forth. They not only found pictures, but for weeks
afterwards the students, without any coercion, spent much of their free
class time searching the Bible itself for clues; they left the computers aside
and delved into the sacred text for themselves. Eventually, I asked them
to include in this, now very large, poster some of the scriptural passages
they had found from the Old Testament that prefigured the meaning of
Baptism and also from the New Testament that described the meaning of

---

11 In this field, the works of Jean Daniélou hold a special place, including *The Bible and
the Liturgy*.

12 Benedict XVI, *Verbum Domini* (Libreria Editrice Vaticana, 2010), § 52. [Afterwards VBD]

13 Ibid., §52.

14 Ibid., §54.

Baptism. These children had begun to engage with the Bible through the Liturgy, and they found this study both captivating and moving. Every class I have tried it with since has reacted to this assignment in more or less the same way.

WHAT DOES MYSTAGOGY LOOK LIKE IN CATECHETICAL PRACTICE?

It is not possible here to give a fully articulated set of activities for what a mystagogical strategy might look like. Instead, I will conclude by sharing another story. Some years ago I was invited to present a talk on the Eucharist to a group of teachers. When I arrived at the school, I discovered that I would be speaking first to a group of eight-year-old children preparing for their First Communion. Fortunately, the school had an atrium of the Catechesis of the Good Shepherd. I was unprepared but keen to do a little experiment with mystagogy. I greeted the children and I asked them to watch me as I moved around the room, laying out the catechetical materials used for reflecting on the Mass: the model altar, some vessels, and some linens. Then I set up four biblical dioramas: the Annunciation, the Last Supper, the Empty Tomb, and the material for the True Vine. After that, I asked the children to walk around and look at what I had done because, I said, there was a connection between everything I had set up. When they returned to their places after ten minutes, I asked them what they had discovered. One child began by saying, as I had expected, that each article in the altar corner reminded her of something in the scripture dioramas; but after that, for the next forty-five minutes, I listened, dumbfounded, to specific examples they had discovered. One child after another told me almost every connection that had taken a lifetime for me to find for myself. Once they understood what was being asked of them, there was no stopping them. Only the insistent ringing of the recess bell could end the session. This encounter changed my approach to catechesis for good. I understood in that moment why the Church considers mystagogy to be the most effective of catechetical strategies.

10
The Scriptures and Typology
Looking for "the Golden Thread"

Closely associated with the process of mystagogy is the related discipline of typology. It was St. Augustine who referred to God's action in the world as a "golden thread" which allows us to make meaning of apparently unconnected events. Whereas mystagogy studies these links between the liturgical symbols and the plan of God in the Scriptures, typology looks for the connections between what may seem at first to be unconnected events in the Bible itself. Typology is an ancient (and still current) method of biblical interpretation; indeed, it can be said to have begun with the Old Testament prophets who began to assign meanings and make connections between Biblical events and their significance in the past, present, and future. Typology is a method that can begin with the events of the New Testament and look for antecedents in the Old Testament. Alternately, it can begin with the Old Testament and read it in the light of New Testament revelation. In both cases, the typological method keeps permanently in view the unity of the Divine Plan: God has known what He was doing from the beginning and there are discernible signs of this in the text. Cavalletti's explanation is helpful here: "In some way, the plant to be born is already present in the seed. Though they seem to be two distinct entities, the plant and the seed are intrinsically connected."[1] Typology as a tool of biblical interpretation seeks to draw attention to the whole sweep of salvation history from the Creation to the Parousia (the time when all is fulfilled in the Kingdom of God).

THE VOCABULARY OF BIBLICAL TYPOLOGY[2]
The vocabulary and concepts used in biblical typology are largely drawn from the works of St. Ambrose of Milan. This technical vocabulary

---

1 Sofia Cavalletti, *The History of the Kingdom of God. From Creation to Parousia. Part 1* (Chicago: Catechesis of the Good Shepherd Publications, 2012), 16.
2 For a more detailed description of the vocabulary of Typology, see Enrico Mazza, *Mystagogy* (New York: Pueblo, 1989), 14–22.

is complex, but it offers necessary distinctions for understanding the typological method.

Mystery (*Mysterium*). For St. Ambrose, the reading of the scriptures could never be reduced to a mere listing of facts. The mysterium is essentially a search for the divine reality underlying the facts. When we discover something of the mysterious purpose of God, we have begun to engage with the scriptures in a typological manner.

Figure (*Figura*). The figure is a significant religious event which reveals in some way the mysterious presence of God. It points to (or *prefigures*) in a general way something in the future. Figures of what is to come can be found in both the Old and New Testament, but they can only be fully understood once they are fulfilled. A figure works by setting up a dynamic relationship between the two events and prevents them from being seen in isolation from each other. The "truth" already exists within the figure, but it is yet to unfold. It locates the events in salvation history in a kind of movement from what is *less* to what is *more* complete. It directs the mind forward to its completion. In this sense, the first man, Adam, is said to be a figure of Christ, the one who is to come. (See Romans 5:14)

Shadow (*Umbra*). While the term *figure* can be applied to both Old and New Testament events, *shadow* can only be used to describe the relationship between an Old and New Testament. In this sense, the New Testament reality is thought of as "casting a shadow" into the past. The real meaning of the past event is not self-contained but was to have a fulfilment in a time yet to come. For example, the Passover Lamb is a *shadow* of Christ, the Lamb of God.

Appearance (*Species*). The appearance (or *species*) describes something in terms of what it looks like externally. Appearances are not necessarily the whole story, but nor are they therefore false. Rather, some things are provisional in relation to the future. In the Bible, something can be described belonging to the same species as something else if it bears any kind of similarity it.

Image (*Imago*). St. Ambrose only uses the term *image* to refer to what is made known by Divine Revelation. He teaches (as does the *Catechism*) that human beings have access to the otherwise inaccessible spiritual world by means of images. In this sense, the idea of the *imago* points directly to Christ, since this is the way the invisible God reveals himself as in this verse from Colossians: "He is the image of the unseen God, the firstborn of all creation" (Colossians 1:15). The *imago* is not simply another way of talking about *species*. There is a connection in the natures of the image and the imaged. (In technical terms, we say there is an ontological connection between the two.) The *imago* actually participates in the reality it signifies. It is correct to say that that the *imago* not only participates in reality, but it is also real in itself. It is the projection into visibility of the reality's inmost essence. In Ambrose's theology, Baptism forms the image of God (*imago Dei*) in a particular sacramental way, which we call "likeness."

Likeness (*Similitudo*). Genesis 1:26 links the terms *image* and *likeness*: "Let us make man in our own image, after our likeness." Hence the terms image and likeness (*imago* and *similitudo*) are regarded as complementary: they are distinct from each other, but they belong together. As explained above, *imago* is about an ontological connection, something that exists in the very nature of things. In contrast, likeness (*similitudo*) is the term Ambrose uses to describe Christ's sacramental presence in the Christian. *Similitudo* is what takes place in the sacraments of Baptism and the Eucharist, by which the image of God is formed in Christians. (We might call it the presence of sanctifying grace, the life of Christ within us, but Ambrose does not use this language to describe it.)

Type (*Typus*). The term *type* is never used to describe a sacrament or a prefiguration of the Eucharist. It is about the figurative realities found in the history of salvation. The type is a real event or person which points to a deeper meaning beyond it. For all practical purposes, a type is identical with a figure. There are subtle distinctions that will be made by scripture scholars and sacramental theologians, but these need not concern us at this level.

APPLYING TYPOLOGY TO THE READING OF THE BIBLE

The Second Vatican Council's document on Divine Revelation, *Dei Verbum,* pointed to the unity of all scripture as "the interpretative means of reading it."[3] This makes the method of typology a particularly suitable method of interpretation. It has three stages:

1. A reality that is yet to come: the Parousia in which the Kingdom of Heaven will be finally established.
2. The reality that has already taken place.
3. The reality we are living in now.

It is worth noting that any study of typology that does not look beyond

3 See Vatican Council II, *Dei Verbum* (Vatican City: Libreria Vaticana Editrice, 1965) § 3, 13.

our present reality towards a fulfilment that is yet to come is merely an academic study devoid of hope. Its purpose should always be to draw us nearer to the mystery of God. Typology teaches us to look at the Bible as part of an entire plan of God, the past, the present, and fulfilment in the future.

The continual celebration of the Eucharist has made it easier to see the way in which events of the past are being lived in the present. This is the nature of the biblical and the subsequent sacramental understanding of *memorial*. The apostles are instructed by Christ to celebrate the Eucharist as a memorial: "Do this as a memorial of me" (Luke 22:19). Cavalletti puts it this way:

> The celebration of memorial annihilates time in some way, making present today the events of the past, events which, without the celebration of memorial would be lost forever. The memorial also projects events toward the end times and, in so doing, prepares us for the completion of history.[4]

There is a striking similarity between the notions of typology and memorial in that they both attempt to set us free from the constraints of time by unifying the work of God into a single moment of recollection; through this we can begin to see the unity of the divine plan. The celebration of a memorial in the Eucharist makes present — using concrete realities and words from the scriptures — the events of salvation history that have already been achieved and points us to their fulfilment. In a similar way, a typological interpretation of the scriptures permits us to view that biblical text that is read in the present as part of a "golden thread" linking events of the past present and future. Cavalletti identified five typologies as being fundamental to our study of the scriptures; without these, we will have insufficient background to understand what Christ is teaching. These typologies are: the Creation, the Fall, the Flood, Abraham, and the account of Moses and the Exodus, which will now be explained briefly.

THE CREATION STORY: ADDRESSING THE PASTORAL DIFFICULTIES FIRST

There is a particular pastoral aspect that applies to the Creation accounts in the Book of Genesis that needs to be addressed before anything else. Many children (and adults) can be confused about the Church's stance

---

4 Sofia Cavalletti, *The History of the Kingdom of God. From Creation to Parousia Part 1*, 22.

concerning whether or not the accounts are true. There are two extremes to be avoided from a Catholic perspective. The first is the notion that these accounts are stories put together by a pre-scientific culture, and that they have been superseded by our contemporary "superior" understanding. The opposite view is also a problem and it comes from fundamentalist Christians: that the Creation accounts are true in every detail. Neither of these positions represents the Catholic view. The *Catechism of the Catholic Church*, in addressing the biblical account of the Fall, clearly expresses the approach of the Church: "The account of the fall in *Genesis* 3 uses figurative language, but affirms a primeval event, a deed that took place at the beginning of the history of man."[5]

These two elements are essential to a Catholic understanding: the events are real, but the language is poetic. This is something that needs to be explicitly put forward. How do we present what is true in a way that people understand it? The history of literature demonstrates that human beings are more likely to understand deep truths if it is presented to them in stories or images. The English writers J.R.R. Tolkien and C.S. Lewis have quite dramatically demonstrated this through their *The Lord of the Rings* and the *Chronicles of Narnia*.

TYPOLOGY OF CREATION

A Christian typology of Creation must attend to the two accounts of creation found in the first and second chapters of *Genesis* in terms of the connection with salvation history. The question to be raised is how each account fits in with the overall plan and points us towards its fulfilment at the Parousia.

There are two specific typologies to consider, although more are possible. The first concerns the relationship of Adam, who is the first-born of all human creation, and Christ, first born of the new creation. In the plan of God, Adam is not the complete story: he is a *shadow* of one who is to come. The plan is not clear at this point, but it comes into much sharper focus at a later stage with the coming of Jesus who is the new man, the first-born of the new order of Creation. A striking contrast is made between Adam as the sinner and Jesus, who restores the relationship with God that was damaged by sin.

In 1 Corinthians 15:45, St. Paul speaks of Adam as being a man of the earth (referring both to his origin and the material used in creating him — the dust

---

5 CCC § 390. See also GS, § 13.

of the ground). He and his descendants are "dust." By contrast, Christ is the heavenly man and those who are united to him by faith become "heavenly" as well. His resurrection constitutes a second creation, which is a re-creation of the first one, but at a higher level. Those who began by carrying within themselves the image of the first earthly man will now carry the image of the new heavenly man. We are aware that the final unfolding of the reality has not yet arrived, as we continue to pray in the Lord's Prayer, "thy kingdom come." The prophets, too, indicated that something more wonderful was to be expected, as in this passage from Isaiah: "I will create a new heavens and a new earth. The things of the past shall not be remembered or brought to mind" (65:17). The mysterious language of the Book of Revelation also indicates that there are more wonderful things that are yet to be.

TYPOLOGY OF THE FALL

The biblical account of the Fall can be found in Genesis 3. While it may seem familiar, it is advised that the account be read aloud, as there are a number of elements in it that are likely to strike the reader as interesting and even unfamiliar. Adam and Eve, the first parents, by disobeying God, bring sin and suffering into the world. Once it is clear that the images are being offered in figurative language, it will be possible to begin exploring the meaning of some apparently strange ideas. Who is the serpent? What is the significance of the trees of knowledge of good and evil, the tree of life? Why do Adam and Eve hide themselves after their sin? Who has caused this? Is the damage permanent? Any number of questions can arise. These meanings are veiled in mystery. They are shadows that have not yet become clear.

As we move to the New Testament, we meet a "new Adam": Jesus. Whereas in the account of the Fall, we notice that a tree is involved in causing great damage, in the Gospels another kind of tree is used to provide wood for the cross: "The tree of man's defeat becomes the tree of victory: Where life was lost, there life has been restored through Jesus Christ" [Preface of the Triumph of the Holy Cross]. In Genesis, Adam and Eve experience their nakedness before God and are ashamed. With the coming of the Sacrament of Baptism, they are "clothed in Christ," as symbolized by the white baptismal garment. Now they need no longer feel ashamed.

This points to a new reality yet to come. St. Paul observes in 1 Corinthians 15:22 that, just as all die in Adam, so too will we be brought to life in Christ. In verse 26, he goes on to say that the last enemy to be defeated is death.

TYPOLOGY OF THE FLOOD

It is a little surprising that the story of Noah's Ark (Genesis 6–9) is so popular with parents of young children. Perhaps the idea of gathering a lot of animals together in one place is an attractive proposition. The real story, however, is far from suitable for young children, and should probably not be attempted until they are at least ten years of age. It is a perplexing story in which people are called to account for their sins. Nevertheless, it has very important truths to teach us.

The account of the Flood makes it clear that sin is a serious matter and can damage not only our spiritual life, but will have consequences for the physical world as well. God certainly seems in these passages to be concerned about the good order of his Creation. In the account of creation in Genesis, the first element to bring forth life is water. On this occasion, however, the very element that supports and sustains life brings destruction on the wicked. The sin of the men descended from Adam has resulted in a near universal destruction, with one exception: Noah, the man who walks with God, together with his family, is saved. The waters of the flood destroy everything else, but Noah becomes the one through whom a new humanity will be descended. With Noah, we see the emergence of something else that is new: a covenant between God and man.

There are many images that emerge from the shadows of this story when Christ the savior is revealed in the Gospel. Just like Noah, a new humanity is to take its origin from Christ. The means chosen for this again involves the element of water, in the sacrament of baptism, but this time the water incorporates both possible meanings. It symbolizes destructive power — the death of Christ on the Cross — as well as life-giving properties — the resurrection to a new life, sustained by grace. The Sacrament of Baptism heralds the individual defeat of sin and the beginning of a new life in all those who receive it.

The future reality is also indicated here, the time when all things are made new and God will be all in all. Again, it is the prophet Isaiah who puts words to our future expectations:

> I am now as I was in the days of Noah when I swore that Noah's waters should never flood the world again. So now I swear concerning my anger with you and the threats I made against you. For the mountains may depart, the hills may be shaken, but my

love for you will never leave you and my covenant of peace with
you will never be shaken. (54:9–10)

THE TYPOLOGY OF ABRAHAM

There can be little doubt that the story of Abraham is at the same time
among the most important and confronting of the key Old Testament
typologies. It can be found in Genesis 12–22. Much material of great
importance is put forward in the story. There is the role that the gift of
faith, which must have been divinely given for Abraham to respond in the
way he did, and for him to be referred to ever after as the father in faith.
There is the promise that Abraham will be the father of a great nation, and
the all the peoples would be blessed in him, combined with the covenant
of circumcision. There is the miraculous birth of his son Isaac, long after
his wife Sarah had passed her child-bearing years. There is the intervention of the priest king Melchizedek, who offers gifts of bread and wine.

Yet, in any presentation of the story of Abraham, one event stands out
in the imagination of the children: the requirement that Abraham sacrifice his son. It is a moment that I have enjoyed presenting many times to
the students, because of the reaction it invariably receives. Most classes
are completely outraged by it—does this mean that this father has to kill
his son because God told him to? That's terrible; surely this can't be what
God wants…, etc. I can usually make the outrage last for about twenty
minutes as child after child joins in. But in the end, it permits a dramatic
intervention that makes the true meaning clear. Yes, I tell them, it certainly
is a terrible thing for a father to have to sacrifice his son, but in the end,
Abraham did not have to do it. Even so, centuries later, there was a father
who really did have to sacrifice his son. Silence usually falls as the children
realize that I am talking about God the Father and Jesus. Abraham and
Isaac are but shadows of the real sacrifice that must be made.

Once it becomes clear that Abraham and Isaac appear to be distant
shadows of Christ and the Father, the parallels begin to be evident. The
Letter to the Hebrews is full of these connections, and makes one of them
very clear indeed: since Isaac received back his life as if from the dead, he
represents a foreshadowing of the resurrection (Hebrews 11:19). Abraham's
offering of Isaac, then, is seen as preparing the way for Christ's offering
to the Father.

Again, it is the prophet Isaiah who provides words to indicate the final
future reality of these dramatic events: "Nations shall walk by your light and

kings by your shining radiance....They all gather and come to you: Your sons from far away and your daughters in the arms of their nurses" (60:3–4).

MOSES AND THE EXODUS TYPOLOGY

Some of the best-known and most critically important typologies of the Old Testament can be found in the Book of Exodus. The story of Moses has been made popular by various movies over a long period of time, and should be well known. Even so, reading the story aloud, little by little, and allowing children to explore it in smaller chunks is a very valuable activity and will place them in direct contact with the scriptures. There are three key images that are vital from this story. The first and most important is the Passover lamb, an innocent victim who is sacrificed and whose blood is placed on the doorposts of the Israelites to save them from the angel of death. After this, the Israelites continue to celebrate this feast as the Passover. This image looks not only forward, but back to previous images of a sacrificed lamb, as, for example, to Abel (Genesis 4:4). The second key event is the crossing of the Red Sea. By a miraculous intervention, the Israelites are able to leave behind them the life of slavery in Egypt and set out across the waters to begin a new life on the other side. Finally, we have the onerous journey across the desert, during which the people are miraculously sustained with a food that seems to come down every night from the sky.

Most children will be sufficiently familiar with these images to come up with fulfilments in the future. The innocent lamb sacrificed at the Passover points to the Lamb of God, Jesus Christ: another innocent victim whose life is sacrificed for the sake of the people. The Easter liturgy itself indicates the next connection, that between the crossing of the Red Sea and the Sacrament of Baptism. In both cases, the participants leave behind an old life and are miraculously offered the opportunity of a completely new life on the other side of the waters. Finally, it almost does not need saying that the heavenly food that descends each night and sustains them on their journey is a shadow of the Holy Eucharist.

Finally, the prophet Isaiah again offers an insight into the final fulfilment of these shadows and images: "In the desert, prepare the way of the Lord! Make straight in the wasteland a highway for God!...The glory of the Lord shall be revealed and all mankind shall see it together; for the mouth of the Lord has spoken" (40:3–5).

11

Prayer

Personalizing the Relationship with God

Whereas all of the other key dimensions by which we are inserted into the mystery of the Trinity (the scriptures, the sacraments, and doctrinal teaching) are mediated to us through the Church, prayer is the dimension by which we make these realities personal. That does not mean that the Church has nothing to say to us about what prayer is about, but it does mean that an individual's prayer forms the bedrock of his or her personal relationship with Christ. It is the point at which we come to God ourselves, say what we want to say, ask what we want to ask or simply remain in the presence of the one we must regard as our own special friend. Without this personal dimension of prayer, this ongoing conversation with one who is always present to us, our spiritual life can seem cold and distant. It is well to begin by briefly exploring what the Church has to tell us about what prayer is.

The Catechism of the Catholic Church identifies six different aspects of prayer, which we will now refer to briefly.[1] The first is blessing and adoration. "Because God blesses the human heart, it can in return bless him who is the source of every blessing."[2] The *Catechism* then considers the prayer of petition. "Forgiveness, the quest for the Kingdom, and every true need are objects of the prayer of petition."[3] Intercession is a form of prayer directed beyond oneself to the needs of others. "Prayer of intercession consists in asking on behalf of another. It knows no boundaries and extends to one's enemies."[4] Another essential part of prayer is thanksgiving. "Every joy and suffering, every event and need can become the matter for thanksgiving which, sharing in that of Christ, should fill one's whole life: 'Give thanks in all circumstances' (1 Thess 5:18)."[5] Finally, we have the prayer of praise.

---

1 See CCC, § 2626–2649.
2 Ibid., § 2645.
3 Ibid., § 2646.
4 Ibid., § 2647.
5 Ibid., § 2648.

"The prayer of praise is entirely disinterested and rises to God, lauds him, and gives him glory for his own sake, quite beyond what he has done, but simply because HE IS."[6] A fully developed prayer life will eventually incorporate all of those aspects in a dynamic ongoing conversation that becomes more and more part of our daily existence, but this is not the way it starts. Relationships usually develop slowly and go through many phases of closeness and separation.

PRAYER AND THE YOUNG CHILD

In dealing with a young child (in fact with anyone) who has little experience of prayer, there is a very simple starting point. Begin by asking the child to close their eyes and thank God for something good that they have. Tell them that God is so powerful that He can even read their thoughts; they don't need to say their prayer aloud, God will hear them anyway. If this is being done in a classroom situation, there is another step that can be used which dramatically enhances the value of what is being done. Light a candle, pick up the Bible, and read Psalm 23:1–2: "The Lord is my shepherd, I shall not want; he makes me lie down in green pastures." Then extinguish the candle and let them experience a very brief period of silence. Tell them that if they want to thank God for something, they can say it in their minds, or they can say it aloud by starting with these words: "Thank you, God, for…" In most classes of young children, there is usually no problem with having someone speak. Once the first one has started, many others will follow. The problem can sometimes be getting them to stop. Something important happens here. If we understand young children at all, we will realize that they have spent much of their lives exploring the world around and are generally fascinated by that they see. When they are asked to say thanks for these things, you are opening a floodgate: young children are experts in this area and are more than happy to link what they have experienced with gratitude to the God who created it for them. This is usually the best starting point for an ongoing relationship of prayer. It is an easy matter for them to make the next connection. If God has already given us good things, we can ask him to give us more of what we need, and, at that point, we have added the prayer of petition to the repertoire.

The task of the adult is not to lay down rigid rules about how the child is to pray. We need only provide some simple guidance about how they might

6 Ibid., § 2649.

approach it, and then leave them to develop their own ongoing dialogue with God. We need to create the conditions in which prayer can arise, including the opportunity for silence and the encouragement to begin. In the area of prayer development, many adults can make the mistake of believing that young children are not capable of enjoying "silence" and using it for prayer. On the contrary, if they are working at something they enjoy — painting, sand modelling, drawing, and the like — they should be told about the possibility of using these moments for communicating with God in prayer. This, more than anything else, will create that inner peace which moves the heart towards God and allows children to begin the habit of listening in a way that can detect the unspoken "voice of God." Another way of supporting young people in the development of the necessary dispositions for prayer is to encourage them to slow down in their movements. If they are encouraged to walk very slowly from one place to another (with the adult modelling how to do this) they will create that calmness from which prayer springs so naturally. Here, some of the traditional prayer gestures and postures are very helpful. The sign of the cross, performed slowly and deliberately instead of quickly and routinely, is capable of focusing the attention very effectively. The act of taking holy water is likewise an effective means of placing themselves in the presence of God. Simple gestures like, bowing, kneeling, or genuflecting are also useful strategies for encouraging the development of the conditions of prayer.

As children get older, they should be offered opportunities for further growth in their habits of prayer. Even from their earliest stages, there are some very basic prayers that will help them to pray. Short phrases from the scriptures, from the Mass, or from well-known hymns are also helpful. The Our Father, Hail Mary, and Glory Be to the Father should be part of their experience from their earliest times; they should be able to hear them and eventually repeat them, even if they are not yet capable of understanding. Children will often need words to express what they are feeling. The scriptures are full of images and prayer formulae of this kind. Sometimes children do not necessarily understand what they are saying, but the sound of the phrase attracts them. Blessed John Henry Newman made the observation that most people "know" more than what they are able to express. He called this "implicit reason." This is especially true of children. They will often have a relationship with God that exists on this deep level, but is not yet able to be expressed in an articulate form. They will recognize words and phrases that are linked to God, but they will not be able to tell you why or how they know this. Cavalletti's advice regarding scriptural images of this kind is quite simple: "Offer them rich food, but not too much of it." Let them savor the beauty of the words, and then let them grow into the meaning as the relationship with God develops. What we want to do is give them words to express what they are thinking; they should have access to beautiful, rich images, but only a little at a time. Other complex vocal prayers should not be introduced until later. From the time that they can independently read, children should be allowed the opportunity of using the scriptures in their prayer. The gospels and the psalms hold a particular place in this development of prayer.

Wherever possible, a physical space should be set up, either in a classroom or a home, which is set aside for prayer. There is no set rule for the setting up these spaces or for deciding what should be there; this is very much according to individual preference. The space should contain items that those using it find meaningful and helpful in drawing their attention to God in prayer. The following list may help in getting started with what might be useful: a crucifix and a statue or Our Lady; a table covered by a cloth in the liturgical color of the season; a Bible, together with a candle; a box of prayer cards and short phrases from the psalms of the gospels; some holy cards of the saints or images from the Bible; a Mass booklet; some lives of the saints. Really, you are only limited by your imagination. The important thing is that the children see that prayer is important to you. The space can also serve as the place used for prayer in common. As children advance in age, more possibilities can be offered, such as more complex prayers. Other suggestions might be *lectio divina* or the opportunity of praying with sacred art.

I gave my own children a simple rule of thumb for working out how much of each day they needed to devote specifically to designated prayer on their own. I said that whatever age they were, they should be spending at least that number of minutes in prayer each day. Of course, this does not replace the time spent in family prayer together or the silent conversation that should be going on for much of the day. Your own ideas about the children in your care are likely to be the most suitable for you.

12

The Indispensable Role of the Family[1]

From the Documents of the Church

The relationship between the Catholic school and its parents and families is founded upon two principles. First, parents are acknowledged as the primary educators of children; therefore, the school is bound by the law of subsidiarity in respect of the education of their own children.[2] Second, schools must help equip parents for the work of education.[3] The Church teaches that without respect for the family it is impossible to promote the dignity of the person.[4] A school manifests that respect by the help and support it offers its families, by its promotion of family life, and by accommodating the family's irreplaceable contribution to community life. "The family is a divine institution that stands at the foundation of life of the human person as the prototype of every social order."[5] The school, though it is a valuable institution, cannot lay claim to this same dignity; it is there to meet the needs of families rather than the other way around.

However, while it is true that parents are the *first* educators of their children, they are not the *only* educators of their children. Families are responsible for close and vigilant cooperation with both civil and Church authorities in this important area of education.[6] Equally important is the insistence that "in the education of children, the role of the father

---

1 The contents of this chapter have been adapted from my "Report on Religious Education in the Diocese of Parramatta," 2014.

2 Vatican Council II, *Gravissimum Educationis* (1965), § 3. [Afterwards GE] Subsidiarity means that a higher or less local authority should not take responsibility for something that can be handled effectively at the more local level. See also: *Circular Letter to the Presidents of Bishop's Conferences on Religious Education in Schools* (2009), § 8. [Afterwards RES]

3 *The Catholic School on the Threshold of the Third Millennium* (1997), § 20. [Afterwards CTM] See also: *The Religious Dimension of Education in a Catholic School* (1988), § 42, 43.

4 *Compendium of the Social Doctrine of the Catholic Church* (2004), § 185.

5 Ibid. (2004), § 211.

6 Ibid. (2004), § 240.

and that of the mother are equally necessary."[7] This is not to denigrate the efforts of single parents; it is simply to affirm an ideal. The Church proposes the concept *communio* — a word which lacks a precise equivalent in English, but expresses the spirit by which we build a community. The Second Vatican Council's Constitution on the nature of the Church, *Lumen Gentium*, teaches that "the children of God constitute one family in Christ," characterized by mutual charity and oneness in praise of the Trinity. Through this, they fulfil their vocation within the Church.[8]

SAMPLE RESEARCH LITERATURE RELATED TO THE ROLE OF FAMILIES AND COMMUNITY-BUILDING

A vast *corpus* of research on the contribution of families to education exists. Three representative studies will be examined here, understanding, of course, that in this ever-expanding field, more studies could be quoted. The three sources quoted are *The Grant Longitudinal Study of Adult Development* (Vaillant, 1977; Vaillant, 2002; Vaillant, 2013); *Disappearing Fathers, Destabilized Families* (Anatrella, 2009); and *School Community Leadership: The Perspective of Primary School Principal* (Spry and Graham, 2007).

THE HARVARD GRANT STUDY OF ADULT DEVELOPMENT[9]

The *Harvard Grant Study of Adult Development* may be the best-known longitudinal study ever undertaken; it charted the development of 268 sophomore men at Harvard University over seven decades; its breadth and depth is, at present, unequalled. Participants were evaluated every two years through surveys and medical records. Originally intended to study healthy aging, it eventually also provided researchers with a wealth of data apropos emotional health. Much of this data reveals the long-term effects of the quality of family life in the individual's early years. The relevant findings are summarized as follows:

1. The levels of warmth and love in the childhood relationship with both the father and the mother were extremely important, but each affected the child differently. Father-son relationships tended to affect overall life-satisfaction. For example, men

7 Ibid. (2004), § 242.
8 *Lumen Gentium*, § 51.
9 See George E. Vaillant, *Triumphs of Experience: The Men of Harvard* (Harvard: Harvard University Press, 2012).

at age 75 who had had warm childhood relationships with their fathers were less anxious, enjoyed vacations more, and had higher life-satisfaction levels than those who had not. Mother-son relationships, however, were found to affect career success. Men who had had warm childhood relationships with their mothers earned $87,000 on average per year more than those who had not. They were also significantly less likely to develop Alzheimer's disease.

2. Sibling relationships mattered. Men who had had good sibling relationships when they were young made $51,000 per year more on average than those with poor relationships.

3. Though a basic level of childhood financial security was necessary for long-term prosperity, it remained true that IQ and socio-economic status influenced success less than did relationships with parents.

4. The good was more influential than the bad. Men who had close, warm relationships with a small number of people in an otherwise dysfunctional family often coped relatively well in the long term.

5. Increasing the number of social connections (i.e. building community) increased longevity, decreased stress, and increased happiness.

6. Dramatic change was possible and happiness could be found at any time. For example, one of the study's unhappiest candidates became one of the happiest, largely because he pursued a determined and thoughtful quest for authentic love.

7. Happiness increased when individuals committed to caring for others. (This is not without its challenges; to genuinely care for others one has to find ways to cope with disappointments in relationships.)

Obviously, this study restricted itself to the apparently non-religious aspects of happiness, yet its findings are compatible with the Church's teaching about the value and importance of families. For schools, the lesson is clear. Families help children to achieve happiness in adult life and to educate children without reference to the family is to ignore one of the most significant aspects of human development.

DISAPPEARING FATHERS, DE-STABILIZED FAMILIES[10]

Mgr. Tony Anatrella is a priest and an academic psychoanalyst who specializes in social psychiatry. His article, "Disappearing Fathers, Destabilized Families," examines the roles of both mother and father in the formation of a family. Anatrella argues that the mother role and father role — which are available to persons other than biological mothers and fathers — are the two poles of operation in a family. The father role helps the child to adjust to the present reality; the mother role opens children to possibilities. The roles do not need to be absolutely fixed and will vary according to the talents and personalities of the parents; nonetheless, children are best served where both poles of activity exist in healthy tension.

Legitimate variations notwithstanding, the essence of the father role is to provide stability and to be the measure against whom a child works out his or her own identity. The father role is directed at helping the child face the world as it is, rather than creating an artificially safe environment. Thus, the person who exercises the father role should not just be a second mother. Conversely, the essence of the mother role is to surround the child with a relatively self-contained, pleasant, and happy experiences. The mother protects children from the fear of abandonment and offers a sense of well-being. The mother's role tends to emphasize the closeness; the father's role, otherness.

The Apparent Contradictions in Mother/Father Dimensions of Parenting. The apparent paradox between the father role and the mother role is, at its deepest level, no paradox at all. There are innumerable examples of apparent paradoxes in Christian virtue. Consider, for example, the tension between justice and mercy. Christian virtue consists of the right exercise of both virtues, not the erasure of one for the sake of the other. The same holds true for the roles of father and mother within the family.

Cultural Challenges: Consequences of the Retreat of Fatherhood. Anatrella identifies the retreat from the fatherly role as the core of contemporary social problems, for it is the father who must liberate the child from the sense of omnipotence that he or she can develop in the security of the maternal influence. The father teaches the child that he is not the master of the house and limits the demands the child can place upon the mother. Anatrella argues that some fathers, though physically present, are absent

---

10 Tony Anatrella, "Disappearing Fathers, Destabilized Families," in *Communio International Catholic Review* (Summer, 2009): 309–28.

from their real role. They may have absented themselves through lack of confidence, through selfishness, or as a result of their own poor formation. They may also have absented themselves because of a mistaken belief that all parenting must be maternal; perceiving correctly that they cannot do what the mother does, they retreat from parenting altogether, not realizing that they have a complementary talent to offer.

A certain contemporary television portrayal of fathers seems to celebrate this retreat. These characters are portrayed as incompetent in matters to do with education, teenagers, or relationships, and are almost always placed in odious contrast with mothers. In accepting the denigration of their proper adult role, their status is reduced to that of a child — yet another of the competent mother's children. Through these portrayals, children are then encouraged to look on fathers as weak and ineffectual, dominated by the mother, or overwhelmed by circumstances.

Consequences of the Retreat from the Father Role. Anatrella states that those who lack fatherly parenting are more prone to drug and alcohol abuse and lack respect for social conventions and the law; he offers the example of an out-of-control teenager who has stolen a car and caused significant damage. An exaggerated exercise of the mother role falsely protects the child from facing the consequences of his choice, preferring instead to defend the antisocial behavior and teenager. The extension of the safe, enclosed, and protective environment of childhood does in fact diminish independence and responsibility in adulthood.

SCHOOL COMMUNITY LEADERSHIP: THE PERSPECTIVE OF PRIMARY SCHOOL PRINCIPAL[11]

Spry and Graham examined the dimension of school leadership which encouraged the development of the community. In using the word, "community" they draw attention to the work of a number of theorists, from Dewey onwards, who, in the early twentieth century expressed the view that schools should be seen as genuine communities. More recently, Sergiovanni (1994) proposed the replacement of the idea of a school as a formal organization with the idea of the school as a community with a network of "felt inter-dependencies." Spry and Graham noted that the idea of community has found its way into the policy documents of most

---

11 G. Spry and J. Graham, *School Community Leadership: The Perspective of Primary School Principal,* AARE 2006 International Education Research Conference (Adelaide: Papers Collection, 2007).

Australian Catholic schools, but in general, principals are unclear about what this implies, and competing views of community are found in educational literature.

Spry and Graham reviewed some of these ideas using the foundational insights of the German sociologist, Ferdinand Tönnies, who distinguishes between *organization* and *community*. In the Tönnies model, a *community* is "a real social relationship of obligation or mutual dependence."[12] The *organization*, by contrast, is an "artificial collective of human beings... they are essentially separated in spite of all the unifying factors...each person is competitively working towards a personal agenda, rather than cooperating with others for the common good."[13]

Both models have their limitations when applied to the modern school, and so a third possibility is proposed, informed by the moral philosophy of personalism and characterized by themes such as subjectivity, autonomy, human dignity, community, participation, and solidarity.[14] (Such terms will be familiar to students of the writings of Pope John Paul II, who enlisted many personalist concepts to express the Catholic understanding of Trinitarian Christocentricity.) According to this view, "It is only in relation to others that we exist as persons; we are invested with significance by others who have need of us."[15]

Spry and Graham also refer to "servant leadership," which focuses on altruism, simplicity, and self-awareness, but they note that this can be manipulated by followers. Another model, "transforming leadership" — in which leaders influence others by inspirational motivation — has also been part of the contemporary discussion; but this too, where the appearance of cooperation masks resentment, is open to manipulation. The two research questions were as follows: *How do principals conceptualize the Catholic primary school as community? How do principals describe their leadership role in building the Catholic primary school as community?*

In response to the first question, *the concept of the school as a community*, the primary school principals involved in the study identified four characteristics and one observation that marked a Catholic school community:

---

12 F. Tönnies, *Community and Society*, C. Loomis, ed. and trans. (East Lansing: Michigan State University Press, 1957), 20.

13 Ibid., 74.

14 See J. Whetstone, "Personalism and Moral Leadership: The Servant Leader with a Transformational Vision," *Business Ethics: A European Review*, 11(4), (2002): 385–92.

15 See J. Macmurray, *Persons in Relation* (London: Harper and Harper, 1961), 211.

1. *Unity and common ground.* Those involved in a Catholic school community needed to be working together in pursuit of the same ends. This, according to the principals, is not easy to achieve.

2. *Care and compassion.* Catholic school communities should be marked by an emphasis on care and compassion. This was not found easy in an individualistic society.

3. *Parental partnership.* Catholic school communities accept the important role to be played by parents in the school. At the same time, the principals involved were concerned that parents should not overstep the mark and attempt to impose their own personal agendas on the community.

4. *Embedded in the parish and in Catholic practice.* The relationship with the Catholic Church is considered integral to the development of the community. The principals identified two levels. Firstly, religious practice needs to be expressed in prayer, ritual, and worship. Second, it is necessary to have a strong connection between the school and the parish. The school was seen as participating in the mission of the Church by offering spiritual support to the members of the school community.

5. *Observation.* In reflecting on these four themes, the principals saw these concepts as ideal rather than reality.

Principals were optimistic about their roles, but they believed it required intense effort. They suggested the following strategies: facilitating communication; developing a strong people-focus in relationships; openness to the place of families and family life; making efforts to link the parish and school; and supporting the needy. The consensus of this group was that conversation, communication, and dialogue were the most important tools for building community leadership. The principals' responses suggested that they preferred to conceptualize their schools according to the real-social-relationships model rather than to the organization model. Their focuses were on "mutual binding to a common goal, shared values, and shared conception of being."[16] At the same time, the actual research data showed that principals were confronted with the opposite reality—an emerging culture of the Catholic school built according to the

---

16 T. Sergiovanni, *Building Community in Schools* (San Francisco: Jossey-Bass, 1994), 6.

organization model. Personally committed to the social-relationships model of community and to the language of Personalism, they were constrained by a context which dragged them continually to the organization model. Three recommendations were made:

1. Development of policy at diocesan and school levels in respect to the Catholic school as community.
2. A role-making process to clarify the role of the principal as school community leader.
3. Professional development in respect to contemporary models of community and leadership.

SUMMING UP

In summary, contemporary research affirms the Church's official teaching about families and communities. The Church adds to this research her own spiritual wisdom; she recognizes the value of the philosophy and sociology, but draws us beyond community to *communio,* a family of God united by mutual charity and made one through the worship of the Trinity. *Communio* arises, not from business models and skills, but from every aspect of the Christian endeavor, every aspect of the school life that promotes what is true, beautiful, and good; every act of faith, hope, and love; every moment spent in prayer, worship, and acts of kindness towards others. The pastoral letter of the NSW Bishops has already given clear guidance in these areas.

The *Grant Study* makes an incomparable contribution to our understanding of the impact of families of the future success and happiness of children. By following a cohort for seven decades, it offers evidence-based conclusions that no other study has been able to emulate. This study allows us to put the impact of the school into perspective and to understand the importance of family relations in the area of education. Its conclusions are compatible with Catholic teaching regarding the family. These are areas in which schools can genuinely assist families in coming to understand what they have to offer to their children. Specific areas of parenting can be addressed as part of the school's education role in helping parents to help their own children.

Tony Anatrella's findings are representative of many studies which highlight the importance of the distinct roles of mothers and fathers; and he specifies *roles* rather than *persons* in this important parenting mix.

Here, too the school is able to help those who care for children with these important, but very simple insights. Catholic schools can be at the forefront of encouraging the fruitful contribution of both roles in the educational process. There is much that can be learned from research studies such as the one undertaken by Spry and Graham. Schools must take seriously their role as communities, rather than mere functional organizations. Specific practical measures for community-building can be drawn from these studies; nevertheless, the Catholic school, like the entire Church, is directed towards building *communio.* All aspects of its life — its teaching, pastoral care, promotion of beauty, worship — contribute something indispensable to this project. The task will never be finished; neither can it be pursued separately from any other aspect of the school's life.

Part II

Principles of Religious Education for the Classroom

13
Effective Teaching Practices[1]

INTRODUCTION

In relation to methods for teaching religious education, there are two principles which must be kept in mind. First, the Church does not specify a particular teaching method for religious education and catechesis; a variety of methods is encouraged.[2] The modern tendency to reduce human activity to a process, whereby a correct procedure leads to completely predictable outcome, cannot be fully applied to the Catholic faith, which is first and foremost a relationship — indeed an *intimate relationship* — with Christ.[3] The acquisition of a specific content follows from and draws its relevance from this relationship. The second principle is closely related to the first. No methodology, however effective, can dispense with the part played by the teacher, whose own life must give witness to the message proclaimed.[4] Not only is a program taught; a faith is lived and witnessed-to in such a way that the students find it both challenging and attractive.

Religious education includes significant dimensions from philosophy and theology. Both disciplines seek the truth. Philosophy proceeds from what human reason can attain, while Catholic theology draws its data from the revelation of God in Christ, handed on and elaborated (but not altered) by the Church. While both of these disciplines make their own distinctive contributions, they are not so separated that they cannot influence one another in allowing human beings to reach the truth. In the project of Catholic education, there are some lines of philosophical inquiry that reject revealed truth and even the possibility of attaining any truth at all. Contemporary expressions of these ideas include relativism and

---

1 This section on effective teaching practices first appeared in a report I prepared for the Diocese of Parramatta, identifying good contemporary practices that could be used in religious education.

2 GDC, 155.

3 CT, 5.

4 GDC, 156.

the view that the universe is unintelligible and void of meaning. Though people are free to follow these ideas if they so choose, they cannot form the basis of a Catholic education in any discipline.

INSIGHTS FROM CONTEMPORARY LEARNING THEORY

In terms of a philosophy of religious education, contemporary learning theory has much to offer by way of professional insights into the skill of teaching. Indeed, educational professionals are encouraged to take this line by the *General Directory of Catechesis*. The Church

> assumes those methods not contrary to the Gospel and places them at its service.... Catechetical methodology has the simple objective of education in the faith. It avails of the pedagogical sciences and of communication, as applied to catechesis.[5]
>
> It seems that the best of modern contemporary learning theory is substantially compatible with the educational vision of the Church. There is an enormous variety of educational writing that could be cited, but this chapter will confine itself to some of the best practices currently used in the field. It will be useful at this point to identify key, research-based teaching practices that would be helpful to incorporate into a religious education program. The list cannot be exhaustive; there will be other effective approaches that could also be used, and the landscape of learning theory is ever-expanding: new and effective teaching and learning practices always coming to light.

A SURVEY OF SOME EFFECTIVE CONTEMPORARY TEACHING AND LEARNING PRACTICES

Self-reported Grades. This practice consists of asking the student's advice about the current state of their own learning. Research indicates that students are quite good at understanding what they know and don't know. A meta-analysis conducted on 209 studies by Kuncel, Crede, and Thomas (2005) indicated that students had a very accurate understanding of their achievements levels across a wide range of subjects.[6] In his exposition of

5 Ibid., 148.
6 N.R. Kuncel, M. Crede, and L.L. Thomas, "The Validity of Self-reported Grade-point Averages, Class Ranks, and Test Scores: A Meta-analysis and Review of the Literature," *Review of Educational Research*, 75 (1), (2005): 63–82.

this phenomenon in his master classes, Hattie explains further that highly effective learning takes place when students present accurate information of this kind to the teacher and the teacher then responds by providing incrementally appropriate learning materials which can be accessed independently by the student. The student is given the freedom to spend exactly the amount of time needed on each material to gain mastery, and then move on. The effect size, which is 3.6 times the expected average, is likely to be achieved because of this precise focus on the exact need of the individual. [7]

Developmentally-appropriate Programs. From studies conducted by Naglieri and Das (1997)[8] and Sweller (2008)[9] together with many studies that have preceded these, it is clear the when teachers know the typical way in which students think at their particular developmental stage is likely to be the most important determining factor which teachers exercise in their choice of material for students. In other words, the teaching/learning experiences will be far more effective if they are designed to meet the stage of development of the learner and focus on their necessary developmental tasks. This will naturally capture their interest and attend to the pre-existing dispositions of the student. The *Early Years Report* of the Canadian province of Ontario has made a good start in bringing together the research in relation to all of the major developmental needs of children up to the age of seven. There is also longstanding support for this practice in the educational method of Maria Montessori, whose work in this field began in 1907 and has continued to be developed through action research by the world-wide Montessori education community up to the present. (These stages have already been described in more detail earlier in this book.) Hattie claims that the effect size of this practice is 1.2 — three times the expected average.[10]

Formative Evaluation. Teachers have a significant impact in the teaching/learning program, and so it is essential that they be open to improving the program through appropriate evaluation. One highly effective way of improving any system is through formative evaluation. Fuchs and Fuchs

---

7 See John Hattie, *Visible Learning* (New York: Routledge, 2009), 43–44.

8 J.A. Naglieri, and J.P. Das, "Intelligence Revised: The Planning, Attention, Simultaneous, Successive (PASS) Cognitive Processing Theory," in R.F. Dillon (ed.), *Handbook on Testing* (Westport: CT, Greenwood Press, 1997), 36–163.

9 J. Sweller, "Cognitive Load Theory and the Use of Educational Technology," *Educational Technology*, 48 (1), 32–34.

10 See John Hattie, *Visible Learning*, 297.

$(1986)^{11}$ demonstrated the effectiveness of using an evidence based model of systematic formative data in place of simple teacher judgement. Hattie has cited a further thirty studies to corroborate this effect, yielding an effect size of 0.9.[12]

Microteaching. Microteaching usually refers to the process whereby teachers deliver lessons to small groups of students, thus making them better able to gauge the responses of the students to the impact of what they are offering. Hattie identified over four hundred studies demonstrating the effectiveness of this teaching practice, and has identified its effect size as 0.88.[13] It also has an impact on the future practice of teachers in training. Metcalf (1995)[14] argued that when teachers engaged in this kind of teaching, it had significant impacts on the effectiveness of their teaching, and this did not diminish over time.

Reciprocal Teaching. One of the most effective ways of learning anything is to have to teach it to someone else. The research of Rosenshine and Meister (1994)[15] has demonstrated this, and a further thirty-eight studies quoted in Hattie's meta-analysis lend further weight to the practice, giving it an effect size of 0.74.[16] The need to do this will often provide a motivation to succeed at a particular task that would otherwise be lacking. The learning program will be significantly enhanced if the students are challenged to take responsibility for teaching something to someone else.

A note of caution is needed here. Those who benefit most from this strategy are usually not those who are already highly competent; rather, it is those who have not yet struggled to a fully developed understanding who will be helped by this process. On another level, it is often the case that highly competent students do not succeed in teaching their peers. There are a number of reasons for this. The competent student, not seeing the difficulties that others experience, may move too quickly through the task. Alternatively, competent students may have their own agenda — to demonstrate their intellectual superiority over those they are teaching.

---

11 L.S. Fuchs, and D. Fuchs, "Effects of Systematic Formative Evaluation: A Meta-analysis," *Exceptional Children*, 53 (3), 199–208.

12 See John Hattie, *Visible Learning*, 181.

13 See ibid., 112–113.

14 K.K. Metcalf, "Laboratory Experiences in Teacher Education: A Meta-analytical Review of Research." Paper presented at the Annual Meeting of the American Educational Research Association, San Francisco, 1995.

15 B. Rosenshine and C. Meister, "Reciprocal Teaching: A Review of the Research," *Review of Educational Research*, 64 (4), (1994): 479–530.

16 See John Hattie, *Visible Learning*, 203–04.

Teacher–Student Relationships. A very large corpus of educational research has consistently found in favor of the effectiveness of building good student/teacher relationships, described in the literature: the so called "person-centered teacher." Cornelius-White (2007) has identified 119 studies incorporating 2,439 schools, 14,851 teachers and 355,325 students in which 1,450 positive effects were based on this characteristic.[17] Hattie cites "agency, efficacy, respect by the teacher for what the student brings to the class…and allowing the experiences of the child to be recognized in the classroom."[18] He claims that these person-centered variables result in classrooms where there is more engagement, minimal resistant behaviors and respect for self and others and gives it an effect-size of 0.72.[19]

Spaced vs. Massed Practice. Much of current educational practice is based on what might be called the "unit model" in which a large amount of time is devoted to mastering a particular set of skills and knowledge. Once this is finished, however, the field rarely, if ever, covered again. This approach is referred to as "massed practice." Research findings have consistently called this practice into question, demonstrating that there is a better way of organizing a program, known as "spaced practice." As the words imply, this requires the spreading out of the tasks over time. This does not mean simple repetitive drill and practice which can be monotonous and largely meaningless. It is about deliberative practice, by which students return to the same material in different and interesting ways — possibly even adapted to their own advancing age and growing confidence — thus deepening their understanding. (The model of the regular cycle of the Liturgical year, when used properly, would be an example of an effective use of spaced practice.) In Hattie's words, "it is the frequency of different opportunities rather than spending more time on a task that makes the difference to learning."[20] He suggests that the proper use of spaced practice will yield an effect size of 0.71.[21]

The Impact of Movement on Learning and Cognition. In the early 1960s, Held and Hein published their classic research on the impact of moment on learning.[22] Two kittens, one designated the leader and the other the

17 J. Cornelius-White, "Learner-Centred Teacher-Student Relationships are Effective: A Meta-analysis," *Review of Educational Research*, 77 (1), (2007): 113–43.
18 John Hattie, *Visible Learning*, 118.
19 Ibid., 118–19.
20 Ibid., 185.
21 Ibid., 185–86.
22 R. Held and A. Hein, "Movement Produced Stimulation in the Development of Visually Guided Behaviour," *Journal of Comparative and Physiological Psychology*, 56 (5), (1963): 872–76.

follower, were only let out of a dark room for three hours a day. During this time, the leader-kitten was fitted with a harness and needed to drag around a cart with the follower-kitten. After three months, both kittens were tested. The leader kitten had developed normal vision, the follower, despite being exposed to exactly the same visual stimuli, had serious vision problems. This work began a great deal of research in the impact of movement on learning. There is now a large body of research that indicates the importance of fine motor tactile activity. In the area of judgement, for example, Glenberg and Kaschak (2002),[23] Ochs, Gonzales, and Jacoby, (1996),[24] McNeill (1992),[25] Kraus and Hadar (1999)[26] demonstrate in a variety of ways that movement and cognition are closely aligned. Memory also, it seems, is significantly improved when connected with fine motor movement as demonstrated in the research of Cohen (1989),[27] Engelkamp, Zimmer, Mohr, and Sellen (1994),[28] Noice, Noice, and Kennedy (2000)[29] and Laird, Wagener, Halal, and Szegda (1982).[30] In summing up, Lillard writes: "there is abundant research showing that movement and cognition are closely intertwined. People represent spaces and objects more accurately, make judgements faster and more accurately, remember information better and show superior social cognition when their movements are aligned with what they are thinking about or learning."[31] It seems, then, that a program that restricts movement too narrowly or does not permit tactile engagement with real objects also restricts learning significantly.

Choice and Perceived Control. Nowhere is it disputed that freedom is a foundational, constitutive element of authentic human life and development. Even as children, human beings function best if they are given a

23 Glenberg and Kaschak, "Grounding Language in Action," *Psychonomic Bulletin & Review*, 9 (3), (2002): 36–41.

24 E. Ochs, P. Gonzales, and S. Jacoby, "Collaborative Discovery in a Scientific Domain," *Cognitive Science*, 21 (2), (1996): 109–46.

25 See D. McNeill, *Hand and Mind* (Chicago: University of Chicago Press, 1992).

26 Kraus and Hadar, "The Role of Speech Related Arm/Hand Gestures in Word Retrieval" in L. S. Messing & R. Campbell (eds.), *Gesture, Speech and Sign* (New York: Oxford University Press, 1999), 93–116.

27 R.L. Cohen, "Memory for Action Events: The Power of Enactment," *Educational Psychology Review*, 1 (1), (1989): 57–80.

28 J. Engelkamp, H.D. Zimmer, G. Mohr, and O. Sellen, "Memory of Self-performed Tasks: Self-performing during Recognition," *Memory and Cognition*, 22 (1), (1994): 34–39.

29 H. Noice, T. Noice, and C. Kennedy, "Effects of Enactment by Professional Actors at Encoding and Retrieval," *Memory*, 8 (6), (2000): 353–63.

30 J.D. Laird, J.J. Wagener, M. Halal, and M. Szegda, "Remembering What You Feel: Effects of Emotion on Memory," *Journal of Personality & Social Psychology*, 42 (4), (1982): 646–57.

31 A.S. Lillard, *Montessori: The Science behind the Genius*, 56.

degree of choice in order to manage their own circumstances. The capacity to use this freedom develops over time, and with very young children, choices must necessarily be limited. If the capacity to make simple choices is entirely absent, however, the learning process is significantly diminished. Recent research has affirmed the value of making limited choices available to students. Some examples include the studies of Ryan and Deci (2000),[32] Iyengar and Lepper (1999),[33] Markus and Kitayama (1991).[34] While agreeing with this as a general principle, other research indicates that unlimited free choice will actually have a negative effect on learning, as per the studies of Iyengar and Lepper (2000)[35] and Schwartz (2004).[36] Another benefit of limited choice is an increase in students' capacity to concentrate deeply and for long periods of time; this is supported by the research of Ruff and Rothbart (1996),[37] Cumberland-Li, Eisenberg, and Reiser (2004),[38] Carlson, Moses, and Hicks (1998).[39] It appears that some degree of limited choice dramatically enhances results at every level; this applies to a religious education classroom as much as to any other human learning activity.

   Inadequacy of Extrinsic Rewards and Motivation. During the early 1970s, educational psychology began to turn away from what had, up to that time, been a prevailing focus on behaviorism, which is the notion the human beings are shaped primarily through reward and punishment. This idea was challenged by studies such as that of Lepper, Greene, and Nisbett (1973),[40] which began to indicate that this emphasis could actually result in less motivation among students. A large meta-study by Deci *et*

---

32 R.M. Ryan, and D.L. Deci, "Self-determination Theory and the Facilitation of Intrinsic Motivation, Self-development, and Well-being," *American Psychologist*, 55 (1), (2000): 68–78.

33 S.S. Iyengar, and M.R. Lepper, "Rethinking the Value of Choice: A Perspective on Intrinsic Motivation," *Journal of Personality and Social Psychology*, 76, (1999): 349–66.

34 H.R. Markus, and S. Kitayama, "Culture and the Self: Implications for Cognition, Emotion and Motivation," *Psychological Review*, 98, (1991): 224–53.

35 S.S. Iyengar, and M.R. Lepper, "When Choice is De-motivating: Can One Desire too much of a Good Thing?," *Journal of Personality and Social Psychology*, 79 (6), (2000): 995–1006.

36 See B. Schwartz, *The Paradox of Choice.* (New York: Harper Collins, 2004).

37 See H.A. Ruff, and M.K. Rothbart, *Attention in Early Development: Themes and Variations* (New York: Oxford University Press, 1996).

38 A. Cumberland-Li, N. Eisenberg, and M. Reiser, "Relations of Young Children's Agreeableness and Resiliency to Effortful Control and Impulsivity," *Social Development*, 13 (2), (2004), 193–212.

39 S.M. Carlson, L.J. Moses, and H.R. Hicks, "The Role of Inhibitory Processes in Young Children's Difficulties with Deception and False Belief," *Child Development*, 69, (1998): 672–91.

40 M.R. Lepper, D. Greene, and R.E. Nisbett, "Undermining Children's Intrinsic Interest with Extrinsic Reward: A Test of the 'Overjustification' Hypothesis," *Journal of Personality and Social Psychology*, 28 (1), (1973): 129–37.

al. (1999)[41] provided clear evidence of the ultimately negative impact of a reward-and-punishment-based system in sustaining motivation to learn. At the same time, other studies demonstrate that, where it is necessary to motivate students to complete very low interest tasks, some rewards can be helpful, as per the work of Cameron, Banko, and Pierce (2001).[42] Nevertheless, it does seem that the use of extrinsic rewards undermines the most potent student motivator — success. Those who work only for reward will need to be offered ever-greater rewards. Those who are encouraged by their own success are more likely to persist in the face of difficulties.

Regarding religious education, the application is clear — if the task is essentially intimacy with Christ, it should be seen as a free relationship aiming at mutual love. The idea that students should participate in this relationship to receive extrinsic rewards will actually undermine the notion of genuine love. Even in human relationships, the friend who uses another to gain reward is not regarded as a true friend at all. While there is always a place for spontaneous gift-giving, this should never be presented in terms of reward and punishment.

Learning from Peers. Educational research identifies three different aspects of successful peer learning: imitative learning, peer tutoring, and collaborative learning. Each one of these has a valuable contribution to make to learning. It seems that different developmental ages favor different peer learning models or combinations of these models. Bandura, Ross, and Ross (1963)[43] offered the now-classic research demonstrating the value of learning through observation and imitation of peers — by simply watching the way others do things, students improve their own competence. Subsequent studies have consistently confirmed the value of this approach. These studies include those of Carpenter, Akhtar, and Tomasello (1998),[44] Chartrand and Bargh (1999),[45] and Gergely, Bekkering,

41   E.L. Deci, R. Koestner, and R.M. Ryan, "A Meta-analytical Review of Experiments Examining the Effects of Extrinsic Rewards on Intrinsic Motivation," *Psychological Bulletin*, 125, (1999): 627–68.

42   J. Cameron, K.M. Banko, and W.D. Pierce, "Pervasive Negative Effects of Rewards on Intrinsic Motivation: The Myth Continues," *Behaviour Analyst*, 24 (1), (2001): 1–44.

43   A. Bandura, D. Ross, and S.A. Ross, "Imitation of Film-mediated Aggressive Models," *Journal of Abnormal & Social Psychology* 66 (1), (1963): 3–11.

44   M. Carpenter, N. Akhtar, and M. Tomasello, "Fourteen through 18-month-old Infants Differentially Imitate Intentional and Accidental Actions," *Infant Behaviour and Development* 21 (1998): 315–330.

45   T.L. Chartrand, and J.A. Bargh, "The Chameleon Effect: The Perception-Behaviour Link and Social Interaction," *Journal of Personality and Social Psychology*, 76 (1999): 893–910.

and Kiraly (2002).[46] Results from peer-tutoring programs, particularly those sessions adapted to the age of the students and tightly structured to achieve a particular purpose, have a double effect. Such programs not only benefit those receiving assistance, but also the tutors themselves. Studies demonstrating this include those of Gauvain and Rogoff (1989),[47] Greenwood, Terrey, Utley, Montagna, and Walker (1993),[48] Fantuzzo and Ginsburg-Block (1998),[49] and Gauvain (2001).[50]

√ While peer-tutoring implies a one-to-one relationship, collaborative learning involves groups of students working together. A number of studies demonstrate that collaborative approaches can help people to learn better in certain circumstances; this goes beyond academic achievement, to include social development as well. Not all studies show this improvement, and there seem to be some limiting factors. For example, very young children do not seem to benefit from collaboration of this kind. Furthermore, if the material to be studies is especially unfamiliar, students seem to benefit more from observation and imitation before progressing to collaboration.⌋

√ It also seems that the success of collaborative learning can be considerably greater if students are allowed to work with friends. The studies demonstrating the effectiveness of the various aspects of collaborative learning include Flavell (1999),[51] Azmitia and Crowley (2001),[52] Rogoff, Bartlett, and Turkanis (2001),[53] and Aronson (2002).[54]

---

46 G. Gergely, H. Bekkering, and I. Kiraly, "Rational Imitation in Pre-verbal Infants," *Nature*, 415 (6873), (2002): 755.

47 M. Gauvain and B. Rogoff, "Collaborative Problem Solving and Children's Planning Skills," *Developmental Psychology* 25 (1), (1989): 139–51.

48 C.R. Greenwood, B. Terrey, C.A. Utley, D. Montagna, and D. Walker, "Achievement, Placement and Services: Middle School Benefits of Classwide Peer Tutoring Used at the Elementary School," *School Psychology Review*, 22 (3), (1993): 497–516.

49 J. Fantuzzo and M. Ginsburg-Block, "Reciprocal Peer Tutoring: Developing and Testing Effective Peer Collaborations for Elementary School Students" in K. Topping & S. Ehly (eds.), *Peer-assisted Learning* (Mahawa, N.J.: Lawrence Earlbaum, 1998), 121–44.

50 M. Gauvain, *The Social Context of Cognitive Development* (London: Guilford, 2001).

51 J.H. Flavell, "Cognitive Development: Children's Knowledge about the Mind," *Annual Review of Psychology* 50 (1999): 21–45.

52 M. Azmitia and K. Crowley, "The Rhythms of Thinking: The Study of Collaboration in an Earthquake Microworld" in K. Crowley, C. D. Schunn, and T. Okada (eds.), *Designing for Science: Implications for Everyday, Classroom, and Professional Settings* (Mahawa, NJ: Lawrence Earlbaum, 2001), 51–81.

53 B. Rogoff, L. Bartlett, and C.G. Turkanis, "Lessons about Learning as Community" in B. Rogoff, C.G. Turkanis, and L. Bartlett (eds.), *Learning Together: Children and Adults in a School Community* (New York: Oxford University Press, 2001), 3–17.

54 E. Aronson, "Building Empathy, Compassion, and Achievement in the Jigsaw Classroom" in J. Aronson (ed.), *Improving Academic Achievement: Impact of Psychological Factors in*

Inquiry/Project-based Learning. Inquiry-based learning has become prominent in recent years. It attempts to harness the interest of the students and gives them the freedom to discover ever-greater dimensions of knowledge. This approach has much to recommend it, especially its capacity to encourage independence in learning. Clearly, it comprises many of the abovementioned teaching practices and would serve as a very effective instrument in an overall teaching-and-learning strategy. However, one *caveat* must be addressed, especially concerning religious education. Some of the more radical exponents of inquiry-learning can be dismissive of the notion of "essential content" and some argue that this is determined by the interests of the students.[55] For religious education, content is not an irrelevant consideration. On the contrary, using educationally appropriate means, it is important to present at least a basic summary of the deposit of faith (*depositum fidei*). Students must also remember this content.[56] Expressions of this concern are not limited to the field of religious education. Kirschner, Sweller, and Clark (2006) demonstrated the ineffectiveness of inquiry or problem-based learning strategies where students worked with new or complex material.[57] Clark (1989) noted that even when students express preference for this approach, they do not learn as effectively as they would from direct instruction.[58] Lundeberg (1987) as well as Pressley and Afflerbach (1995) indicated that mastery of a variety of learning strategies — not just inquiry-based strategies — was necessary for developing expertise across different domains.[59] Samuelstuen and Braten (2007) confirmed that students benefit more from using a variety of learning approaches.[60] Small (2003) demonstrated the fallacy of radical constructivism's epistemology and pointed to the unhelpful

---

Education (San Diego: Academic Press, 2002), 209–25.

55 Reggio Emilia method is an example of an educational approach that takes this view of content.

56 See CT, 56.

57 See P.A. Kirschner, J. Sweller, and R.E. Clark, "Why Minimal Guidance during Instruction Does Not Work: An Analysis of the Failure of Constructivist, Discovery, Problem-based, Experiential and Inquiry-based Teaching," *Educational Psychologist* 41 (2), 75–86.

58 See R.E. Clark, "When Teaching Kills Learning: Research on Mathematics" in H.M. Mandl, N. Bennett, E. de Corte, and H.F Friedrich (eds.), *Learning and Instruction: European Research in an International Context. Vol. 2* (London: Pergamon, 1989), 1–22.

59 See M.A. Lundeberg, "Metacognitive Aspects of Reading Comprehension: Studying Understanding in Legal Case Analysis," *Reading Research Quarterly* 61 (1), (1987): 94–106.

60 See M.S. Samuelstuen, and I. Braten, "Examining the Validity of Self-reports on Scales Measuring Students' Strategic Processing," *British Journal of Educational Psychology*, 77 (2), (2007): 351–78.

confusion between the legitimate and well-established *learning* process (by which human beings *construct* knowledge by relating component parts) and the *teaching* strategy involved in problem-based learning.[61] Phillips (1995) concluded that the issue should be considered from the learner's perspective. The *construction* of knowledge by an individual benefits more from direct instruction and does not need inquiry methods to achieve the best result.[62] John Hattie, the world's most cited educational researcher, expresses the frustration of those who have pointed out the shortcomings of radical constructivism and the over-dependence on inquiry learning:

> Every year I present lectures to teacher-education students and find that they are already indoctrinated with the mantra "constructivism good, direct instruction bad." When I show them the results of these meta-analyses, they are stunned, and they often become angry at having been given an agreed set of truths and commandments against direct instruction.[63]

In other words, while inquiry-based learning is an excellent tool for use in an existing framework of knowledge, there are significant problems where it is used to establish that basic framework. The cognitive load (the number and complexity of intellectual demands on the learner) in establishing the data to be used is beyond the capacities of inexperienced learners if they are left to establish this simply using their own inquiries. With regard to religious education, this means that students need to be comfortable and proficient with the basic content of their faith before they should be asked to undertake further inquiry. Inquiry learning has much to offer, but it cannot carry the whole load of teaching the essential content of the Catholic faith.

---

61 See R. Small, "A Fallacy in Constructivist Epistemology," *Journal of Philosophy of Education* 37 (3), (2003): 483–502.

62 N.B. Phillips, C.L. Hamlett, L.S. Fuchs, and D. Fuchs, "Combining Classwide Curriculum-based Measurement and Peer Tutoring to Help General Educators Provide Adaptive Education," *Learning Disabilities Research and Practice* 8 (3), (1995): 148–56.

63 John Hattie, *Visible Learning*, 204.

14
The Pedagogy of God

As early as the second century, St. Irenaeus of Lyons drew attention to the fact that God seemed to have a particular way of teaching human beings, a pedagogy of God. This is regarded as an insight of such importance that it is specifically referred to in the current *Catechism of the Catholic Church*.[1] It could perhaps be described best as a pedagogy of gift and response. There is a striking parallel in human experience that can illustrate this point very well: the process of courtship. At the moment when we begin exploring a relationship with another with a view to marriage, we normally find ourselves drawn to a particular person, whom we may not know very well. It is usually the young man who must take the initiative and start the relationship, but there is quite a risk involved. What if the other person does not respond? That will feel like a rejection. There is no way around it, however; this is a risk we must take.

When I was in this position myself, I received some very good advice. I was told that the best way to start such a relationship was to offer a gift (a very small gift; you don't want to appear "desperate"!). A single rose was a good place to start. The response that comes back from this first tentative step will tell us whether or not our feelings might be reciprocated. This is exactly what I did. To my delight, the gift was well received, and was followed by another in return! And so it continued all through our courtship. The gifts became more and more considered and valuable, and so were the responses. Finally, one day I believed that I was ready for the greatest gift of all—I was going to offer the best thing I had to give: myself, as a gift in marriage. To my great joy, it was accepted and reciprocated. Forty years later, we are still striving to give the gift of ourselves to each other. The similarities to biblical revelation are striking. God did not give himself to humanity immediately; he began by offering small gifts and waiting for the response. Along the way, it is possible to trace the rising value of what was offered; this will be explored more fully in some of the following paragraphs.

---

1 CCC, § 53.

Taking its cue from the *Catechism,* the *General Directory of Catechesis* draws attention to this fact that the Church has learned a particular form of pedagogy from God himself.[2] The goal of this pedagogy is nothing less that "communion with the Trinity." This should be considered the best method of communicating the faith. The purpose of the Pedagogy of God is to gain wisdom and knowledge from the faith, but also from personal liberation in Christ. The pedagogy of God proceeds slowly, with sufficient time allowed for reflection on the meaning of each stage, followed by an invitation to respond. We can follow it through the stages of biblical revelation. Throughout the Old Testament, it is clear that God communicates himself progressively and in stages. We see the slow unfolding of the Plan of God through various key events: the Covenants with Noah and Abraham; the Law and the election of Israel as a nation; the linking of divine and human wisdom in the Psalms; the ongoing reflection of the prophets on the meaning of God's plan. At each point, we learn a little more, not only about God, but about what it means to be human and created in the image of God.

After centuries of revelation, the moment finally arrives when God is ready to reveal himself fully and give himself as a gift to the world. God comes to the world himself, taking on human nature as Jesus Christ. In this way, God gives us the *New Law.* Jesus not only *teaches* us; he actually *saves* us by making it possible to live with the same kind of life that God has himself—the life of grace. At the same time, there is a unique human being, a young woman who alone in the history of the world has been prepared so that she is capable of responding to the gift in such a way that God can become a man. Through his ministry, Jesus teaches us; through the paschal mystery—his death and resurrection—Jesus saves us and makes the life of grace available to us. The plan is not concluded with the death and resurrection of Christ; he has given an ongoing role to the Church he founded. It must hand on, progressively, the meaning and the person of Jesus Christ through the action of the Holy Spirit.

There are four key elements of this task:

1. <u>Sacraments</u> / **Liturgy (Body).** The Church must ensure that the holy mysteries fully revealed by God (the *Mysterion*) are passed on. These are the redemptive mysteries about God's actions in the world that we read about in the Bible. They are recalled and made present through the

---

2 GDC, § 139–47.

sacraments, the sacred signs and words expressed in the Liturgy of the Church. Because all of these signs are designed to be sensed, we can say that they are designed to appeal to the senses in the body of the human person.

2. The Scriptures (Heart). The Church must ensure that the record of what God has revealed is passed on in the written word — the scriptures. These must be accurate and authentic, acknowledging that the Holy Spirit is the author. The scriptures give an accurate account of the words and actions of God in the world. It is here that we come to know Christ and to understand what he has done for us. The proper human response to this is gratitude and love. When properly understood, the scriptures touch the heart and bring forth love.

3. The Tradition / Doctrine (Mind). The Church must also pass on all the authentic insights that it has learned from centuries of reflection. This is called the *Traditio (Tradition)* and includes such treasures as the creeds and the doctrines which give insights into how we might understand what has been revealed. Because tradition is designed to help us make sense of what God has done from what we have sensed and loved, it is directed mainly at the mind.

4. Prayer (Personal Integration of the Mystery). There is a further role for the Church beyond formation and information: all of those who want to grow in the life of grace must develop their own intimate dialogue with Christ. This personal dialogue of salvation between God and individual human persons is called prayer.

THE LITURGICAL SPIRAL CURRICULUM

The idea of continually returning to the same themes on a seasonal basis is far from new. Ancient Israel had its seasonal feasts which came around every year and drew the attention of the people to the many different gifts and blessings that they had received from God. Each time they returned to a feast, they sought deeper meanings as their reflections proceeded over a lifetime. This is an excellent model, and one that has been used by the Church from the beginning. If it is to be used as the basis for ongoing education in the faith, it is well that this process be used as the basis of a genuine catechetical curriculum for families, parishes and schools. This would bring the whole community into an awareness that there is a progressive deepening of the same foundational themes. The key themes almost cry out for recognition and should be based on the major feasts of the Church, which in themselves draw attention to the Plan of

God. They are, of course, Christmas (the coming of Christ as the culmi-
nation of divine revelation), Easter (the death & resurrection of Christ),
and Pentecost (the sending of the Holy Spirit to sustain the presence of
Christ in the Church).[3]

Term 4. The focus of this term is twofold. In the first part, the previous
Church year needs to be brought to a conclusion. The focus will be on
death and everlasting life, concluding with the celebration of the final goal
of heavenly glory in the feast of Christ the King. The second half of the
term returns to a study of the unfolding plan of God in history: salvation
history. This could begin with a focus on some major themes of the Old
Testament, such as the history of the covenants, the Exodus, and various
prophets. This is an ideal time for looking at the prefiguring events which
point to the coming of Christ. For younger children, it is important to
make a judgement about how much of the Old Testament they may be
capable of understanding. It is far more important at this level to put the
emphasis on the Infancy Narratives—the Annunciation, Visitation and
the Birth of Christ—with some further extension into the Presentation
of Christ in the Temple and the coming of the Magi at the Epiphany.

Term 1. The focus of the term at the beginning of the year is the feast
of Easter. This has a number of dimensions. In the early part of the term,
the focus needs to be on the liturgical season of Lent. As well as the usual
ascetical challenges, the main reflections should follow the ministry of
Christ: those things that Jesus said and did to proclaim the kingdom of
God. This would include the miracles of Christ, the parables, and other
reflections on the Kingdom. Towards the end of the term the focus should
shift to the Paschal mystery. Beginning with Palm Sunday the program
moves through the other key events of Holy Week—the Last Supper,
the suffering and death of Christ on Good Friday and the great events
associated with the resurrection.

Term 2. The main focus of this term are the related feasts of Ascension
and Pentecost. This functions differently. Whereas Christmas and Easter
serve as the culminating point, Pentecost is the starting point. The coming
of the Holy Spirit brings into focus the role of the Church in sustaining the
presence of Christ on the earth. There are two major ways in which this is

---

3 In practical terms, the school year is divided into four terms. In order to preserve the logic
of the unfolding Church year, the usual Australian school terms have been arranged in the order
that they would occur in the northern hemisphere, but preserving the names that would normally
be used. For details of Liturgical Spiral Curricula in the US and Australia, see appendix 1 and 2.

accomplished, and it is the first of these — the Sacraments — which should form the focus of activities at this time. It is relatively simple to make the connection between the feast of the Ascension and Baptism: in the Great Commission Christ commanded his apostles to baptize. The other two Sacraments of Initiation are likewise relatively simple to link with the feast days that celebrate great mysteries. The Eucharist can be seen as the fulfilment of Christ's command at the Last Supper to celebrate his ongoing presence in this way. The Sacrament of Reconciliation can take its starting point from the appearance of Christ to the Apostles on Easter Sunday night, when he breathed on them and told them to "receive the power to forgive sins." The Sacrament of Confirmation can follow quite naturally from the Feast of Pentecost. The remaining sacraments, Anointing of the Sick, Marriage, and Holy Orders, also fit naturally into the desire of Christ to remain among his people in a way that touches on every human need.

Term 3. There is another way in which Christ must remain present on the earth until the end of time. He is present in us; in our actions and behavior towards others. This brings out two related dimensions. First, we are meant to be progressively transformed into the likeness of Christ; this implies moral effort. The study of Christian morality finds a natural place at this point. Second, we are meant to be agents of change in the world around us. This is the place for placing a particular emphasis on the social teaching of the Church. Challenges to develop one's own spiritual life in support of these projects, changing ourselves and helping others, indicates where the life of prayer can receive its proper focus.

Other Considerations. Throughout the course of the year, there are significant celebrations of saints and aspects of Church teaching which do not fit strictly into the usual tenor of the liturgical season. They follow anniversaries, as in the lives of the saints, the Annunciation and the Visitation. In some cases, such as Trinity Sunday, Corpus Christi, Sacred Heart, and the special feasts of Our Lady under various titles, the date is chosen for another reason. These should be celebrated at the appropriate time, and the rest of the program needs to be fitted around these. All solemnities of the Church calendar should be remembered every year and acknowledged in the curriculum by way of preparation. The celebration of other locally relevant memoria will depend on the needs and interests of the children and the local community. Finally, there is always a danger, when following the broad structure of the liturgical year, of going over the same material at the same simplistic level every year. The opposite problem can also cause difficulties, that is, presuming that the students know more than they really do and therefore taking them into areas that are beyond their capacity. The only effective way to use a spiral curriculum is to enter into the same central mysteries at deeper and deeper levels, taking careful note of the real situation of each individual. There are two appendices in this work that have been provided for the purpose of helping those responsible (parents, priests, teachers, or administrators) to decide on a particular level of content.

In 2013, Pope Francis drew attention to some highly significant aspect of the task in two documents: the encyclical *Lumen Fidei* and the apostolic exhortation *Evangelii Gaudium*. In *Lumen Fidei* (Light of Faith) many significant points are reiterated, but one of these stands out in relation to catechesis. Pope Francis identifies the key element in handing on the Catholic Faith in the following terms:

> The Church, like every family, passes on to her children the whole store of her memories. But how does this come about in a way that nothing is lost...? What is communicated in the Church...is the new light born of an encounter with the true God.... There is a special means for passing down this fullness...a means capable of engaging the entire person, body and spirit, interior life and relationships with others. It is the sacraments, celebrated in the Church's liturgy. The sacraments communicate an incarnate memory, linked to the times and places of our lives, linked to all our senses.[4]

There could be no clearer statement about the important role that is played by the Sacraments in the whole process of religious education and catechesis. The Sacraments are to be considered the primary means of passing on the faith; the way in which Christ is to be made present in this and every other time in history until the end of the world.

Evangelii Gaudium (*The Joy of the Gospel*) covers a wide variety of themes, but there are specific areas where some very clear statements are made about the catechesis. The most compelling of these statements concerns an ancient insight that needs to be re-stated more clearly: "We have rediscovered the fundamental role of the first announcement or

---

4 LF, § 40.

kerygma ...Jesus Christ loves you; he gave his life to save you; and now he is living at your side every day to enlighten, strengthen and free you."[5] All Christian formation, Pope Francis insists, consists of "entering more deeply into the kerygma."[6] Perhaps the *kerygma* need to be printed on a brass plaque in displayed in every place where catechesis is being pursued. If we were to analyze it line by line, it begins with the fundamental bedrock of the Christian faith: the assurance that Christ loves us. The second proposition makes clear the depth of this love: "he gave his life to save us." The third statement — that Christ is now at our side every day — makes the implicit claim that, through the sacraments, we have daily access to the Lord, who is "at our side." The final proposition — that the purpose of the divine presence is to strengthen, heal, and free us — demonstrates that human beings are not yet ready for their final goal, but need strengthening, healing, and freeing. This implies both the need for moral effort on the part of human beings, and the assurance of divine assistance — grace — through our ever-present savior. All programs of catechesis must contribute in some way to these essential goals. Also in *Evangelii Gaudium,* Pope Francis stresses the need for what he terms mystagogical renewal, which he then explains: "This basically has to do with two things: a progressive experience of formation involving the entire community, and a renewed appreciation of the liturgical signs of Christian initiation....Many manuals and programs have not yet taken sufficiently into account the need for a mystagogical renewal."[7] In so doing, Pope Francis echoes the findings of the earlier 2007 apostolic exhortation, *Sacramentum Caritatis.*[8]

To sum up, Pope Francis has been clear as to what direction religious education and catechesis should be taking at this time. Religious education needs to begin with the reality that God loves, cares for and protects us. There needs to be an emphasis on "mystagogy," on working through the concrete liturgical signs we find in the sacraments. Finally, religious education requires a suitable environment, an attractive presentation, and the integration of every dimension of the person within a community journeying towards God. The sacraments are particularly well adapted to passing on the Faith of the Church.

---

5 EG, § 164.
6 Ibid., § 165.
7 Ibid., § 166.
8 See SC, § 67.

15
Classroom Methods for Religious Education / Catechetics

The documents of the Church make it clear that it is wise to allow a variety of methods to be used in passing on the Catholic Faith. The specific means chosen are likely to correspond with the talents of the teacher or catechist. In 2013, however, Pope Francis came very close to indicating a preferred method, while still maintaining the need for variety. The method, of course, is the ancient catechetical strategy of mystagogy referred to in the previous chapter. Even so, there are some basic principles in this area that need to be part of any method chosen, starting with the most obvious fact that the method selected should account for the differing ages and other needs of the students.[1] As we have already noted, *The General Directory for Catechesis* describes the methodology of catechesis in terms of a "pedagogy of God" which "receives its characteristics from the Holy Spirit."[2] These characteristics include:

1. A "dialogue of salvation" between God and the person
2. the principle of the progressiveness of Revelation and its adaptation to different persons and cultures
3. the centrality of Jesus Christ, "a pedagogy of the incarnation"
4. the community experience of faith
5. a pedagogy of signs, where words and deeds, teaching and experience are interlinked
6. a pedagogy drawing on the power of truth[3]

Verbum Domini insists that the pedagogy of the Church in presenting the faith has always unfolded the scriptures against the backdrop of the

---

1 GDC, § 177–81.
2 Ibid., § 143.
3 See GDC, § 143.

liturgical year.[4] This emphasis on the inseparable role that the scriptures and the Liturgy play in catechesis has already been referred to in the previous chapter. Another long held intuition made explicit in *Evangelii Gaudium* is that every form of catechesis should also involve the "way of beauty." Hence, "every expression of true beauty can thus be acknowledged as a path leading to an encounter with Christ."[5] The Church is also quite explicit about the fact that the personal contribution of the parent, teacher, or catechist. No methodology, however effective, can dispense with the part played by the teacher, whose own life must give witness to the message proclaimed.[6] In terms of intellectual content, "discovery" is cited as an important pedagogical tool and one that is in accord with the "realist" philosophical view of the Catholic Church regarding the existence of objective reality, as opposed to subjectivist and relativist interpretations.[7] Continuing this intellectual theme, Pope John Paul II, in *Catechesi Tradendae,* made a very strong statement about the value of "memory." He insisted that the purpose of any catechetical methodology is to fix in the memory, intelligence, and heart the essential truths that must impregnate the whole of life.[8] Teachers are encouraged to ensure that certain basic ideas are committed to memory through appropriate educational means.[9] The texts that are committed to memory should be gradually understood in depth, to become a source of Christian life on the personal and community levels.[10] In determining whether a catechetical methodology is helpful, then, in so far as it is capable of embracing all of these necessary principles, it can be considered suitable. If any of these elements is missing, it would be advisable either to choose a different methodology or to attempt to incorporate the missing elements if it is possible to do so.

In the remaining part of this chapter, I will describe and analyze two methodologies that have been found to be useful. One is a Montessori-based method, the other is an analytical method. Both of these approaches incorporate the inductive and deductive approaches which the *General Directory*

---

4 VBD, § 52.

5 EG, § 167.

6 GDC, § 156.

7 See Congregation for Catholic Education, *Religious Dimension of Education in a Catholic School* (Vatican City: Libreria Editrice Vaticana, 1998). [Afterwards RDEC]

8 GDC, § 44.

9 CT, § 56.

10 GDC, § 154.

for Catechesis considers essential. An inductive method "corresponds to a profound urge of the human spirit to come to a knowledge of unintelligible things by means of visible things." An inductive method precedes and leads on to a deductive method "which explains and describes facts by proceeding from their causes." The deductive synthesis, however, has full value only when the inductive process is completed.

MYSTAGOGICAL CATECHESIS: A MONTESSORI-BASED METHOD

The two best-known Montessori-based methods are *Catechesis of the Good Shepherd* and *Godly Play*. There are considerable similarities between the two methodologies, but also significant differences. I do not intend at this point to argue the relative merits of these two systems. What I have set out below is a method I am describing as *Mystagogical Catechesis*. This attempts to draw attention to how one might implement the call of the contemporary Church for a "mystagogical renewal."[11] Essentially, it is a modified form of the *Catechesis of the Good Shepherd* approach which, in my judgement, has significant advantages in linking the sacraments with the scriptures and so presenting a Catholic view of reality.

The work of Gianna Gobbi and Sophia Cavalletti was referred to above, so I will only recall it briefly here. Through continued research and observation, Gobbi and Cavalletti developed a method of religious education based around scripture, sacraments/liturgy, and salvation history. Each of these aspects is carefully related to each of the other aspects to form an integral whole. One of the central insights is the matching of presentations to the developmental-sensitive period of the children. This method places a very strong emphasis on the independence of the child, and after initial training, children could conceivably work in an atrium even if their teacher is not present. The process goes through a series of essential stages.

1. Preliminary Stage: Setting the Scene. *The Learning Environment.* One of the key components of this method is an acknowledgement that the environment itself has a role in instructing the learner. To work successfully, there must be some preliminary setting up of a learning environment. This can work in any classroom setting. Essentially, it entails a careful thinking through of the content likely to be relevant for the age group in question. This must include not only the typical work which might need to be provided for typical students of the level, but also provision for those

---

11   See EG, § 166.

who need simpler material, and for those who need more advanced material. Everything needs to be ready so that the students can have access to whatever level they need to work at. Each learning goal needs a range of materials that will allow the student to work independently, or in groups.

Grace and Courtesy Procedures. Another essential preliminary task consists of teaching students the processes for successfully working in the space. The teacher should introduce these procedures on the very first school day of the year and continue to insist on them throughout the year. While it is true that the students are likely to settle into these procedures quickly, they need to be implemented firmly but kindly at all times. These procedures are not significantly different from those needed in any contemporary classroom. They include:

- Appropriate ways to move within the classroom
- Consideration for others — e.g., taking turns in using the materials
- Levels of noise: not silence, but speaking quietly in order not to disturb others
- Response to signals
- Care of the materials and the environment

Setting Up Response Tools. The last preliminary task requires the setting up of student response tools. After presenting the basic content of a lesson, teachers often need to come up with some other activity that allows the students to continue working with the concept they have learned. In a Montessori environment, these responses are not specified for each activity. The students are free to choose from a range of response tools that they have been shown how to use independently. Teachers are always adding to this range of tools, but some of the more common ones for younger children include:

- Use of the materials that have been presented in class
- Water-color painting sets
- Drawing tools: paper, pencils, etc.
- Independent relevant reading material, including Bibles and saints lives
- Opportunities for writing a response, reflection, poem, or prayer
- Material for play-dough modelling
- Opportunities for quiet prayer and reflection in the prayer corner

- Templates for computer investigation projects
- Learning journal
- A variety of task cards associated with particular materials

2. Introducing New Content and Materials. Once all of the preliminary work has been completed, it will be possible to move to the introduction of new content. This is not a lengthy task. Begin by briefly presenting to the children a material that is designed to give a basic understanding of a particular theme. The style of this presentation will depend on the age of the children and their observable needs. Once the presentation is over, the teacher proposes open-ended questions to allow the children to begin thinking about the material. These questions usually begin with the words: "*I wonder...*" This frees the children from needing to provide an accurate answer. The teacher allows the students to propose many and varied answers and does not normally intervene. The exception to this rule occurs when the children take the discussion in a directly contrary path to the true meaning of the story. The presentations can be supported by simple instruction booklets that teachers can use, but when the teachers become confident of the process, these booklets can be discarded, and the teachers can present the material in their own way, still covering the same essential content.

In general, initial presentations are made during the appropriate liturgical season. For example, the story of the Last Supper is presented in Holy Week, before Easter. The story of the Birth of Christ is presented just before Christmas, etc. In a mystagogical approach of this kind, attempts are made to make strong links between the biblical account and the Liturgy/Sacraments. If a sacramental theme is being presented, this will be followed or preceded from the biblical account that it is drawn from.

The presentation can be given to a whole group of children or to individuals. It must be emphasized, however, that this presentation should not be seen as the traditional "class lesson" in which the teacher attempts to meet the needs of all students in a single session. Most of the learning will come after the presentation, when they reflect on the meaning in their own way. For this reason, the teacher should not attempt to answer too many questions or to extend the session beyond ten to fifteen minutes.

Further Reflection. Each material is presented to the whole group only once. After this, the children given a degree of freedom to choose what they would like to do next from the range of designated responses or from the materials already presented. The majority of the religious education time is given over to allowing the children to work on something that has captured their interest and meets their needs. The teacher's role during these ongoing reflection periods is to watch what the children are working on and to assist them if they do not seem to have understood the meaning. This may involve presenting it again, one to one. The teacher also looks for "gaps" in what is being chosen and intervenes where necessary to ask the students to look at something they have not considered.

Fixing in Mind and Memory. There remains one further aspect of the process that needs to be completed: the way in which these experiences are made permanently present in the mind through the training of the memory. In previous generations, a great deal of effort went into the doctrinal propositions that encapsulated religious experiences for those learning about their faith. Comprehensive catechisms based on questions and answers (such as the American *Baltimore Catechism* or the British *Penny Catechism*) were composed for this purpose. In the immediate aftermath of the Second Vatican Council, these tools were often discarded without properly attending to the valuable contribution that an updated version might have contributed.

Clearly, a program whose focus was on the learning of intellectual propositions had two significant problems. First, without proper instruction, this may not have reached the heart of the student in a way that encouraged conversion. This accusation can be made of any method: all programs, in the end, are only as good as those who teach from them. Essentially, then, this is not a valid criticism. The second problem, however, is more serious and was articulated very well by Cardinal Henri de Lubac in 1942.[12] He was not concerned so much with the fact that the faith was being memorized in short formulae, but with the impression given that the mystery of God could be contained in such propositions. He was rightly concerned that those who had completed a course of study in school and learned all of their catechism answers by heart might believe that their knowledge of God was now sufficient. This was a timely warning with an important truth to be considered. Nevertheless, it simply means that one must be aware in learning off propositions that they only offer a basic outline of the mystery of God. Lifelong reflection remains a necessity.

---

12 See Henri de Lubac, "Internal Causes for the Weakening and Disappearance of the Sense of the Sacred." Re-published in *Josephinum Journal of Theology*, 18, 1 (2011): 37–50.

I would like to contend that a program of religious education that does not ultimately offer suitable compressed propositions for summarizing essential content fails to do the job required by the Church. It is not difficult to come across suitable compressed formulae of faith that can be associated with the experiences that have been reflected on. So long as the teacher is careful to make it clear that there is more to the mystery than the words being used, this will not be a problem. I have already referred to the support given for this need in *Catechesis Tradendae* by Pope John Paul II, who made it clear that:

> A certain memorization of the words of Jesus, of important Bible passages, of the Ten Commandments, of the formulas of profession of the faith, of the liturgical texts, of the essential prayers, of key doctrinal ideas etc., far from being opposed to the dignity of young Christians, or constituting an obstacle to personal dialogue with the Lord, is a real need.[13]

While a mystagogical catechesis such as *Catechesis of the Good Shepherd* has a great deal to offer, unless it finally reaches into some form of memorization of doctrinal propositions, it cannot be said to present the Faith according to the mind of the Church. Might I say, however, that this is not difficult? All it requires is that the experiences of each reflection be associated with a key prayer, liturgical text, or doctrinal proposition. In my experience of the *Catechesis of the Good Shepherd*, this is already done, but it could be improved.

Mystagogical Catechesis Methodology
SUMMARY

1. Set up the environment

2. Establish procedures of "Grace and Courtesy"

3. Set up procedures for using response tools

4. Present the material

5. Follow up with open-ended questions

6. Allow children to work with materials or responses

7. Follow up with children who need specific input

8. Relate each work that is reflected upon with a suitable doctrinal proposition

13 CT, § 55.

REPORT CARD FOR MYSTAGOGICAL CATECHESIS

CATEGORY	EXCELLENT	ADEQUATE	NEUTRAL	FAIL	COMMENT
Accounts for a mystagogical perspective.	X				Makes continual links between the signs and symbols of liturgy and sacraments with the revelation of the mystery of God in Scripture.
Facilitates a dialogue between God and the person.	X				Allows a great deal of time for the student to reflect on the meaning of the signs, and makes provision for the child to engage in personal and community prayer.
Incorporates the principle of the progressiveness of Revelation and its adaptation to different persons and cultures.	X				Careful attention is paid to the developmental needs of the student, offering individual materials to meet their current personal level of development.
Is Trinitarian and Christo-centric, incorporating "a pedagogy of the incarnation."	X				Allows the student to follow the needs of body, heart and mind to encounter the persons of the Trinity, while beginning always with Christ.
Provides for the community experience of faith.	X				Is always conducted in a group of students who are also learning about God. Conducted in a Catholic school, parish or family.
Uses a pedagogy of signs, where words and deeds, teaching and experience are interlinked.	X				Particular emphasis is placed on the ability of sacred signs to be the means by which the Holy Spirit communicates with the individual child.
Uses "discovery" as a pedagogical strategy and draws on a realist pedagogy of the truth.	X				Places emphasis of "wonder," which is described as "an attentive gaze at reality."
Unfolds the Scriptures against the backdrop of the Liturgical year and the Sacraments.	X				The program is structured around the celebration of the liturgical year, drawing the attention of the students to the whole Plan of God.
Is genuinely a "way of beauty."	X				The environment "teaches" and so particular attention is paid to the simplicity and beauty of the physical context in which the program unfolds.
Makes provision for the teacher as "witness."	X				Emphasizes that Christ is the teacher, and both student and teacher are seeking to know more about the mystery of God.
Makes deliberate provision for committing essential ideas to memory through appropriate educational means.			X		This has been a weakness in this program. If specific attention is paid to this, it can be easily achieve to an excellent degree.
Aims to put students not only in touch, but in intimacy with Jesus Christ.	X				While allowing the students to discover this for themselves, every effort is made to allow them to come to their own personal intimacy with Christ, the Good Shepherd.
Reflects the Kerygma.	X				Places and integrated emphasis on every dimension of the kerygma.

HERMENEUTIC CIRCLE METHOD

The Hermeneutic Circle method is an updated version of the so-called "Munich Method" of catechesis. The student is situated within the "hermeneutic circle" of the Catholic faith community and develops its teaching from this perspective. The Hermeneutic Circle Method uses suitable contemporary educational methods, but also incorporates elements of catechesis throughout its stages. This method can be adapted for use with any content- or text-based program. The method has four basic stages, as follows:

1. **Introductory Stage.** In this phase, the teacher determines what level of religious knowledge can be found in the particular class of children. Typically, there will be a textbook series with a structured content which proceeds from year to year, building on what went before. This content should be used by the teacher so that what the class knows can be brought out using these appropriate prompts. A very broad "open-ended" question such as "what did you learn last year?" is likely to be met with the standard response "nothing." While this is no doubt very good for the humility of the previous teacher, it is not usually accurate! Typical techniques by which teachers can activate the prior knowledge of the students include such techniques as "brainstorming," whereby the teacher proposes a series of topics and ask the students to tell something of what they know. Alternatively, if there is a comprehensive set of questions and answers that the students are meant to know, these can be asked directly. One of the most effective ways of getting the best out of the students, however, is to ask them to create a piece of art that expresses what they know. This really engages them in thinking and reflecting. It also allows the teacher to engage with students individually while they are completing their artwork.

2. **Present New Content.** Once you have determined what the students already know, you are in a position to know what emphasis will need to be placed on the development of the program. Usually, there will be a textbook with a topic, but the teacher must determine how best to address this material for the particular class.

Prior to beginning a new presentation, it is worth considering the environment in which the content will be delivered. In contemporary classrooms, it may be necessary to pay careful attention to the atmosphere; sometimes a different learning space, appropriate music, availability of individual pieces of art, and the like will help set an appropriate mood which prepares the students better for what you are going to do.

a. Identify the Key Content. In order to focus the attention of the students on essentials, it is useful to identify the topic that you intend to cover. This may be done quite simply with a brief statement or series of statements which will also serve as a finally summary of what they are expected to know once they have finished. Given the availability of beautiful artwork on many internet sites, it may also be useful to offer them an image which incorporates the content that you want to convey artistically. Some teachers use a large number of different works of art on the same subject, asking the students to talk about what they can "see."

b. Proclaim the Word of God. The primary means of offering new content in faith is proclamation, particularly from the scriptures, but also from Tradition. Both of these have a privileged place in catechesis. There is an educational "temptation" that afflict teachers: the temptation to "explain" before the student has had the opportunity to encounter the Word of God personally. There is little doubt that the student will not understand the full meaning of what has been presented—but neither will the teacher! The truth is that in this matter, we are dealing with a mystery; it is the Holy Spirit who passes on the faith. It is important, then, to allow the students to hear the Word of God for themselves before it is interpreted, however effectively, by someone else.

c. Explain the Key Content. Once the topic has been identified and proclaimed and the students have had the opportunity to engage with it for themselves, the time comes for the teacher to offer a plausible and authentic explanation of what it might mean. This should never conflict with the doctrinal teaching of the Church. The teacher explains the content using whatever method is deemed appropriate for the class. If the textbook contains an exposition of the topic, this can be used as part of the explanation. As the goal of this task is essentially cognitive, any appropriate strategy for building comprehension can be employed at this point. This includes all of the strategies described in the effective teaching practices chapter.

3. **Reflection and Synthesis of the New Content.** When the students have had the opportunity to gain a basic familiarity with the new content, they should then be given the opportunity of reflecting more personally on what they have learned and how it might affect their lives. A selection of related activities should be provided to allow them the time and the supportive structure to do this. Apart from describing the task and organizing activities, the teacher should not be unduly intrusive at this point. Artistic

or "hands-on" activities which allow the students to reflect while engaging in creative artwork are very appealing for many students. Journal writing can be very effective for students who like writing while they think: be aware, however, that not all students enjoy this task, and it is best not to force it on them if there is another suitable activity available. Some students reflect best through discussion, by talking things out with someone else. If this is a possibility, it should be used as part of the repertoire of activities. Research projects (either online or in the library) may appeal to some students, together with the opportunity to read appropriate literature in support of the content.

Above all, however, time and space should be set aside for personal prayer. This may be the only opportunity some students have of enjoying the silence necessary for encountering God and listening for his "voice." The use of key scripture passages, liturgical texts, creedal formulations, and traditional prayers may help link the children's reflections with the sources of Catholic faith: Scripture and Tradition, through which the Word of God is transmitted. The whole synthesizing and reflecting process might conclude with a suitable liturgy, if this is appropriate. Alternatively, there could be a sharing of responses if children volunteer their thoughts and reflections.

4. Assessment. The Hermeneutic Circle method lends itself to contexts which require "assessment" as part of the religious education process. This is an entirely legitimate demand, and is in keeping with the requirements of Congregation for Catholic Education's guiding documents, which insist that religious education needs to be seen as a subject with the same systematic demands and rigour as other disciplines.[14] The level of assessment will be determined at a local level and will depend on the imperatives of the relevant school system. There are alternatives, however, to the traditional paper test.

14 See RES, § 18.

CATEGORY	EXCELLENT	ADEQUATE	NEUTRAL	FAIL	COMMENT
REPORT CARD FOR HERMENEUTIC CIRCLE METHOD					
Accounts for a mystagogical perspective.			x		Capable of accounting for a mystagogical perspective, but this is not inherent. It will depend on the texts or program used.
Facilitates a dialogue between God and the person.	x				The importance of incorporating the spiritual dimension of dialogue is evident in the structure of the methodology.
Incorporates the principle of the progressiveness of Revelation and its adaptation to different persons and cultures.			x		Dependent on the content of the program used.
Is Trinitarian and Christo-centric, incorporating "a pedagogy of the incarnation."			x		Dependent on the content of the program used.
Provides for the community experience of faith.		x			The community dimension is implicit in the synthesizing stage.
Uses a pedagogy of signs, where words and deeds, teaching and experience are interlinked.			x		This methodology places emphasis on the proclamation of an intellectual content. There is space for incorporation of a pedagogy of signs, but this will depend on the skill of the teacher rather than the direction of the methodology.
Uses "discovery" as a pedagogical strategy and draws on a realist pedagogy of the truth.			x		Capable of using "discovery," but this is not inherent in the program.
Unfolds the Scriptures against the backdrop of the Liturgical year and the Sacraments.			x		The methodology could be organized to bring out this perspective, but it is not inherent.
Is genuinely a "way of beauty."		x			Some attention is directed to the "way of beauty," but much more could be done.
Makes provision for the teacher as "witness."	x				A great deal in this methodology depends on the witness of the teacher.
Makes deliberate provision for committing essential ideas to memory through appropriate educational means.		x			This methodology pays attention to the need for assessment, but more could be done to support the essential role of memory.
Aims to put students not only in touch, but in intimacy with Jesus Christ.	x				This is clearly the aim of this program.
Reflects the Kerygma.			x		Capable of incorporating this perspective.

16

Catholic Education, Religious Education, and Catechesis in the Documents of the Church Since Vatican II

INTRODUCTION

This review surveys and categorizes the teaching of the Catholic Church concerning the Church's educational project since the Second Vatican Council. It is set out under four broad headings:

1. The Essential Characteristics of a Catholic School. These characteristics constitute the context in which the religious education program is to be delivered: its vision and mission. The documents identify the overall purpose of Catholic education in the evangelizing mission of the Church: the mediation between faith and culture. The emphasis is placed on the central importance of the human person both as an individual and in relationship with others. A degree of religious freedom must be afforded to those in Catholic educational settings who are not Catholic, but this is not to infringe on the right of the Catholic institution to present its teaching. Particular attention is paid to the role of the "community" in achieving the aims, as well as the role of parents as "first educators." The documents consistently assert that a distinguishing feature of Catholic education is that it has a particular concern for the poorest and weakest in society.

2. The Formation of Personnel. The documents make strong claims about the conduct and formation of those involved in the project of religious education. Those who work in this field are expected to be committed to the task as sincere believers. The work they do in this area is not under their own auspices, but is to be performed on the basis of a mandate (whether formal or implied) from the local Church authorities. They need to be well formed, both professionally and personally, and to be offered further formation and professional development as they proceed.

3. The Organization of the Curriculum. An important twofold distinction that runs through many of the documents concerns the functions of religious education and catechesis. The former is seen as the systematic presentation of religious knowledge. There is an insistence that religious education be systematic and rigorous, attaining the same academic status as other subjects pursued at school. On the other hand, catechesis is primarily about personal formation in the Christian life. More recent documents also insist that any presentation of the Christian message be done in terms of a category described as "Trinitarian Christocentricity"; that is, Christ is to be considered the center of the proclamation, and this must ultimately be ordered to the Trinity, "*to* the Father, *through* the Son, *by* the Holy Spirit." Some documents issued prior to the *Catechism of the Catholic Church* offer outlines of basic content. Those issued subsequent to the *Catechism* insist that this document be used as the basic standard for identifying the essential doctrinal content.

Issues of methodology are also addressed, with advice offered that the presentation needs to be adapted to suit the age and needs of the recipients. Beyond this, Church documents acknowledge that the choice of methodology need not be prescribed, and leave the choice to local authorities.

4. The Contemporary Challenge of Intercultural Dialogue. In 2013, the Congregation for Catholic Education published a groundbreaking document, *Educating to Intercultural Dialogue in Catholic Schools: Living in Harmony for a Civilization of Love*. This is the first official comprehensive guidance offered by the Church to its schools to assist them in making an appropriate response to contemporary challenge of cultural pluralism.

PART 1: THE ESSENTIAL CHARACTERISTICS OF A CATHOLIC SCHOOL

Catholic Identity and Mission: An Overview. The identity and mission of Catholic education (and in particular, Catholic schools) can be classified under three categories: its nature and goals; its means of operation; and its distinguishing characteristics.

Nature and Goals. According to Pope Benedict XVI, the Church's deepest nature is expressed in her threefold responsibility: proclaiming the word, celebrating the sacraments, and exercising the ministry of charity.[1] The project of Catholic education necessarily embraces all three of those

---

1 Benedict XVI, *Deus Caritas Est* (Vatican City: Libreria Editrice Vaticana, 2005), § 25. [Afterwards DCE]

dimensions. Catholic schools must be aware of the risk of losing sight of the reasons why they exist. They must not unthinkingly conform to the expectations of a society marked by the values of individualism and competition.[2] The documents of the Church consistently locate the mission of Catholic education within the framework of its universal mission to evangelize: "Go out to all the world and tell the Good News."[3] The Church has a deep conviction that it is only in the Christian message that people of our time can find answers to their questions and energy for their commitment to human solidarity.[4] At its heart, the identity of the Catholic school is grounded in its role in the evangelizing mission of the Church and directed to the complete formation of the students.[5]

The Catholic school is always to be seen as part of the Church's mission because of its teaching activity, in which faith, culture, and life unite in harmony.[6] It is encouraged to promote a wisdom-based society, to go beyond knowledge and educate people to think, evaluating facts in the light of values.[7]

A Catholic school is institutionally linked with the bishop of the diocese, who guarantees that that the education be grounded in the principles of the Catholic faith and imparted by teachers of right doctrine and probity of life.[8] The Catholic school is described as "a place of integral education of the human person through a clear educational project of which Christ is the foundation, directed at creating a synthesis between faith, culture and life."[9] The purpose is to bring about a

---

2 Congregation for Catholic Education, *Educating for Intercultural Dialogue in Catholic Schools* (Vatican City: Libreria Editrice Vaticana, 2013), § 56. [Afterwards EID]

3 Paul VI, *Evangelii Nuntiandi* (Vatican City: Libreria Editrice Vaticana, 1975), § 49, 72. [Afterwards EN]

4 Ibid., § 3.

5 Congregation for Catholic Education, *The Catholic School on the Threshold of the Third Millennium* (Vatican City: Libreria Editrice Vaticana, 1997), § 11. [Afterwards CSTM] See also Congregation for Catholic Education, *The Religious Dimension of Education in a Catholic School* (Vatican City: Libreria Editrice Vaticana, 1988), § 33. [Afterwards RDEC] See also John Paul II, *Ecclesia in Oceania* (Vatican City: Libreria Editrice Vaticana, 2001), § 32. [Afterwards EO]

6 Ibid., *Circular Letter to the Presidents of Bishops' Conferences on Religious Education in Schools* (2009), § 5. [Afterwards RES]

7 Ibid., *Educating to Intercultural Dialogue in Catholic Schools: Living in Harmony for a Civilization of Love* (2013), § 66. [Afterwards EID]

8 Ibid., § 6, 7.

9 Ibid., *Educating Together in Catholic Schools: A Shared Mission between Consecrated Persons and the Lay Faithful* (Vatican City: Libreria Editrice Vaticana, 2007), § 3. [Afterwards ETCS] See also CSTM, § 3.

Christian vision of the world through the interweaving of reason and faith.[10] What marks an educational institution as Catholic is its reference to a Christian concept of life centered on Jesus Christ.[11] It is the intention of the Church that those who have been baptized become ever more aware of their gift of faith, learn to worship God in spirit and in truth, and conform their lives in the principles of justice and truth.[12] It is intended that the Catholic educational project be continually working towards its goal by a Christian vision of reality.[13] The education offered by Catholic schools flows from their witness to the Gospel and their love for all that is free and open.[14]

To this end, Catholic schools attempt to create an atmosphere animated by the Gospel spirit of freedom and charity.[15] This project should not be seen as narrowly closed in on itself, since education, by its nature, requires openness to other cultures without the loss of one's own identity.[16] Even so, the Church insists that "Jesus Christ has a significance and a value for the human race and its history, which are unique and singular, proper to him alone, exclusive, universal, and absolute."[17] The religious dimension of this school climate is expressed through celebration of Christian values in Word and Sacrament, individual behavior and friendly interpersonal relationships.[18] This should lead to a clear realization of the identity of a Catholic school and the courage to follow all the consequences of its uniqueness.[19] Moreover, the implementation of a real educational community, built on the foundation of shared projected values, represents a serious task that must be carried out by the Catholic school.[20]

The Means. The integral formation of the human person determines the structure of the Church's educational programs which must look to Christ himself as the fullness of humanity.[21] Pope Benedict XVI, addressing

10   ETCS, § 12, 14.

11   EID, § 17.

12   Vatican Council II, *Gravissimum Educationis* (Vatican City: Libreria Editrice Vaticana, 1965), § 2. [Afterwards GE] See also RDEC, § 98.

13   Congregation for Catholic Education, *The Catholic School* (Vatican City: Libreria Editrice Vaticana, 1977), § 39. [Afterwards TCS]

14   EID, § 61.

15   GE, § 8.

16   EID, Introduction.

17   Ibid., § 16.

18   RDEC, § 25.

19   TCS, § 66.

20   ETCS, § 5.

21   EO, § 32.

Catholic religion teachers in 2009, made it clear that Catholic education requires the enlargement of rationality to the deeper questions of what is true and good by linking theology, philosophy, and science. While the autonomy of each discipline must be respected, it is necessary to be aware of the intrinsic unity that holds them together.[22] The Church's primary means of passing on the faith is assigned to the sacraments, properly understood and celebrated: "There is a special means for passing down this fullness. It is the sacraments, celebrated in the Church's liturgy."[23] This aspect of the task is considered so foundational that Catholic faith is described as having a sacramental structure which links us with Christ: "The awakening of faith is linked to the dawning of a new sacramental sense in our lives as human beings and as Christians, in which visible and material realities are seen to point beyond themselves to the mystery of the eternal."[24]

If the Catholic school is to be means of education in the modern world, there are some fundamental characteristics regarding its identity which must be strengthened:[25]

1. The human person is central to the Catholic educational project, and the vital relationship with the person of Christ is where the full truth about humanity is to be found.[26] Catholic schools must be aware of the dangers of bureaucratic formalism, the consumerist demands of families, and the unbridled search for external approval.[27]

2. Catholic schools must reject the contemporary pervading and enervating neutrality with regard to Christian values and offer a clear understanding of the Christian vision of life and what it means to be human.[28] Secularization in the West carries the extreme danger of marginalizing religious experience to the private sphere and losing religion's contribution to intercultural dialogue.[29]

---

22 Benedict XVI, *Address to Catholic Religion Teachers* (Vatican City: Libreria Editrice Vaticana, 2009). [Afterwards CRT]

23 LF, § 40.

24 Ibid., § 40.

25 CSTM, § 8.

26 Ibid., § 9.

27 EID, § 56.

28 Ibid., § 10.

29 Ibid., § 9.

Characteristics. The documents identify a number of important features that need to be associated with Catholic education generally and Catholic schools in particular. Before all else, however, there must be a spirit of unity that links educators and students in a communion of love.[30] Catholic schools must be seen as being communities of fraternal relationships and places of research dedicated to deepening and communicating truth in various scholarly disciplines.[31] There may be a strong temptation to treat the school like a company or business, but if Catholic schools are to be successful, "those who lead them must be able to invoke the school's reference values and move the school in this direction."[32] Four distinctive characteristics of a Catholic school are specified: educational climate; personal development; relationship of Gospel and culture; illumination of all knowledge with light of faith.[33] Each of these needs to be ordered toward the realization of a Christian vision of life. An important distinguishing feature of Catholic education ought to be that it is open to all and attentive to the demands of justice, especially in regard to the poorest and weakest in society.[34] Catholic schools also have an ecumenical dimension whereby the students are prepared for living in contact with non-Catholics, affirming their Catholic identity while respecting the faith of others.[35] Finally, there is an acknowledgement that Catholic education is a long-term project and consequently, the value of the efforts that go into it (particularly in Catholic schools) cannot be measured by immediate efficiency.[36]

The Nature and Goals of Catholic Schools
SUMMARY OF KEY POINTS

- *What marks an educational institution as Catholic is its reference to a Christian concept of life centered on Jesus Christ.[37]*
- *The Church has three primary responsibilities: proclaiming the Word; celebrating the sacraments; and exercising the ministry of charity.[38]*
- *The mission of the Catholic school embraces all three of these dimensions and is*

30 Ibid., § 48.
31 Ibid., § 77.
32 Ibid., § 85.
33 RDEC, § 1.
34 EO, § 32. See also TCS § 58 and CSTM, § 15.
35 CT, § 32.
36 TCS, § 84.
37 EID, § 17.
38 See DCE, § 25.

described as being part of the evangelizing mission of the Church based on the Great Commission of Christ himself: "Go out to all the world and tell the Good News."[39]

- Catholic Schools are institutionally linked to the bishop of the diocese who has the responsibility for their proper functioning.[40]
- The Catholic school is a place of integral education of the human person and its particular project is directed at creating a synthesis between faith, culture and life. It works towards this role by a Christian vision of reality.[41]
- A genuine Catholic education promotes a wisdom-based society. It must go beyond knowledge and educate people to think, evaluating facts in the light of values.[42]
- The religious climate of the school is expressed through the celebration of Christian values in word and sacrament.[43]
- The Catholic educational project seeks always to work in harmony with the nature human person as revealed in Christ.[44]
- The Catholic school can never take a position of neutrality with regard to Christian values or what it means to be human.[45]
- There are four distinctive characteristics of a Catholic school:
  - Its distinctive educational climate.
  - Its emphasis on the personal development of each student.
  - Its emphasis on the relationship between the Gospel and the culture.
  - Its illumination of all knowledge with light of faith.[46]
- Catholic education, by its nature, requires openness to other cultures, without succumbing to the loss of one's own identity.[47]
- Catholic schools have a particular concern for the poor and the weak. They also have an ecumenical dimension.[48]
- The project of Catholic education is "long-term" and so the value of Catholic schools cannot always be measured in terms of immediate efficiency.[49]

39 EV, § 49, 72.
40 RES, § 6, 7.
41 ETCS, § 12, 14. See also TCS, § 39.
42 EID, § 66.
43 RDEC, § 25.
44 EO, § 32.
45 CSTM, § 10.
46 RDEC § 1.
47 EID, Introduction.
48 CT, § 32.
49 TCS, § 84.

THE HUMAN PERSON AND THE MEDIATION OF CULTURE

Many of the documents of the Church regarding education draw attention to two complementary elements: the centrality of the human person as the subject of education, and the mediation of human and Christian culture as the essential object.

Human Person. The documents observe that any genuine educational philosophy must be based on the nature of the human person and account for both physical and spiritual powers of each individual.[50] Catholic education must embrace a new commitment to the individual seen as a "person in communion" and a new sense of his or her belonging to society.[51] As already noted, it is through her educational programs that the Church seeks the integral formation of the human person, looking to Christ himself as the fullness of humanity.[52] Christianity is the religion of God with a human face. Reason is always in need of being purified by faith, and religion always needs to be purified by reason.[53] "God is at work in every human being who, through reason, has perceived the mystery of God and recognizes universal values."[54]

Culture. The Church sees the focus of her pastoral service in the field of education as mediating between faith and culture. This requires the twofold task of being faithful to the Gospel and at the same time respecting the autonomy and methods proper to human knowledge.[55] Hence, the task of education is to guide students through a critical and systematic assimilation of culture.[56] The primary responsibility of a Catholic school is to witness to Christ. In the various situations created by different cultures, the Christian presence must be shown and made clear; that is, it must be visible, tangible, and conscious.[57] Every culture is a way of giving expression to the transcendental aspects of life including reflection on the mystery of the world and of humanity.[58] "The generating nucleus of every authentic culture is constituted by its approach to the mystery of God."[59] In this matter, however, the Church's role is not neutral. What is

---

50 RDEC, § 63.
51 EID, § 46.
52 EO, § 32.
53 EID, § 11.
54 Ibid., § 13.
55 RDEC, § 31.
56 TCS, § 26.
57 EID, § 57.
58 Ibid., § 30.
59 Ibid., § 7.

important is to evangelize culture and cultures: they have to be regenerated by an encounter with the Gospel.[60] The Catholic school is based on an educational philosophy in which faith, culture, and life are brought into harmony.[61] While it is acknowledged that human culture must be taught with scientific objectivity, nevertheless, faith cannot be divorced from culture: the points of contact are established within the human person.[62] Furthermore, in the view of the Church, "the religious dimension is in fact intrinsic to culture. It contributes to the overall formation of the person and makes it possible to transform knowledge into wisdom of life."[63]

The Human Person and the Mediation of Culture
SUMMARY OF KEY POINTS

- *Catholic Education must embrace a new commitment to the individual seen as a "person in communion" and a new sense of his or her belonging to society.[64]*
- *Any genuine educational philosophy must account for both the physical and spiritual powers of each individual human person, looking to Christ himself as the fullness of humanity.[65]*
- *Christianity is the religion of God with a human face. Reason is always in need of being purified by faith, and religion always needs to be purified by reason.[66]*
- *The Catholic school aims to bring faith, culture and life into harmony and to guide students through a critical and systematic assimilation of culture.[67]*
- *The religious dimension is intrinsic to culture and contributes to the formation of the person.[68]*
- *"God is at work in every human being who, through reason, has perceived the mystery of God and recognizes universal values."[69]*
- *"The generating nucleus of every authentic culture is constituted by its approach to the mystery of God."[70]*
- *In the various situations created by different cultures, the Christian presence must be shown and made visible, tangible, and conscious.[71]*

60　EN, § 20.
61　RDEC, § 34.
62　Ibid., § 51.
63　CRT.
64　EID, § 46.
65　EO, § 32.
66　EID, § 11.
67　RDEC, § 34.
68　CRT.
69　EID, § 13.
70　Ibid., § 7.
71　Ibid., § 57.

EVANGELIZATION

As already noted, the Church locates the project of Catholic Education within the overall mission of evangelization. For this reason, it will be useful to explore this in terms of its implications for Catholic education in general and for schools in particular. The Church sees the purpose of its entire activity as an expression of the love that seeks the good of every human being, and this is brought about by means of evangelization through word and sacrament.[72] The 1975 Apostolic Exhortation *Evangelii Nuntiandi* made the claim that the Church exists to evangelize: to preach and teach, to be the channel of grace, reconcile sinners with God and perpetuate Christ's sacrifice in the Mass.[73] The essential kernel of the Good News is the salvation proclaimed by Christ, which is above all liberation from sin and the evil one.[74] Those who have been evangelized are in turn expected to evangelize others.[75]

The 1997 *General Directory of Catechesis* comprehensively sets out the characteristic features of the task of Evangelization. It identifies three broad socio-religious contexts requiring different pastoral approaches:

1. The mission *Ad Gentes — to the pagans;* to those who have never known the Christian message. *Main Tasks*: conversion; developed within baptismal catechumenate.
2. Communities fervent in their faith and Christian living. *Main Tasks*: processes of well-articulated Christian initiation for children and adolescents; further formation for adults.
3. Entire communities have lost a living sense of faith and live lives apart from the Church. This is properly called the "New Evangelization." *Main Tasks*: primary proclamation; basic catechesis.[76]

The *General Directory* describes the tasks associated with Evangelization as fitting broadly onto a continuum whereby one stage is followed by another in a more or less predictable pattern. The point of the continuum on which those being evangelized find themselves will determine the kind of activity to be pursued:

72 DCE, § 19.
73 EN, § 14.
74 Ibid., § 3, 9.
75 Ibid., § 24.
76 GDC, § 58.

1. Christian witness, dialogue and presence in charity
2. Proclamation of the Gospel and the call to conversion
3. The catechumenate (*a time of learning through participation*) and Christian initiation
4. The formation of Christian communities through and by means of the sacraments and their ministers[77]

Witness. A persistent theme of the documents in terms of Evangelization is "witness." The word is used thirty-six times in *Evangelii Nuntiandi* alone: "The first means of evangelizing is the *witness* of an authentically Christian life."[78] "Above all the Gospel must be proclaimed by witness."[79] Those who evangelize, then, must *not* preach themselves or their personal ideas in the name of the Church.[80] The importance of the individual "Person to person" evangelizer is indispensable.[81] Moreover, it is made clear that the evangelizer should have a love of those being evangelized.[82] Evangelization will never be possible without the action of the Holy Spirit.[83] The Catholic school is identified as playing an important role with those committed to their care and they are reminded that catechetical instruction must not be neglected as a means of evangelization.[84] It is made clear that while evangelization begins with a "presence in charity," it must eventually result in the explicit presentation of the message itself. The faith must be preached since faith comes from what is heard and what is heard comes from the preaching of Christ.[85] *Evangelii Nuntiandi*, however, looks beyond the teachers in the school. It proposes that young people well trained in faith must become more and more the apostles of youth.[86]

Evangelization
SUMMARY OF KEY POINTS

- *The Church sees the purpose of its entire activity as an expression of the love that seeks the good of every human being, and this is brought about by means*

---

77   Ibid., § 47.
78   EN, § 42.
79   Ibid., § 21.
80   Ibid., § 15.
81   Ibid., § 46.
82   Ibid., § 79.
83   Ibid., § 75.
84   Ibid., § 44.
85   Ibid., § 42.
86   Ibid., § 72.

of evangelization through word and sacrament.[87]

- *The Church exists to evangelize: to preach and teach and to be a channel of grace, reconciling sinners with God and perpetuating Christ's sacrifice in the Mass.*[88]
- *There are three broad socio-religious contexts for evangelization:*
  1. *To those who have never known the Christian message*
  2. *To those fervent in their faith*
  3. *To those who have lost a living sense of their faith: The New Evangelization*[89]
- *Evangelization proceeds according to a continuum of four successive stages:*
  1. *Christian witness, dialogue and presence in charity*
  2. *Proclamation of the Gospel and the call to conversion*
  3. *The catechumenate and Christian initiation*
  4. *The formation of Christian communities through and by means of the sacraments and their ministers*[90]
- *Catholic schools have an important role to play with those committed to their care and are reminded that catechetical instruction must not be neglected as a means of evangelization.*[91]
- *Those involved in evangelization do so primarily by means of their Christian witness. The initial presence in charity, however, must eventually result in the explicit presentation of the Gospel message.*[92]

THE COMMUNITY DIMENSION

The documents strongly assert the importance of the role of the community in the project of Catholic education. The idea of a Catholic school as a community is theological rather than sociological.[93] It is founded on the concept of *communio*: the eternal mystery, revealed in Christ, of the communion of love that is the very life of God, the Trinity. In practical terms, this means that as a community the Church must practice love and it is necessary that this be organized if it is to be effective in serving the community.[94] The model that school structures must take as their inspiration is the *educating community*, a place of differences living together in harmony.[95]

---

87 DCE, 19.
88 EV, § 14.
89 GDC, § 58.
90 Ibid., § 47.
91 EV, § 42.
92 Ibid., § 21.
93 CSTM, § 18.
94 DCE, § 19.
95 EID, § 58.

Educating Together in Catholic Schools goes so far as to say that, because its purpose is to make human beings more human, a Catholic education can only be carried out authentically in a relational community context.[96] Furthermore, "the Catholic school aims at forming the persons in the integral unity of their being. They must be involved in the dynamics of interpersonal relations that give life to a school community."[97] Human beings are seen as essentially relational and the communion to which they are called has two dimensions—communion with God and communion with other people.[98] In other words, the educational process is "not simply a human activity but a genuine Christian journey; the will of God is found in the work and human relationships of each day."[99]

Consequently, "because of its identity and its roots in the Church, the Catholic school community must aspire to being a community of faith. Neutral or fundamentalist societies and schools, which lack reference values and are uninvolved with any moral formation, do not develop participation."[100] The Catholic school must be able to form ever more profound relationships of communion nourished by a living relationship with Christ and with the Church.[101] Only by giving witness to communion can a Catholic educational community educate for communion.[102] One of the important purposes of a Catholic school is that the students should learn to overcome individualism by living in solidarity with Christ and with others.[103] Catholic schools are also called on to build open communion—to share the fruits of their relationship with Christ and each other in the wider world.[104]

Justice and Poverty. There is a role that the Catholic Church must play in establishing justice. All of humanity is alienated when too much trust is placed in merely human projects, ideologies, and false utopias.[105] Yet, "the just ordering of society and the State is a central responsibility of politics."[106] Isolation is one of the deepest possible forms of poverty and it

96 ETCS, § 12.
97 Ibid., § 13.
98 Ibid., § 5, 9.
99 RDEC, § 48.
100 EID, § 59.
101 ETCS, § 14.
102 Ibid., § 39.
103 Ibid., § 45–46.
104 GDC, § 50–53.
105 EID, § 38.
106 DCE, § 28.

springs from a sense of not being loved or able to love.[107] A fundamental distinction exists in Christianity between what belongs to Caesar and to God, "in other words, the distinction between Church and state, or, as the Second Vatican Council puts it, the autonomy of the temporal sphere."[108] In this sphere, lay Catholics in particular are encouraged to play their part.[109] Even so, "there is no ordering of the State so just that it can eliminate the need for a service of love."[110] Establishing justice is one part of the mission and must be pursued in the context of the whole. The curriculum must help the students reflect on the great problems of our time, including the difficult situation of a large part of humanity's living conditions.[111]

The Community Dimension
SUMMARY OF KEY POINTS

- *The "community" dimension plays a very important role in the project of Catholic education. This is a theological concept: the eternal mystery, revealed in Christ, of the communion of love that is the very life of God, the Holy Trinity.[112]*
- *A Catholic education can only be carried out authentically in a relational community context because its purpose is to make human beings more human.[113]*
- *There are two dimensions to a genuine relational community: one with God and the other towards one another.[114]*
- *One of the important purposes of a Catholic school is that the students learn to overcome individualism by living in solidarity with Christ.[115]*
- *Isolation is one of the deepest possible forms of poverty and it springs from a sense of not being loved or able to love.[116]*
- *The Church, and by extension, the Catholic school, has a role to play in promoting justice. This role must be placed in the overall context of its mission, which is multi-dimensional.[117]*
- *The curriculum must help the students reflect on the great problems of our time, including the difficult situation of a large part of humanity's living conditions.[118]*

107 EID, § 38.
108 Ibid., § 28.
109 See CF, § 15.
110 CF, § 28.
111 EID, § 66.
112 DCE, § 19.
113 ETCS, § 12.
114 Ibid.
115 GDC, § 50–53.
116 EID, § 38.
117 DCE, § 28. See also: CF, § 15.
118 EID, § 66.

RESPECT FOR RELIGIOUS FREEDOM

In Catholic schools, the religious freedom of non-Catholic pupils must be respected. All children and young people must have the same possibilities for arriving at the *knowledge of their own religion* as well as of elements that characterize other religions.[119] The Church's responsibility of practical charity cannot be used as a means of making converts — love is free and cannot be practiced as a means of achieving other ends. This does not mean, however, that God and Christ can be left aside, since often the deepest cause of suffering is the absence of God.[120] Furthermore, those who carry out the Church's ministry of charitable work must not be "inspired by ideologies aimed at improving the world, but should rather be guided by faith which works through faith."[121]

In the context of a Catholic school, respect for religious freedom clearly does not affect the right/duty of the Church "in [its] public teaching and witness to [its] faith, whether by the spoken or by the written word.[122] A Catholic school cannot relinquish its own freedom to proclaim the Gospel; to offer is not to impose.[123]

For students who are non-believers, religious education assumes the character of a missionary proclamation of the Gospel and is ordered to a decision of faith, which catechesis, in its turn, will nurture and mature.[124] A search for whatever favors the integral development of the whole person lies at the heart of the dialogue between faith and various forms of non-religious viewpoints. [125] In dealing with students who come from different faiths or ideological backgrounds, evangelization may not be possible, and attempts should be made at "pre-evangelization," the development of a religious sense of life.[126] Teachers are duty-bound to respect the human person who seeks the truth of his or her own being, as well as to appreciate and spread the great cultural traditions that are open to the transcendent and that articulate the desire for freedom and truth.[127] The Church operates some schools in places where the overwhelming majority

---

119 Ibid., § 18.
120 Ibid., § 31.
121 Ibid., § 33.
122 RES, § 16.
123 RDEC, § 5.
124 GDC, § 75.
125 EID, § 12.
126 RDEC, § 108.
127 EID, § 18.

are not Catholic (e.g., in Thailand). In such circumstances, catechetical activity is necessarily limited and even religious education — when possible — accentuates its cultural character.[128]

Respect for Religious Freedom
SUMMARY OF KEY POINTS

- *In Catholic schools, the religious freedom of non-Catholic pupils must be respected.*
- *The service offered to non-Catholics in Catholic schools is one of practical charity and freely given. It is not pursued for any other purpose.*
- *All children and young people must have the same possibilities for arriving at the knowledge of their own religion as well as of elements that characterize other religions.[129]*
- *For students who are non-believers, religious education assumes the character of a missionary proclamation of the Gospel and is ordered to a decision of faith.*
- *A Catholic school cannot relinquish its own freedom to proclaim the Gospel; to offer is not to impose.*

THE PRIMARY ROLE OF THE FAMILY

The documents of the Church consistently and unequivocally assert the role of the family as critical and primary:[130] "The family is a divine institution that stands at the foundation of life of the human person as the prototype of every social order."[131] In the education of children, the role of the father and that of the mother are equally necessary.[132] The relationship is irreplaceable and inalienable. It is impossible to promote the dignity of the person without showing concern for the family.[133] The role of the family is therefore incapable of being entirely delegated or usurped by others.[134] The sacrament of marriage gives to this educational role the dignity and vocation of being really and truly a "ministry" of the Church.[135] The role of parents in the education of their children is

---

128 GDC, § 260.

129 EID, § 18.

130 GE, § 3.

131 Pontifical Council for Justice and Peace, *Compendium of the Social Doctrine of the Catholic Church*, (Vatican City: Libreria Editrice Vaticana, 2004), §211. [Afterwards CSD]

132 Ibid., §242.

133 Ibid., § 185.

134 John Paul II, *Familiaris Consortio* (Vatican City: Libreria Editrice Vaticana, 1981), § 36. See also: RES, § 2–4.

135 Ibid., § 38, 40.

held to be so decisive that "scarcely anything can compensate for their failure in it."[136]

Parents are the *first* educators, not the *only* educators, of their children. It belongs to them, therefore, to exercise with responsibility their educational activity in close and vigilant cooperation with civil and ecclesial agencies.[137] It is for these reasons that Catholic schools are bound by the principle of subsidiarity in respect of the role of parents in the education of their children.[138] A school must treat its families with due respect must not deny them their essential place and dignity, allowing them to make their unique contribution to the community.[139] Consequently, schools need to provide concrete support to parents to enable them to play their role as first educators.[140] Furthermore, the partnership between a Catholic school and the families of the students is essential if the goals of the school are to be achieved. Schools should initiate meetings and other programs which make parents conscious of this role.[141]

The Primary Role of the Family
SUMMARY OF KEY POINTS

- *The family is a divine institution that stands as the prototype of every social order.[142]*
- *It is impossible to promote the dignity of the person without showing concern for the family.[143]*
- *Parents are the primary educators and, for this reason, the school is bound by the law of subsidiarity in respect of the education of their own children.[144]*
- *Schools need to provide concrete support to parents to enable them to fulfil this role, including meetings and programs to help equip them for the task.[145]*
- *In the education of children, the role of the father and that of the mother are equally necessary.[146]*

---

136 Ibid., § 36.
137 See CSD, § 240.
138 RES, 8.
139 CSD, §186.
140 CSTM, § 20. See also RDEC, § 42, 43.
141 RDEC, § 42, 43.
142 CSD, § 211.
143 See CSD, § 185.
144 GE, § 3. See also RES, § 8.
145 CSTM, § 20. See also RDEC, § 42, 43.
146 CSD, §242.

PART 2. FORMATION OF PERSONNEL

Teachers and Catechists. The documents of the Church have much to say on the subject of the teachers and catechists working in Catholic education.

Professionally Trained. In terms of their professional preparation for the task, those who work in Catholic education are required to have a solid professional formation, since inadequacy in this area undermines the formation of students and the teacher's own capacity to witness.[147] There is also a realistic awareness of the current demands of the teaching profession, where continuous rapid transformation leads to the premature aging of knowledge, requiring educators to constantly update the content and methods of the subject area. This professional commitment also applies to religious education.[148] Educators in Catholic schools are encouraged to be "well prepared interlocutors, able to awaken and direct the best energies of the students towards the search for truth and the meaning of existence. Real education is not possible without the light of truth."[149]

Personal Witness. A good school is where the teachers, as a group, know how to become something more than a mere recognized *corps*, in which the members are bound together by ties of mere bureaucracy.[150] During his address to Italian teachers of religious education, Pope Benedict XVI addressed the qualities needed in Catholic teachers: "In him [St Paul] we recognize the humble and faithful disciple, the courageous herald, the gifted mediator of Revelation. These are characteristics to which I invite you to look to nourish your identity as educators and witnesses in the world of the school."[151] The documents of the Church consistently call for this kind of personal commitment and conviction from teachers, who are meant to carry out their task "in communion with Christ."[152] Catholic schools require people not only to know how to teach or direct an organization; they also must bear authentic witness to the school's values.[153] Teachers, as witnesses, need to be willing to account for the hope that nourishes their own lives by living the truth they propose to their pupils.[154] The effectiveness of religious education is closely tied to the personal witness

---

147   ETCS, § 21, 22. See also GE, § 8; RDEC, § 42, 43.
148   ETCS, § 23–24.
149   Ibid. § 2.
150   EID, § 82.
151   CRT.
152   CT, § 9.
153   EID, § 80.
154   ETCS, § 38.

given by the teacher.[155] It depends primarily on the teachers whether or not the Catholic school achieves its purpose.[156] Indeed, the project of the Catholic school is convincing only if carried out by people who are deeply motivated, because they witness to a living encounter with Christ.[157]

The Catholic school should be able to count on the unity of purpose and conviction of all its members.[158] The effectiveness of the Catholic school will be significantly enhanced if the students experience the love and care of committed educators.[159] For this reason, those responsible for hiring teachers and administrators in Catholic schools are advised to take account of the faith life they are hiring.[160] One further consequence is that "the power of evangelization will find itself considerably diminished if those who proclaim the Gospel are divided among themselves.[161]

Opportunities for Spreading the Gospel. Not only should teachers be personally and professionally committed, but they should also be "sensitive to finding opportunities for allowing their students to see beyond the limited horizon of human reality."[162] Together with and in collaboration with the family, schools provide possibilities for catechesis that must not be neglected.[163]

Spiritual Formation. Given that they are acting on behalf of the Church in their school communities, Catholic educators need a formation of the heart as well as the mind if they are to contribute effectively to the project of religious education.[164] "Educators must be willing to develop knowledge and be open to updating methodologies, but open also to spiritual and religious formation."[165]

The Mandate from the Church. Teachers never act on their own behalf in offering religious teaching in a Catholic school; they are transmitting Christ's teaching and not their own.[166] When lay people work in this field, it is by way of invitation to cooperate more closely with the apostolate

---

155 RDEC, § 96. See also EO, § 33.
156 CSTM, § 19.
157 ETCS, § 4.
158 TCS, § 59.
159 CSTM, § 18.
160 EO, § 33.
161 EV, § 77.
162 RDEC, § 51.
163 Ibid., § 66.
164 ETCS, § 25, 34–37.
165 Ibid., § 20.
166 CT, § 6, 16.

of the bishops, a mandate of an apostolic undertaking.[167] The essential element of the mandate is union with those whom the Holy Spirit has assigned to lead and guide the Church.[168]

Teachers and Catechists
SUMMARY OF KEY POINTS

- *Catholic schools require people not only to know how to teach or direct an organization; they also must bear authentic witness to the school's values.[169]*
- *The effectiveness of the religious education program is closely tied to the personal witness given by teachers.[170]*
- *Teachers must have a solid professional formation. Inadequacy in this area undermines the success of their work with students and their ability to witness to their faith.[171]*
- *As in other subject areas, religious education teachers must be continually updating their professional qualifications.[172]*
- *Religious education teachers should have a personal commitment to their role enabling them to carry it out "in communion with Christ."[173]*
- *Those responsible for hiring teachers and administrators in Catholic schools are advised to take account of the faith life of those they are hiring.[174]*
- *All teachers in a Catholic school should be "sensitive to finding opportunities for allowing students to see beyond the limited horizon of human reality."[175]*
- *Catholic educators need a formation of the heart as well as the mind if they are to contribute effectively to the project of religious education.[176]*
- *When lay people work in this field, it is by way of invitation to cooperate more closely with the apostolate of the bishops as a mandate of an apostolic undertaking.[177]*

PART 3: THE ORGANIZATION OF THE CURRICULUM

Catechesis and Religious Education. One of the key questions that theorists working in the field of Catholic Education have been grappling with since the

---

167   TCS, § 71.
168   Ibid., § 72.
169   EID, § 80.
170   RDEC, § 96. See also EO, § 33.
171   ETCS, § 21, 22. See also GE, § 8; RDEC, § 42, 43.
172   Ibid., § 20.
173   CT, § 9.
174   EO, § 33.
175   RDEC, § 51.
176   ETCS, § 20.
177   TCS, § 72.

Second Vatican Council is the relationship between catechesis and religious instruction (referred to more commonly in Australia as religious education).

Catechesis. In *Catechesi Tradendae*, catechesis is described as "an orderly and systematic initiation into the revelation that God has given of Himself to humanity in Christ Jesus, a revelation stored in the depths of the Church's memory and in Sacred Scripture and constantly communicated from one generation to the next by a living, active *traditio*."[178] Its definitive aim is not simply the conveying of knowledge, but intimacy with Christ.[179] Furthermore, catechesis implies the ongoing communication of supernatural life which, in the words of *Evangelii Nuntiandi*, "finds its living expression in the seven sacraments and in the radiation of grace and holiness which they possess."[180]

Religious Education. It is quite clear that the Church insists on making a distinction between religious education and catechesis. In the context of a school, religious education needs to be seen as a subject with the same systematic demands and rigour as other disciplines.[181] By the same token, other subjects in the curriculum should be taught according to their own methodology, and not as mere adjuncts of faith.[182] Religious education is different from and complementary to catechesis, as it conveys knowledge on the identity of Christianity and Christian life.[183]

In distinguishing the task of religious education from catechesis, *The Religious Dimension of Education in a Catholic School* gives this clarification:

> The aim of the school however, is knowledge. While it uses the same elements of the Gospel message, it tries to convey a sense of the nature of Christianity, and of how Christians are trying to live their lives. It is evident, of course, that religious instruction cannot help but strengthen the faith of a believing student, just as catechesis cannot help but increase one's knowledge of the Christian message.

Catechesis, however, is described by the same document in this way:

178 CT, § 22.
179 Ibid., § 5.
180 EN, § 47.
181 RES, § 18.
182 TCS, § 39.
183 RES, § 17.

The distinction comes from the fact that, unlike religious instruction, catechesis presupposes that the hearer is receiving the Christian message as a salvific reality. Moreover, catechesis takes place
within a community living out its faith at a level of space and time
not available to a school: a whole lifetime.[184]

Some have used these passages to argue that in the context of contemporary Catholic schools, only religious education and not catechesis
is possible since many of the students are not receiving the message as
a salvific reality. Moreover, the school is not capable of being present in
the lives of students for a whole lifetime. This view has been strongly
advocated and is now widely represented in Australian Catholic schools.

While the case for separating catechesis from religious education may
be argued logically from the two passages quoted above, this can only be
done by isolating these passages from their context. There is, in fact, no
warrant from the actual documents of the Church for this approach. A
distinction is proposed: not a complete separation of the two elements. In
order to demonstrate this, it will be necessary to quote extensively from the
relevant documents in order to clarify the context. The simplest example
can be drawn from the quotation immediately above. By including the
two sentences that immediately precede those quoted, it becomes clear
that the connection between the two tasks is just as important as the
distinction between the two:

> *There is a close connection, and at the same time a clear distinc-
> tion, between religious instruction and catechesis, or the handing
> on of the Gospel message. The close connection makes it possible
> for a school to remain a school and still integrate culture with the
> message of Christianity.* The distinction comes from the fact
> that, unlike religious instruction, catechesis presupposes that
> the hearer is receiving the Christian message as a salvific reality.
> Moreover, catechesis takes place within a community living out
> its faith at a level of space and time not available to a school: a
> whole lifetime.[185]

---

184 RDEC, § 68.
185 Ibid.

It is further evident from the very next paragraph that it is intended that the Catholic school continue to play a specific role in the domain of catechesis:

> The distinction between religious instruction and catechesis does not change the fact that a school can and must play its specific role in the work of catechesis. Since its educational goals are rooted in Christian principles, the school as a whole is inserted into the evangelical function of the Church. It assists in and promotes faith education.[186]

Furthermore, the relationship of catechesis and religious education is seen as complementary: "It is evident, of course, that religious instruction cannot help but strengthen the faith of a believing student, just as catechesis cannot help but increase one's knowledge of the Christian message." The religious education offered in schools should also coordinate with the catechetical activities offered elsewhere: "religious instruction in the school needs to be coordinated with the catechesis offered in parishes, in the family, and in youth associations."[187]

Within the overall curriculum in a Catholic school, religious education is meant to play a role in influencing the development of religious values:

> One important result of religious instruction is the development of religious values and religious motivation; these can be a great help in obtaining the willing participation of the students. But we must remember that religious values and motivation are cultivated in all subject areas and, indeed, in all of the various activities going on in the school, one way that teachers can encourage an understanding of and commitment to religious values is by frequent references to God.[188]

Even *The Religious Dimension of Education in A Catholic School* — the document which makes the clearest case for a distinction between catechesis and religious education — envisages that a religious education teacher will be forming students in religious truth and values using an Christological approach:

186 Ibid., § 69.
187 Ibid., § 70.
188 Ibid., § 107.

Teachers learn through experience how to help the students understand and appreciate the religious truths they are being taught, and this appreciation can easily develop into love. A truth which is loved by the teacher, and communicated in such a way that it is seen to be something valuable in itself, then becomes valuable to the student. One advantage of the Christological approach to religious instruction is that it can develop this love more easily in young people. The approach we have suggested concentrates on the person of Jesus. It is possible to love a person; it is rather difficult to love a formula. This love for Christ is then transferred to his message which, because it is loved, has value.

But every true educator knows that a further step is necessary: values must lead to action; they are the motivation for action. Finally, truth becomes fully alive through the supernatural dynamism of grace, which enlightens and leads to faith, to love, to action that is in accord with the will of God, through the Lord Jesus, in the Holy Spirit. The Christian process of formation is, therefore, the result of a constant interaction involving the expert labor of the teachers, the free cooperation of the students, and the help of grace.[189]

Further reference to the documents only serves to underscore the relationship between catechesis and religious education, while at the same time affirming the legitimate distinction between the two. Religious education and catechesis are at the same time distinct and complementary, and the Catholic school's purpose is the students' integral formation.[190] The essential task of education remains the formation of the human person in its totality, particularly as regards the religious and spiritual dimension.[191]

There is a necessary connection between the scholastic teaching of religion and the essential deepening of faith. Catholic teachers cannot legitimately avoid giving witness in the classroom that God is the essential reference point in their own lives.[192] The relationship between catechesis and religious education is one of distinction and complementarity. While

189 Ibid., § 107.
190 Ibid., § 70.
191 RES, § 1.
192 CRT.

it is necessary to clearly distinguish between the two, it is just as important to ensure that they continue to work in harmony.[193] The *General Directory for Catechesis* is quite insistent that, when given in the context of the Catholic school, religious education must be complemented by catechesis and other forms of ministry.[194]

It may be useful to sum up this issue with an analogy. It would appear that what is being proposed in the documents is a distinction like the one between the left and right hands of the same person: both hands working on the same project. Nowhere is it envisaged that the tasks are so separate that the analogy for them would be two different people, with one delivering catechesis and the other religious education.

Catechesis and Religious Education
SUMMARY OF KEY POINTS

- *The Church insists on making a distinction between religious education and catechesis. In the context of a school, religious education needs to be seen as a subject with the same systematic demands and rigour as other disciplines.[195]*
- *The definitive aim of catechesis, on the other hand, is intimacy with Christ and ongoing induction into the life of the Church.[196]*
- *What is proposed here is a distinction, not a formal separation of the two tasks.[197]*
- *In the Church's view, the distinction between religious education and catechesis does not change the fact that a school can and must play its specific role in the work of catechesis.[198]*
- *A suitable analogy for explaining the distinction would be the cooperation of the left and right hand — each one with a different role to play but working together.[199]*

TRINITARIAN CHRISTOCENTRICITY

The documents of the Church insist that Christ be seen as the foundation of the whole educational enterprise in a Catholic school.[200] Furthermore, in the view of the Church, Jesus Christ not only transmits the word of God: he is the Word of God. The project of educating in the Catholic faith

193 GDC, § 73.
194 Ibid., § 74.
195 RES, § 18.
196 CT, § 5.
197 RDEC, § 68.
198 Ibid., § 69.
199 GDC, § 73.
200 TCS, § 34.

is therefore completely tied to him. This centrality of Christ is referred to as "Christocentricity."[201] Christian anthropology insists that the ability of human beings to create culture derives from their being created in the image and likeness of God, a Trinity of Persons in communion.[202] Made in the image of the Trinity, all human persons are relational by nature.[203]

The Church teaches that Christ leads us to the innermost mystery of God: the mystery of the Holy Trinity, the central mystery of Christian faith and life.[204] Hence by association, every authentic mode of presentation of the Christian message must always be Christocentric-Trinitarian: "Through Christ to the Father in the Holy Spirit....If catechesis lacks these three elements or neglects their close relationship, the Christian message can certainly lose its proper character."[205] In fact, the Church views all of it charitable activities "as a manifestation of Trinitarian love. 'If you see charity, you see the Trinity,' wrote St. Augustine." [206]

Trinitarian Christocentricity
SUMMARY OF KEY POINTS

- *Jesus Christ not only transmits the word of God: he is the Word of God. The project of educating in the Catholic faith is therefore completely tied to him.[207]*
- *Christ leads us to the innermost mystery of God: the Holy Trinity, the central mystery of Christian faith and life.[208]*
- *Every authentic mode of presentation of the Christian message must always be Christocentric-Trinitarian: Through Christ to the Father in the communion of the Holy Spirit.[209]*
- *The ability of human beings to create culture derives from their being created in the image and likeness of God, a Trinity of Persons in communion.[210]*
- *Made in the image of the Trinity, all human persons are relational by nature.[211]*

---

201   GDC, § 98.
202   EID, § 34.
203   Ibid.
204   RES, § 99.
205   GDC, § 100.
206   DCE, § 19.
207   GDC, § 98.
208   RES, § 99.
209   GDC, § 100.
210   EID, § 34.
211   Ibid.

SOURCE AND SOURCES OF DIVINE REVELATION

The documents of the Church insist that the Good News first proclaimed by the witness of life will sooner or later need to be proclaimed by the word of life.[212] Hence, catechesis and religious education necessarily follow from the initial witness.

This subsequent proclamation draws its content from the Word of God transmitted in Tradition and Scripture.[213] The Second Vatican Council's dogmatic constitution, *Dei Verbum*, clarified the Church's teaching about the sources of divine revelation by identifying Jesus Christ himself as the mediator and fullness of revelation, while Scripture and Tradition are to be seen as the authentic sources of our knowledge of Christ.[214] For the purposes of religious education and catechesis, then, the basic data is to be found in the scriptures and in the Creed (which is described as an exceptionally important expression of the living heritage of the Church).[215]

The scriptures are given a particular emphasis in the project of Catholic education. Pope Benedict XVI has been especially insistent on this need to "rediscover the centrality of God's Word in Catechesis."[216] He refers to the encounter of Jesus with the disciples on the road to Emmaus as a model of catechesis based on the explanation of the scriptures which Christ alone can give.[217] The pope's words to religious education teachers underscore the importance he places on the scriptures: "One of the main aspects of your teaching is of course the communication of the truth and beauty of the word of God and knowledge of the Bible is an essential element of the curriculum for teaching the Catholic religion."[218]

The Apostolic Exhortation *Verbum Domini* makes it clear that it is not just reading the scriptures with an independent mindset that is envisaged here, but rather, that "catechesis will be all the richer and more effective for reading the [Biblical] texts with the mind and the heart of the Church."[219] The same document draws attention to the importance of the relationship between Scripture and Tradition as it is set forth in the *Catechism of the*

212 EV, § 22.
213 CT, § 27.
214 See GDC, § 1.
215 CT, § 27, 28.
216 See VBD, § 74.
217 Ibid.
218 CRT.
219 VBD, § 74.

Catholic Church.[220] Hence, to achieve what the Church has in mind, religious education teachers need to be given careful training in the sacred scriptures and in the *Catechism of the Catholic Church*.[221] *Verbum Domini* also refers to an essential and indispensable link between the Liturgy and Scripture, so much so that neither can be properly understood without reference to the other:

> To understand the word of God, then, we need to appreciate and experience the essential meaning and value of the liturgical action. A faith-filled understanding of sacred Scripture must always refer back to the liturgy, in which the word of God is celebrated as a timely and living word: in the liturgy the Church faithfully adheres to the way Christ himself read and explained the sacred Scriptures, beginning with his coming forth in the synagogue and urging all to search the Scriptures.[222]

Source and Sources of Divine Revelation
SUMMARY OF KEY POINTS

- *The proclamation of the Good News draws its content from the Word of God transmitted in Tradition and Scripture.*[223]
- *"A faith-filled understanding of sacred Scripture must always refer back to the liturgy, in which the word of God is celebrated as a timely and living word."*[224]
- *Jesus Christ himself is the mediator and fullness of revelation, while Scripture and Tradition are to be seen as the authentic sources of our knowledge of Christ.*[225]
- *The scriptures, read with the mind of the Church, are given a particular emphasis in the project of Catholic education.*[226]
- *There is a vital relationship between Scripture and Tradition as it is set forth in the Catechism of the Catholic Church, so teachers need careful training in both.*[227]

---

220 Ibid.
221 Ibid., § 111.
222 VBD, § 52.
223 CT, § 27.
224 VBD, § 52.
225 See GDC, § 1.
226 VBD, § 74.
227 Ibid., § 111.

ESSENTIAL CONTENT

In *Evangelii Gaudium*, Pope Francis draws attention to the role of the *kerygma* in articulating the foundational content of the Christian message: "Jesus Christ loves you; he gave his life to save you; and now he is living at your side every day to enlighten, strengthen and free you."[228] Benedict XVI makes the link between human and religious formation. Religious education cannot be considered as some optional extra that can be added to an existing secular program — the whole curriculum of the Catholic school should be directed toward the integral development of the human person, in which religious education is integrated organically. "The religious dimension is not some kind of superstructure, it is an integral to being human; it makes the human person more human."[229] This concern is reflected in other documents as well: "Efforts must be made in putting together the school curriculum to avoid fragmentation by placing the human person — a material and spiritual being — at the center."[230] Schools must promote two levels of learning — cognitive and relational — taking into account not only the content, but also attitudes and ways of respecting diversity. These approaches must cultivated empathy and collaboration.[231] In *Lumen Fidei*, it is made clear that what the Church is handing on is not solely a doctrinal content for which a book or the repetition of an idea might suffice. There must be an encounter with the true God which touches the whole person.[232]

In terms of the content of religious education and catechesis, a highly detailed program is not specified by the Church, but some outlines are provided for overall guidance. In addition, the *Catechism of the Catholic Church* is mandated as the standard reference for doctrinal presentations. That said, there is an expectation that catechesis and religious education should be "systematic, deal with essentials, be integral and sufficiently complete."[233] It must convey the truth, which must never be hidden or betrayed if evangelization is to be successful.[234] There are three outlines of essential content to be found in *The General Directory for Catechesis, Catechesi Tradendae*, and *The Religious Dimension of Education in a Catholic School*.

228 EG § 164.
229 CRT.
230 RDEC, § 55.
231 EID, § 69.
232 LF, § 40.
233 CT, § 21.
234 EN, § 78.

In the *General Directory of Catechesis,* the following tasks are identified as being fundamental. Further clarification of the meaning of each one can be gained from reading the document itself if this is required.

The fundamental tasks of catechesis include:[235]

1. Promoting knowledge of the faith
2. Liturgical education
3. Moral formation
4. Teaching to pray
5. Education for Community Life
6. Missionary initiation

In *Catechesi Tradendae,* John Paul II provides a brief list of basic essentials:

1. humanity's creation and sin
2. God's plan of redemption and its long, loving preparation and realization
3. the incarnation of the Son of God
4. Mary Immaculate, Mother of God, ever Virgin, assumed into heaven
5. her role in the mystery of salvation
6. the mystery of lawlessness at work in our lives
7. the power of God freeing us from it
8. the need for penance and asceticism
9. the sacramental and liturgical actions
10. the reality of the Eucharistic Presence
11. participation in divine life here and hereafter[236]

The same document also identifies specific aspects of the Christian message that are regarded as so important that they should be committed to memory.[237] "Far from being opposed to the dignity of young Christians, or constituting an obstacle to personal dialogue with the Lord, [such memorization] is a real need, as the synod fathers forcefully recalled."[238] These aspects are:

---

235 GDC, § 85, 86.

236 CT, § 30.

237 Bishop Geoffrey Jarrett (Diocese of Lismore) has responded to this request by identifying the specific details required proposed by this passage and has published them in a brief pamphlet titled *For Mind and Memory.*

238 CT, § 55.

1. A certain memorization of the words of Jesus
2. Important Bible passages, such as the Ten Commandments
3. The formulas of profession of the faith
4. The liturgical texts of the essential prayers
5. Key doctrinal ideas[239]

The Religious Dimension of Education in a Catholic School has an outline which is useful in identifying what needs to be included in a basic but comprehensive program of religious education and catechesis. It is divided into two parts: "The Christ Event and the Christian Message" and "The Christian Life."

The Christian Event and the Christian Message

Preliminary. Vatican II advised that the task of the teacher is to summarize Christology and present it in everyday language.[240] This should be preceded by:

1. some basic ideas about Scripture (especially the Gospels);
2. an acquaintance with Divine Revelation and the Tradition that is alive in the Church.

Outline. With this base, the class begins to learn about the Lord Jesus:

1. his message
2. his deeds
3. the historical fact of his resurrection
4. the mystery of his divinity
   - for more mature students this can be expanded to include:
   i. Jesus as Savior, Priest, Teacher, and Lord of the universe
   ii. At his side is Mary his Mother, who cooperates in his mission.[241]

- The reliable way to bring young people closer to the mystery God is the way indicated by the Savior: "Whoever has seen me, has seen the Father."[242]
- Students learn much about the human person from science, but science has nothing to say about mystery. Teachers should help students begin to

---

239 Ibid.
240 RDEC, § 74.
241 Ibid.
242 RDEC, § 75.

discover the mystery within the human person.[243]

- Human history unfolds within a divine history of salvation: from creation, through the first sin, the covenant with the ancient people of God, the long period of waiting until finally Jesus our Savior came, so that now we are the new People of God, pilgrims on earth journeying toward our eternal home.[244]
- *Christian Anthropology.* The educational value of Christian anthropology is obvious, since students will discover:

    1. the true value of the human person: loved by God, with a mission on earth and a destiny that is immortal
    2. the virtues of self-respect and self-love, and of love for others
    3. a willingness to embrace life
    4. their own unique vocation as a fulfilment of God's will[245]

- *Ecclesiology.* Ecclesiology has an extremely important educational value: the ideal of a universal human family is realized in the Church.[246]
- *Sacraments and Sacramentality.* Teachers will help students to discover the real value of the Sacraments: they accompany the believer on his or her journey through life.[247]
- *The Last Things.* Reflection on the "Last Things" using the story of Dives and Lazarus (Jn 11:25–27).[248]
- *The Communion of Saints.* Using the Creed as a pattern, the teacher can help students to learn about the Kingdom of Heaven and the Communion of Saints.[249]

The Christian Life

Each truth of faith has ethical implications, but a systematic presentation of Christian ethics is also required.[250]

The First Christian Communities. This study of ethics can be introduced by looking at the first Christian communities where the Gospel message was accompanied by prayer and the celebration of the Sacraments.

Christian Perfection. The Christian perfection to which we are all called is a gift of Jesus through the mediation of the Spirit; but the gift requires

---

243 Ibid., § 76.
244 Ibid.
245 Ibid.
246 Ibid.
247 RDEC, § 78.
248 Ibid., § 80.
249 Ibid., § 81.
250 Ibid., § 82.

our cooperation.[251]

The Virtue of Faith. Students will begin to understand the meaning of the virtue of faith: helped by grace, to give complete, free, personal and affective loyalty to the God who reveals himself through his Son.[252]

A Gift of God. This commitment to Christian living is not automatic; it is itself a gift of God. We must ask for it and wait for it patiently. And students must be given time to grow and to mature.[253]

Expressed in Acts of Religion. The life of faith is expressed in acts of religion. The teacher will assist students to open their hearts in confidence to Father, Son, and Holy Spirit through personal and liturgical prayer.[254]

The Human Person. The human person is present in all the truths of faith: created in "the image and likeness" of God; elevated by God to the dignity of a child of God; unfaithful to God in original sin, but redeemed by Christ; a temple of the Holy Spirit; a member of the Church; destined to eternal life.[255]

Christian Social Ethics. Christian social ethics must always be founded on faith. From this starting point it can shed light on related disciplines such as law, economics and political science, all of which study the human situation, and this is an obvious area for fruitful interdisciplinary study.[256]

Basic elements of a Christian social ethic:

- *The human person*, the central focus of the social order.
- *Justice*, the recognition of the rights of each individual.
- *Honesty*, the basic condition for all human relationships.
- *Freedom*, the basic right of each individual and of society.
- *World peace* must then be founded on good order and the justice to which all men and women have a right as children of God.
- *The goods of the earth* are gifts of God, and are not the privilege of some individuals or groups while others are deprived of them. National and international well-being depend on the fact that the goods of the earth are for all to share in.
- *Misery and hunger* weigh on the conscience of humanity and cry out to God for justice.[257]

251 Ibid., § 95.
252 Ibid., § 82.
253 Ibid.
254 Ibid.
255 RDEC, 84.
256 Ibid., § 88.
257 Ibid., § 89.

Essential Content
SUMMARY OF KEY POINTS

- *What the Church is hands on is not solely a doctrinal content. There must be an encounter with the true God which touches the whole person.*[258]
- *The curriculum of the Catholic school should not be fragmented; the religious dimension is not some kind of superstructure, it is integral to being human.*[259]
- *The Catechism of the Catholic Church is mandated as the standard reference for doctrinal presentations.*[260]
- *The essential content, the kerygma, is summarized thus: "Jesus Christ loves you; he gave his life to save you; and now he is living at your side every day to enlighten, strengthen and free you."*[261]
- *Schools must promote two levels of learning: cognitive and relational taking into account not only the content, but also attitudes and ways of respecting diversity.*[262]
- *An outline of the essential content of a program of religious education cannot be briefly summarized, and readers are referred to the main body of the text for details.*
- *The outlines provided make a two-fold division of content: the Christian event and message; and the Christian Life.*[263]

METHODOLOGY

The documents of the Church do not directly specify a particular methodology for religious education or catechesis. On the contrary, a variety of methods is encouraged:

> The plurality of methods in contemporary catechesis can be a sign of vitality and ingenuity. In any case, the method chosen must ultimately be referred to a law that is fundamental for the whole of the Church's life: the law of fidelity to God and of fidelity to man in a single loving attitude.[264]

More emphasis is placed on the witnessing role of the teacher: "No methodology, however effective, can dispense with the part played by the

258 LF (2013), § 40.
259 RDEC, § 55.
260 EN, § 78.
261 EG, § 164.
262 EID, § 69.
263 Ibid., § 82.
264 CT, § 56.

teacher, whose own life must give witness to the message proclaimed."[265]

In general terms, it is noted that the role of any catechetical method is "to fix in the memory, intelligence and the heart the essential truths that must impregnate the whole of life."[266] This emphasis on memory is reiterated strongly in both *Catechesis Tradendae* and the *General Directory for Catechesis*. It is acknowledged that memorization, pursued in the wrong way, presents certain difficulties, "not the least of which is that it lends itself to insufficient or at times almost non-existent assimilation."[267] Even so, teachers are asked to "put this faculty back into use in an intelligent and even an original way in catechesis, all the more since the celebration or 'memorial' of the great events of the history of salvation require a precise knowledge of them."[268] The *General Directory for Catechesis* is even more directive on the subject, insisting that the use of memory "forms a constitutive aspect of the pedagogy of the faith since the beginning of Christianity."[269] Echoing the teaching of *Catechesis Tradendae*, the document goes on to make a strong case for appropriate memorization:

> The blossoms — if we may call them that — of faith and piety do not grow in the desert places of a memory-less catechesis. What is essential is that texts that are memorized must at the same time be taken in and gradually understood in depth, in order to become a source of Christian life on the personal level and on the community level.[270]

There are other general observations referred to in the *General Directory for Catechesis*. Here, the methodology of catechesis is seen in terms of a "pedagogy of God" which receives its characteristics from the Holy Spirit.[271] These characteristics include a "dialogue of salvation" between God and the person; the principle of the progressiveness of Revelation and its adaptation to different persons and cultures; the centrality of Jesus Christ, "a pedagogy of the incarnation"; the community experience of faith; a pedagogy of signs, where words and deeds, teaching and experience are

265 GDC, § 156.
266 Ibid., § 44.
267 CT, § 56.
268 Ibid.
269 GDC, § 154.
270 Ibid.
271 Ibid., § 143.

interlinked; all drawing on the power of truth.[272] *Verbum Domini* makes the point that the pedagogy of the Church in presenting the faith has always unfolded the scriptures against the backdrop of the liturgical year.[273]

In *Evangelii Gaudium*, Pope Francis is quite explicit in favoring a particular pedagogy, *mystagogic* initiation, as a highly recommended mode of formation. This requires an experience of formation involving the entire community and a renewed appreciation of the liturgical signs of Christian initiation.[274] It also demands "a suitable environment and an attractive presentation, the use of eloquent symbols."[275] Even so, he does not insist that this is the only methodology that can be used. Finally, it is recommended that every form of catechesis should also involve the "way of beauty." Hence, "every expression of true beauty can thus be acknowledged as a path leading to and encounter with Christ. This must not be confused with an *aesthetic relativism* which separates beauty from the *true* and the *good*."[276]

One of the principal reasons for encouraging variety of methods is the obligation to account for the age, intellectual capacity, and developmental stage of the students. The *General Directory of Catechesis* devotes eight articles to this, referring to differing needs for infants and children (including children who are not supported in their faith by family circumstances), for pre-adolescents, adolescents, young adults, the aged, the marginalized, and those in various other groups.[277]

The Religious Dimension of Education in a Catholic School makes a strong case for the use of "discovery" as an important pedagogical tool.[278] Through the discovery process, the "person of Jesus will come alive for the students. They will see again the example of his life, listen to his words, hear his invitation as addressed to them: 'Come to me, all of you....' Faith is thus based on knowing Jesus and following him; its growth depends on each one's good will and cooperation with grace." In highlighting the importance of "discovery" this document is locating authentic pedagogy for catechesis and religious education within the Catholic philosophical tradition of *Realism*, which argues for the objective existence of things which human senses perceive. This is in contrast with many prevalent educational philosophies,

272   See GDC, § 143.
273   VBD, § 52.
274   EG § 166.
275   Ibid.
276   Ibid., § 167.
277   GDC, § 177–81.
278   RDEC, § 74.

which do not accept the existence of objective truth, and insert relativist and subjectivist interpretations in its place. The importance of a "realist" philosophy has been consistently insisted upon in the Catholic tradition, most recently in *Fides et Ratio*, in which Pope John Paul II noted the spread of this phenomenon and contrasted it with a Catholic approach: "In brief, there are signs of a widespread distrust of universal and absolute statements, especially among those who think that truth is born of consensus and not of a consonance between intellect and objective reality."[279]

Finally, it is worth noting that the Church recognizes a role for the media of social communication in Evangelization, catechesis and religious education:

> When they are put at the service of the Gospel, they are capable of increasing almost indefinitely the area in which the Word of God is heard; they enable the Good News to reach millions of people. The Church would feel guilty before the Lord if she did not utilize these powerful means that human skill is daily rendering more perfect. It is through them that she proclaims "from the housetops" the message of which she is the depositary. In them she finds a modern and effective version of the pulpit. Thanks to them she succeeds in speaking to the multitudes.[280]

At the same time, it issues a caution that these media have limitations, in that they lack a personal dimension, and, hence, cannot be used unreservedly:

> In the long run, is there any other way of handing on the Gospel than by transmitting to another person one's personal experience of faith? It must not happen that the pressing need to proclaim the Good News to the multitudes should cause us to forget this form of proclamation whereby an individual's personal conscience is reached and touched by an entirely unique word that he receives from someone else.[281]

279 FR, § 56.
280 EN, § 45.
281 Ibid., § 46.

Methodology
SUMMARY OF KEY POINTS

- *The General Directory for Catechesis describes the methodology of catechesis in terms of a "pedagogy of God" which receives its characteristics from the Holy Spirit.*[282]
- *These characteristics include:*
  - *A "dialogue of salvation" between God and the person.*
  - *The principle of the progressiveness of Revelation and its adaptation to different persons and cultures.*
  - *The centrality of Jesus Christ, "a pedagogy of the incarnation."*
  - *The community experience of faith.*
  - *A pedagogy of signs, where words and deeds, teaching and experience are interlinked.*
  - *A pedagogy drawing on the power of truth.*[283]
- *The pedagogy of the Church in presenting the faith has always unfolded the Scriptures against the backdrop of the liturgical year.*[284]
- *Every form of catechesis should also involve the "way of beauty." Hence, "every expression of true beauty can thus be acknowledged as a path leading to and encounter with Christ."*[285]
- *The Church does not specify a particular methodology for religious education and catechesis; a variety of methods is encouraged.*[286] *More recently, Pope Francis has encouraged the use of mystagogic initiation as a method to be favored.*[287]
- *No methodology, however effective, can dispense with the part played by the teacher, whose own life must give witness to the message proclaimed.*[288]
- *The purpose of any catechetical methodology is to fix in the memory, intelligence, and heart the essential truths that must impregnate the whole of life.*[289]
- *Teachers are encouraged to ensure that certain basic ideas are committed to memory through appropriate educational means.*[290]
- *The texts that are committed to memory should be gradually understood in depth, to become a source of Christian life on the personal and community levels.*[291]

---

282 GDC, § 143.
283 See Ibid.
284 VBD, § 52.
285 EG § 167.
286 GDC, § 155.
287 EG § 166.
288 GDC, § 156.
289 Ibid., § 44.
290 CT, § 56.
291 GDC, § 154.

- *Methods selected should account for the differing ages and other needs of the students.*[292]
- *Discovery is cited as an important pedagogical tool and one that is in accord with the "realist" philosophical view regarding the existence of objective reality, as opposed to subjectivist and relativist interpretations.*[293]
- *Technology and the media of social communication should be incorporated into the program. Nevertheless, there is a personal dimension which these media cannot replace, and this must be born in mind.*[294]

PART 4: INTERCULTURAL DIALOGUE

Introduction. Catholic schools have in Jesus Christ the basis of their operations and must be seen as privileged places of intercultural dialogue.[295] The starting point for such dialogue is a sound understanding of what it means to be a human person. Moreover, we can neither live nor develop our human potential unless we understand that in our inmost nature we are relational beings.[296]

Cultures. The fact of cultural difference must be viewed as a "richness of expression to be understood in terms of the fundamental unity of the human race."[297] The love for all men and women is also a love for their culture and, thus, Catholic schools are intercultural.[298] Yet it must be acknowledged that it is primarily persons, not cultures, who enter into contact with each other—persons who are grounded in their own history and relationships. This guides the idea of dialogue and it is marked with respect, refusing to push the other person into a cultural prison.[299]

Importance of Maintaining Catholic Identity. From a Catholic perspective, faithfulness to one's own Christian identity is the indispensable condition for both interreligious dialogue and adequate intercultural education.[300] "Clarity in dialogue means especially faithfulness to one's own Christian identity,"[301] and intercultural dialogue is most effectively promoted by a confessional teaching of religion. In fact, "if religious

---

292 Ibid., § 177–81.
293 RDEC, § 74.
294 EN, § 45, 46.
295 EID, § 6.
296 Ibid., § 39.
297 Ibid., § 1.
298 Ibid., § 61.
299 Ibid., § 42.
300 Ibid., § 16.
301 Ibid.

education is limited to a presentation of the different religions, in a comparative and 'neutral' way, it creates confusion or generates religious relativism or indifferentism."[302] Dialogue is not a compromise, but "a framework for reciprocal witnessing among believers who belong to different religions."[303]

Inadequate Approaches. The documents of the Church make it clear that *pluralism* is a fact in today's world, and it has been answered by two principal approaches: relativism and assimilation. Both are inadequate, but have some helpful points.[304] The assimilationist approach demands that the other person "adapt" and abandon their cultural reference points.[305] Relativism respects differences, but separates them into autonomous spheres, considering them isolated and therefore making dialogue impossible.[306] This kind of exaggerated tolerance leads to a substantially passive relationship with those of different cultures. In this model, there can be no "self-comparison" with their values nor any sense of developing love for them.[307] Such an approach, "based on an inadequate understanding of tolerance is the basis for a political and social model of multi-culturalism. This offers no adequate solutions for co-existence and does not engage in genuine intercultural dialogue."[308] Moreover, "cultural diversity should be understood within the horizon of the unity of the human race," rather than "the radicalization of identity which makes cultures resistant to any beneficial influence from outside."[309]

Motives and Strategies for Intercultural Dialogue.

Motives. The Church identifies significant benefits for encouraging intercultural dialogue. It is part of being human to desire others to share in one's own goods. Acceptance of the Good News should mean that we want to share what we have discovered — the true face of God in Jesus.[310] The fostering of encounters between different people helps to create mutual understanding, although it ought not to mean a loss of one's own identity.[311] It is fundamental that the Catholic religion, for its part, be an inspiring sign

302 Ibid., § 75.
303 Ibid., § 15.
304 Ibid., § 21.
305 Ibid., § 24.
306 Ibid., § 22.
307 Ibid.
308 Ibid., § 23.
309 Ibid., § 32.
310 Ibid., § 55.
311 Ibid., Introduction.

of dialogue. In fact, "it can be stated absolutely that the Christian message has never been so universal and fundamental as today."[312]

At its very core, this experience of intercultural relationships is aimed at including individuals and peoples in one human family, founded on the fundamental values of solidarity, justice, and peace.[313] Authentic integral humanism is enriched by religion's identity and is able to thereby appreciate religion's great traditions: faith; respect for human life and for the family; respect for community, education, and work.[314] The Church identifies the central challenge of education for the future to allow various cultural expressions to coexist and to promote dialogue so as to foster a peaceful society.[315]

Strategies. The starting point for dialogue must be the two underlying assumptions. First, faithfulness to one's own Christian identity is the indispensable condition for interreligious dialogue, and for adequate intercultural education.[316] The second is that the values of other cultures and religions must be respected and understood. Schools have a vital role to play in this. They must become places of pluralism, sharing universal values, such as solidarity, tolerance and freedom.[317] They must also be open to encountering other cultures and support each person in developing their own identity in an awareness of their cultural tradition.[318] Multiculturalism and pluralism are characteristic traits of our times; thus, teachers must allow their students, in the routine of the classroom, to experience real listening, respect, dialogue, and the value of diversity.[319] Intercultural strategies avoid separating individuals into autonomous spheres. They promote encounter, dialogue and mutual transformation, allowing people to coexist. There are three essential markers of successful formation in interreligious dialogue: integration of students from different cultural backgrounds; interaction facilitating good relationships; and recognition of the other person without imposing one's own view.[320]

Believers can enter into dialogue in a number of ways. Life itself will allow them the opportunity of sharing joys and sorrows in the normal

---

312 Ibid., § 71.
313 Ibid., § 37.
314 Ibid., § 72.
315 Ibid., Introduction.
316 Ibid., § 16.
317 Ibid., § 63.
318 Ibid., § 50.
319 Ibid., § 83.
320 Ibid., § 78.

course of daily events. In their work, they can collaborate for the development of their fellow men and women. Theology and religious experience also offer opportunities for dialogue on an even deeper level.[321] Typically, dialogue unfolds in stages:

1. discovering the multicultural nature of one's own situation
2. overcoming prejudices by living and working in harmony
3. educating oneself "by means of the other" to a global vision and a sense of citizenship[322]

Inter-cultural Dialogue
SUMMARY OF KEY POINTS

- *Intercultural dialogue is most effectively promoted by a confessional teaching of religion.[323]*
- *A presentation of different religions in a comparative and "neutral" way creates confusion and generates religious relativism and indifferentism.[324]*
- *Pluralism is a fact in today's world, but neither a relativist nor assimilationist approach can offer adequate answers.[325]*
- *Cultural diversity must be understood within the unity of the human race and an openness to beneficial influence from other cultures.[326]*
- *The Church identifies the central challenge of education for the future to allow various cultural expressions to coexist and to promote dialogue so as to foster a peaceful society.[327]*
- *Dialogue must begin with faithfulness to one's own Christian identity together with respect for the values of other cultures and religions.[328]*
- *Typically, dialogue unfolds in stages:*
  1. *discovering the multicultural nature of one's own situation*
  2. *overcoming prejudices by living and working in harmony*
  3. *educating oneself "by means of the other" to a global vision and a sense of citizenship [329]*

---

321 Ibid., § 14.
322 Ibid., Introduction.
323 Ibid., § 21.
324 Ibid., § 75.
325 Ibid., § 23.
326 Ibid., § 32.
327 Ibid., Introduction.
328 Ibid., § 16.
329 Ibid., Introduction.

Appendix A

*Organization of Content
in Liturgical Spiral Curriculum,
Kindergarten–Gr. 7
(US Schools)*

KINDERGARTEN AND GRADE 1

THEMES	TIME OF YEAR	TOPICS
The Holy Spirit continues to make Christ present.	AUGUST / SEPTEMBER	**Moral Formation; Prayer**
Focus Solemnity: Pentecost (ongoing)	OCTOBER / EARLY NOVEMBER	**Social Justice; Example of Mary & Saints**

GRADE 1	DOCTRINAL CONTENT
Prayer Set up prayer table See Prayer Development Chart	▪ *Prayer is loving, speaking, listening and singing to God.* [CCC 2590] ▪ *We also pray at Mass, with our families and at school.* [CCC 2694] ▪ *The Bible has a central place in personal and community prayer.* [CCC 2653; 2662] ▪ *Jesus promises that when we gather in his name, he is there with us.* [CCC 1373] ▪ *Jesus wants us to pray often, at any time and in any place.* [CCC 2757] ▪ *The Holy Spirit helps us to pray.* [CCC 741] ▪ *God speaks to us in the Bible, which is the Church's book.* [CCC 141] ▪ *God speaks to us through his Church.* [CCC 100]
Ecclesiology, Kingdom Parables *Repeat:* Good Shepherd*; Mustard Seed*; Leaven* *Add:* Found Sheep*; Good Shepherd and the Wolf*; Pearl of Great Price*	▪ *The Church is a Sheepfold* [LUMEN GENTIUM 1] ▪ *Jesus gives his life for his sheep.* [CCC 754] ▪ *Jesus the Good Shepherd loves us.* [CCC 764] ▪ *Jesus taught us about God's Kingdom using parables.* [CCC 546; 2607]
Moral Formation *Repeat:* Grace Courtesy Procedures*; Setting up of Response Tools* **Practical Life Activities*** *Repeat:* Dusting; Watering Plants; Flower Arranging; Cleaning Surfaces; Sweeping; Rolling a Mat *Add:* Leaf Washing; Polishing	▪ *God helps us to do good.* [CCC 2003] ▪ *When we sin, we are not living the way Jesus taught us. We make choices that are not good which hurt others and ourselves.* [CCC 1745; 1871] ▪ *Jesus wants us to share our good things with others.* [CCC 1926]

KINDERGARTEN
Prayer Set up prayer table* See Prayer Development Chart
Ecclesiology *Introduce:* Good Shepherd* **Kingdom Parables** *Introduce:* Mustard Seed*; Leaven*; Treasure in a Field*
Moral Formation *Introduce:* Grace Courtesy Procedures*; Setting up of Response Tools;*; Drawing; Watercolor Painting; Collage & Pasting; Playdough Modelling; Writing / Modelling in Damp Sand. **Practical Life Activities*** Dusting; Watering Plants; Flower Arranging; Cleaning Surfaces; Sweeping; Rolling a Mat

KINDERGARTEN	GRADE 1	DOCTRINAL CONTENT
Liturgical Gestures, Colors *Introduce:* Sign of the Cross (+ Holy Water)*; Liturgical Colors: Chasuble stands*	**Liturgical Gestures, Colors** *Repeat:* Sign of the Cross (+ Holy Water)*; Liturgical Colors: Chasuble stands* *Add:* Liturgical Calendar*; Genuflection;* Kneeling*	◼ *God is the Father, the Son (Jesus), and the Holy Spirit. We show this in the sign of the cross.* [CCC 261]
Liturgical Furniture, Vessels and Linen *Introduce:* Altar; Altar Cloth; Crucifix; Candles*; Chalice; Cruets; Purificator; Corporal*; Lectern, Lectionary; Tabernacle; Ciborium*	**Liturgical Furniture, Vessels and Linen** *Repeat:* Altar; Altar Cloth; Candles*; Chalice; Cruets; Purificator; Corporal*; Lectern, Lectionary; Tabernacle; Ciborium* *Add:* Finger Bowl; Finger Towel*; Bell; Sanctuary Lamp*	◼ *Every item used in the liturgy reminds us of something important that Jesus did or taught.* [CCC 1075]

KINDERGARTEN AND GRADE 1

THEMES	TIME OF YEAR	TOPICS
God Prepares the World to receive His Son	MID-NOVEMBER / DECEMBER	Salvation History; Infancy Narratives; Advent; Christmas

KINDERGARTEN	GRADE 1	DOCTRINAL CONTENT
Advent *Introduce:* Advent Procession*; Prophecy of the Young Women*; Prophecy of the Town*; Prophecy of the Star and the Scepter*	**Advent** *Repeat:* Advent Procession*; Prophecy of the Young Women*; Prophecy of the Town*; Prophecy of the Star and the Scepter*	◼ *God spent many years gradually preparing His people for the coming of Jesus.* [CCC 69]
Infancy Narratives *Introduce:* Annunciation*; Visitation*; Birth of Jesus; Shepherds and Angels*; Birth of Jesus: Visit of the Magi*; Presentation in the Temple*; Christmas Pageant	**Infancy Narratives** *Repeat:* Annunciation*; Visitation*; Birth of Jesus; Shepherds and Angels*; Birth of Jesus: Visit of the Magi*; Presentation in the Temple*; Christmas Pageant *Add:* Flight into Egypt*	◼ *Mary was asked to be the mother of Jesus, who is God.* [CCC 495; 509] ◼ *Angels are God's messengers.* [CCC 329; 330; 332] ◼ *Jesus, Mary, and Joseph were a family.* [CCC 488] ◼ *God made human beings to live in families. Families can help us to know God better.* [CCC 383] ◼ *Jesus loves us and shows this through our parents and people who care for us.* [CCC 383]

KINDERGARTEN AND GRADE 1

THEMES	TIME OF YEAR	TOPICS	DOCTRINAL CONTENT
Life of Christ **Focus Solemnity: Easter**	JANUARY	Biblical Geography; Gospel Narratives	▪ *God made the world to show his love.* [CCC 315] ▪ *God made us.* [CCC 44; 45; 315] ▪ *God loves us and his work is good.* [CCC 319] ▪ *God makes us to be different from one another. Each of us is special.* [CCC 353]
	FEBRUARY	Lent; Paschal Mystery	▪ *During Lent, the Church reflects on the meaning of Christ's 40 days in the desert.* [CCC 540]
Paschal Mystery	PRIOR TO EASTER	Paschal Mystery; Holy Week	▪ At the Last Supper, Jesus taught us to celebrate the Eucharist. [CCC 1340] ▪ On Good Friday, Jesus died for our sins. [CCC 623] ▪ On Easter Sunday, Jesus rose from the dead to a new and everlasting life. [CCC 656–58]

KINDERGARTEN	GRADE 1
Biblical Geography Creation: Gift of God*; Globe: Locate Israel*; Raised Map of Israel*	**Biblical Geography** *Repeat:* Raised Map of Israel* *Add:* City of Jerusalem;* Puzzle Map of Israel*; Tracing Maps;* Coloring Maps*
Lent Making Promises: Remembering Jesus in the Desert; Mystery of Life & Death: Planting Seeds*; Burying the Alleluia*	**Lent** Making Promises Burying the Alleluia Mystery of Life & Death: Planting Seeds*
Paschal Narratives *Introduce:* Last Supper (Cenacle)*; Resurrection (Empty Tomb)*	**Paschal Narratives** *Repeat:* Last Supper (dramatize): Resurrection (dramatize) *Add:* Palm Sunday (dramatize); Stations of the Cross and Crucifixion (dramatize)

KINDERGARTEN AND GRADE 1

THEMES	TIME OF YEAR	TOPICS
The Holy Spirit continues to make Christ present through the Sacraments. **Focus Solemnity: Pentecost.**	APRIL	**Ascension; Pentecost; Baptism**
	MAY	**Eucharist; Reconciliation**
	JUNE	**Holy Orders; Marriage; Anointing of the Sick**

KINDERGARTEN	GRADE 1	DOCTRINAL CONTENT
Major Feasts *Introduce:* Spreading the Light of Christ: Baptism*; Baptism Introduction*	**Major Feasts** *Repeat:* Pentecost; Ascension; Our Lady Help of Christians *Add:* Sacred Heart; Corpus Christi	▪ At the Ascension, Jesus went back to heaven to prepare a place for us. [CCC 2177] ▪ At Pentecost, Jesus sent the Holy Spirit to Mary and the apostles and to stay always with the Church. [CCC 731–32]
Baptism *Introduce:* Spreading the Light of Christ: Baptism*; Baptism Introduction*	**Baptism** *Repeat:* Spreading the Light of Christ: Baptism*; Baptism Introduction* *Add:* Baptism Collage*; Baptism Articles & Gestures Chart*	▪ The Holy Spirit was given to us at our baptism. [CCC 1266] ▪ At baptism, we are welcomed into God's family, the Church. [CCC 804] ▪ In baptism, we receive God's life (grace). [CCC 1277; 2017; 2023] ▪ Through the new life given at baptism, we can live forever in heaven. [CCC 1212; 1987]
Eucharist *Introduce:* Eucharistic Presence of the Good Shepherd*; Last Supper*; **Mass Moments** Preparing the Chalice (Water and Wine)*; Epiclesis*; Consecration; Offering (Doxology)*	**Eucharist** *Repeat:* Eucharistic Presence of the Good Shepherd* *Repeat:* Preparing the Chalice (Water and Wine)*; Epiclesis;* Consecration*; Offering (Doxology)* *Add:* Sign of Peace*; Washing of Hands (Lavabo)*	▪ Jesus is present with us when we celebrate the Eucharist. (Presence of the Good Shepherd). [CCC 1418] ▪ On Sunday, Catholics go to Mass. [CCC 1193] ▪ At the Last Supper, Jesus taught us to celebrate the Eucharist. [CCC 1340] ▪ Jesus gives himself to us in the Eucharist. [CCC 1406]

GRADES 2, 3, 4

	THEMES	TIME OF YEAR	TOPICS
	The Holy Spirit continues to make Christ present through us. Focus Solemnity: Pentecost.	AUGUST / SEPTEMBER	Moral Formation; Prayer
		OCTOBER	Social Justice; Example of Mary & Saints

GRADE 2	GRADE 3	GRADE 4	DOCTRINAL CONTENT
Prayer *Introduce:* Set up prayer table*; Establish prayer routine*; Study the Our Father each week, phrase by phrase, in prayer time. Memorize formal prayers See Prayer Development Chart	**Prayer** *Repeat:* Set up prayer table*; Establish prayer routine *Add:* Introduce praying with icons See Prayer Development Chart	**Prayer** *Repeat:* Set up prayer table*; Establish prayer routine*; Praying with icons *Add:* Continue memorizing formal prayers See Prayer Development Chart	■ *"Through Christ our Lord" we pray to the Father.* [CCC 2664] ■ *Prayer allows us to listen and respond to God.* [CCC 2590] ■ *We are meant to pray often; every day.* [CCC 2720] ■ *All our prayers bring our minds and hearts to God, or ask for good things from Him.* [CCC 2590] ■ *We grow in relationship with Jesus through prayer.* [CCC 2565] ■ *Jesus prayed often to his Father: by himself and publicly.* [CCC 2599] ■ *In the Our Father, Jesus taught us how to pray.* [CCC 2763]
Moral Formation Revise Grace and Courtesy Procedures Re-establish classroom chores Set Up Classroom Procedures for the Year Maxims of Jesus*; Moral Parables: The Insistent Friend*	**Moral Formation** Revise Grace and Courtesy Procedures Re-establish classroom chores Set Up Classroom Procedures for the Year *Repeat:* Maxims of Jesus*; The Insistent Friend* *Add:* Moral Parables: The Sower*; The Pharisee and the Tax Collector*	**Moral Formation** Revise Grace and Courtesy Procedures Re-establish classroom chores Set Up Classroom Procedures for the Year *Repeat:* Maxims of Jesus*; The Insistent Friend; The Sower*; The Pharisee and the Tax Collector* *Add:* Moral Parables: The Debtors*	■ *The commandments call us to love God and our neighbour.* [CCC 1983] ■ *I have the power to choose.* [CCC 1733]

GRADE 2	GRADE 3	GRADE 4	DOCTRINAL CONTENT
Christian Social Ethics Parables of Mercy: Forgiving Father*; Social Parables: Good Samaritan*; Scripture: The First Christian Community (Acts 2:44–45) Practical: Identify acts of service that can be done for others	**Christian Social Ethics** *Repeat*: Good Samaritan*, Forgiving Father*; The First Christian Community (Acts 2:44–45) *Add*: Lost Coin*; Practical: Identify acts of service that can be done for others	**Christian Social Ethics** *Repeat*: Good Samaritan*; Forgiving Father*, Lost Coin *Add*: Centurion's Servant*; The Great Commission; Practical: Identify acts of service that can be done for others	▪ Our problems can bring us closer to God. [CCC 1508; 1521] ▪ God wants us to turn back to him after we have sinned. This is called "Repentance." [CCC 1490] ▪ Many scripture stories show that Jesus loved and forgave sinners who asked to be forgiven. ▪ Jesus asks us to love one another as he has loved us. [CCC 1970]
Christian Anthropology *Introduce*: Every human being is loved by God	**Christian Anthropology** *Repeat*: Every human being is loved by God *Add*: The obligation of human persons to love others	**Christian Anthropology** *Repeat*: Every human being is loved by God; The obligation of human persons to love others *Add*: Capacity to be active and creative agent.	▪ The commandments call us to love God and our neighbour. [CCC 1983] ▪ By loving God and our neighbour, we journey towards Heaven. [CCC 1051; 1054]
Ecclesiology *Introduce*: Baptism makes us members of the Church; The True Vine*	**Ecclesiology** *Repeat*: Baptism makes us members of the Church; The True Vine* *Add*: Parables of the Kingdom: Pearl of Great Price*	**Ecclesiology** *Repeat*: Baptism makes us members of the Church; The True Vine*; Pearl of Great Price* *Add*: Parables of the Kingdom: Treasure in the Field*	▪ The Church helps us to know Jesus, and to make him known to others. [CCC 851] ▪ We share God's life and love (grace). [CCC 2021] ▪ Grace has been given to us by the Holy Spirit. [CCC 1999] ▪ We need grace to help us do what is right. [CCC 1714; 2021]
Christian Community Life *Introduce*: Care for the least among the brethren (Mt 18,6)	**Christian Community Life** *Repeat*: Care for the least among the brethren *Add*: Christian life requires common prayer (Mt 18,19)	**Christian Community Life** *Repeat*: Care for the least among the brethren; Christian life requires common prayer *Add*: The need for mutual forgiveness (Mt 18,22)	▪ Jesus teaches that whatever we do for the disadvantaged, we do to him. [CCC 1932; MT 25:40] ▪ The Our Father teaches us to forgive others as we have been forgiven ourselves. [MT 6:12]

GRADES 2, 3, 4

THEMES	TIME OF YEAR	TOPICS
Death and Everlasting Life.	EARLY NOVEMBER	Human Person; Family; The Last Things; Eschatology

GRADE 2	GRADE 3	GRADE 4	DOCTRINAL CONTENT
Christian Anthropology *Introduce:* Every human person has a destiny that is immortal.	**Christian Anthropology** *Repeat:* Every human person has a destiny that is immortal.	**Christian Anthropology** *Repeat:* Every human person has a destiny that is immortal. *Add:* The redeemed human person is destined to eternal life.	▪ *God created us with a body and a soul … the hand guided by intelligence.* [CCC 362–68; 382] ▪ *Our immortal soul is a spirit, created directly by God.* [CCC 382] ▪ *The selfish choices of the first people have caused sin and much human suffering to come into our world.* [CCC 1521]
The Last Things *Introduce:* Reflection on the "Last Things" using the story of Dives and Lazarus (Jn 11: 25-27).	**The Last Things** *Repeat:* Reflection on the "Last Things" using the story of Dives and Lazarus (Jn 11: 25-27). *Add:* Those who have died are not separated from us. They, with us, form the one Church, the People of God, united in the "communion of saints."	**The Last Things** *Repeat:* Those who have died are not separated from us. They, with us, form the one Church, the People of God, united in the "communion of saints." *Add:* The good or evil done to each human being is as if done to Christ.	▪ *God brings to heaven those who die in his love.* [CCC 1051] ▪ *The sacraments strengthen and comfort the dying.* [CCC 1525] ▪ *We continue to pray for those who have died.* [CCC 1032] ▪ *By loving God and our neighbour, we journey towards Heaven.* [CCC 1051; 1054] ▪ *Jesus will come again at the end of time.* [CCC 1060] ▪ *Through Jesus's life, death, and resurrection, we have new life.* [CCC 1016]

GRADES 2, 3, 4

THEMES	TIME OF YEAR	TOPICS
God Prepares the World to receive His Son	MID-NOVEMBER / DECEMBER	Salvation History; Infancy Narratives; Advent; Christmas

DOCTRINAL CONTENT

- God's creation is good. [CCC 299; 315]
- Sin came into our world when the first man and woman chose to disobey God. [CCC 390; 415–17]
- In the Old Testament, we are introduced to the stories of God's Chosen People, the Hebrew people of the Holy Land.
- God send prophets to guide and form his people. [CCC 64]
- New Testament reveals the Good News of Jesus to all people.
- Like the shepherds and the magi, we must "kneel" humbly before Jesus, born in a stable in Bethlehem. [CCC 563]
- The Presentation in the Temple reminds us that Jesus was born to be the promised savior. [CCC 529]
- The Flight into Egypt reminds us that Jesus lived his life under sign of persecution. [CCC 530]
- Jesus lived most of his life doing ordinary things, living under the authority of his parents. [CCC 531]

GRADE 2	GRADE 3	GRADE 4
Salvation History Three Moments Chart: Creation Redemption, Parousia*; Advent Procession*, Advent Prophecies*	**Salvation History** Repeat: Three Moments Chart*; Advent Procession*; Advent Prophecies* Add: Timeline Ribbon: Major events of Salvation History*	**Salvation History** Repeat: Three Moments Chart*; Advent Procession*; Advent Prophecies*; Timeline Ribbon* Add: Creation to Parousia Timeline
Infancy Narratives Revise Infancy Narrative directly from the Scriptures: Annunciation*, Visitation*, Birth of Jesus*, Shepherds Angels*, Visit of the Magi* Add: Flight into Egypt*	**Infancy Narratives** Repeat: Individual revision of Infancy Narratives from the Scriptures. Select own response. Add: Art synthesis of the Infancy Narratives: Provide images*	**Infancy Narratives** Repeat: Individual revision of Infancy Narratives from the Scriptures. Select own response. Add: Joyful Mysteries of the Rosary Art synthesis of the Infancy Narratives: Students search for images

GRADES 2, 3, 4

THEMES	TIME OF YEAR	TOPICS
Life of Christ / Focus Solemnity: Easter	JANUARY	Biblical Geography; Gospel Narratives
	EARLY FEBRUARY	Lent; Parables; Miracles
Paschal Mystery	PRIOR TO EASTER BREAK	Paschal Mystery; Holy Week

GRADE 2	GRADE 3	GRADE 4	DOCTRINAL CONTENT
Biblical Geography Introduce: Land of Israel*	**Biblical Geography** Repeat: Land of Israel* Add: City of Jerusalem*	**Biblical Geography** Repeat: Land of Israel*, City of Jerusalem* Add: Flag Maps of Israel*	■ The Gospels tell us about the life and teachings of Jesus. [CCC 68; 561]
The Scriptures Introduce: The Books of the Bible*	**The Scriptures** Repeat: The Books of the Bible* Add: Bible Charts*	**The Scriptures** Repeat: The Books of the Bible*; Bible Charts* Add: Free Reading of the Bible (up to 15 minutes).	■ The Holy Spirit inspired the writers of the Bible. [CCC 81; 136] ■ The Bible comprises the books of the Old and the New Testaments. [CCC 138]
Life of Jesus Introduce: Art Synthesis: Life of Jesus; Luminous Mysteries of the Rosary Focus: Jesus is teacher.	**Life of Jesus** Repeat: Art Synthesis: Life of Jesus; Sorrowful Mysteries of the Rosary Add: Biblical Charts of key events in the life of Jesus. (Children should read the Bible for themselves, then make their own response.) Focus: Jesus is Savior (Christ; Messiah).	**Life of Jesus** Repeat: Art Synthesis: Life of Jesus; Biblical Charts of key events in the life of Jesus. Add: Focus: Jesus is God and man.	■ Jesus loved us so much that he died for our sins. [CCC 629] ■ The Gospels tell us about the life and teachings of Jesus. [CCC 68; 561] ■ Jesus is our Saviour. He has won for us the life of grace. [CCC 1715; 2020]

GRADE 2	GRADE 3	GRADE 4	DOCTRINAL CONTENT
Mary and the Saints *Introduce:* Art Synthesis: Life of Mary*	**Mary and the Saints** *Repeat:* Art Synthesis: Life of Mary* *Add: Focus:* Role of Mary in Mission of Jesus	**Mary and the Saints** *Repeat:* Art Synthesis: Life of Mary* *Add: Focus:* Because Mary is the mother of Jesus, she is the mother of God.	▪ *Mary said "yes" to God by doing as he asked.* [CCC 973] ▪ *Mary is the mother of the Church and our mother.* [CCC 975] ▪ *Mary continues to work through the Church in leading us to Jesus.* [CCC 975] ▪ *Angels are spirits who serve God and act as his messengers.* [CCC 350]
Lent *Introduce:* Making sacrifices to be ready for Easter; Burying the Alleluia*; Changing the prayer table cloth to purple*	**Lent** *Repeat:* Making sacrifices to be ready for Easter; Burying the Alleluia*; Changing the prayer table cloth to purple* *Add:* Temptation of Christ	**Lent** *Repeat:* Making sacrifices to be ready for Easter; Burying the Alleluia*; Changing the prayer table cloth to purple; Temptation of Christ *Add: Typology:* The Passover*	▪ *During Lent and Holy Week, we try to do something in our lives to bring us closer to Jesus.* ▪ *During Lent we remember that Jesus suffered and died for our sins. He rose again from the dead on Easter Sunday.* ▪ *During Lent, we come closer to God through prayer, fasting, almsgiving and making sacrifices.*
Paschal Narratives Easter Triduum: Palm Sunday Revise Last Supper*; Revise Resurrection (Mt 28:1–8)*	**Paschal Narratives** *Repeat:* Resurrection Account (Mt 28:1–8) *Add:* Last Supper: Origin of the Eucharist*; Art Synthesis of the Paschal Narratives	**Paschal Narratives** *Repeat:* Resurrection Account* (Mt 28:1–8); Last Supper: Origin of the Eucharist*, Art Synthesis of the Paschal Narratives *Add:* Glorious Mysteries of the Rosary	▪ *Through Jesus's life, death, and Resurrection, we have new life.* [CCC 1016]
Christian Anthropology The human person is present in all the truths of faith. *Focus:* Christ died to save human beings.	**Christian Anthropology** *Repeat:* Christ died to save human beings. *Add:* The redeemed human person is elevated by God to the dignity of a child of God.	**Christian Anthropology** *Repeat:* Christ died to save human beings. The redeemed human person is elevated by God to the dignity of a child of God. *Add:* The human person is affected by original sin, but redeemed by Christ.	▪ *Jesus is our Lord and Saviour because he gained for us the new life of grace.* [CCC 455; 620–21] ▪ *Jesus Christ is the first to rise forever from the dead. He promised that we too will rise again.* [CCC 655; 658]

GRADES 2, 3, 4

THEMES	TIME OF YEAR	TOPICS
The Holy Spirit continues to make Christ present through the Sacraments. **Focus Solemnity: Pentecost.**	APRIL	**Ascension; Pentecost; Baptism**
	MAY	**Eucharist; Reconciliation**
	JUNE	**Holy Orders; Marriage; Anointing of the Sick**

GRADE 2	GRADE 3	GRADE 4	DOCTRINAL CONTENT
Major Feasts: *Introduce:* Ascension; Pentecost*	**Major Feasts:** *Repeat:* Ascension; Pentecost* *Add:* Corpus Christi	**Major Feasts:** *Repeat:* Ascension; Pentecost* *Add:* Sacred Heart	■ The Holy Spirit gives us grace to guide and strengthen us during life. [CCC 733; 735–36; 747] ■ We celebrate the coming of the Holy Spirit at Pentecost. [CCC 731] ■ At Ascension, we remember that the "visible presence of Christ on earth has now passed into the sacraments." [ST. LEO THE GREAT] ■ We worship Jesus who is present in the Eucharist, the "real presence." [CCC 1377–78, 1418] ■ Feast of the Sacred Heart recalls God's love for us. [CCC 68]
Baptism *Introduce:* Baptism Introduction* *Add:* Gestures*	**Baptism** *Repeat:* Baptism Introduction*, Gestures* *Add:* Symbols and Objects of Baptism*	**Baptism** *Repeat:* Baptism Introduction*, Gestures*, Symbols and Objects of Baptism* *Add:* Baptism: The Rite*	■ Baptism gives us the new life of grace, forgiveness of sins, and the gifts of faith, hope, and love. [CCC 1266; 1279; 1842–44] ■ Baptism is the first and chief sacrament of the forgiveness of sins. [CCC 985] ■ Baptism, Confirmation, and Eucharist are the sacraments of Christian initiation. [CCC 1212]
Reconciliation Briefly revise all relevant parables *Add:* The True Vine*	**Reconciliation** *See also: Moral Formation* Briefly revise all relevant parables* *Repeat:* The True Vine* *Add:* Rite of Reconciliation Cards*	**Reconciliation** *See also: Moral Formation* Briefly revise all relevant parables* *Repeat:* The True Vine*, Rite of Reconciliation Cards* *Add:* Preparation and participation in the sacrament	■ Jesus gave the Church the power to forgive sins. [CCC 986] ■ To receive God's forgiveness in the Sacrament of Penance we must be sorry for our sins and want to avoid them in the future. We must tell our sins to God through the priest. ■ The priest absolves us from our sins and gives us a penance to do. [CCC 1490–91; 1494–95] ■ Forgiveness brings peace. [CCC 1468]

GRADE 2	GRADE 3	GRADE 4	DOCTRINAL CONTENT
Eucharist *Introduce:* Origin of the Eucharist*	**Eucharist** *Repeat:* Origin of the Eucharist* *Add:* Synthesis of the Mass	**Eucharist** *Repeat:* Origin of the Eucharist*; Synthesis of the Mass* *Add:* First Missal*	▪ *Jesus is present when the scriptures are read and the Eucharist is celebrated at Mass.* [CCC 1101; 1408; 1373] ▪ *The Eucharist is the greatest sacrament of Christian initiation.* [CCC 1322; 1407] ▪ *We call the celebration of the Eucharist the Mass. It is the thanksgiving sacrifice of Jesus, offered for the living and the dead.* [CCC 1414] ▪ *The Eucharist is the great memorial of Jesus's sacrifice on the cross.* [CCC 1356; 1358; 1365; 1366]
Gestures of the Mass *Introduce:* The Offering*; Synthesis of Epiclesis and Eucharistic Presence *	**Gestures of the Mass** *Repeat:* The Offering*; Synthesis of Epiclesis and Eucharistic Presence* *Add:* Lamb of God	**Gestures of the Mass** *Repeat:* The Offering*; Synthesis of Epiclesis and Eucharistic Presence*; Lamb of God *Add:* The Mystery of Faith*	▪ *The stories and actions of Jesus are remembered and lived out in the liturgy.* [CCC 1111] ▪ *The Eucharist is the centre of Christian liturgy.* [CCC 1193] ▪ *Through the liturgy, we worship God in our actions and words.* [CCC 1110]
Other Sacraments *Introduce:* Holy Orders	**Other Sacraments** *Repeat:* Holy Orders *Add:* Marriage: The Rite 1	**Other Sacraments** *Repeat:* Holy Orders Marriage: The Rite 1 *Add:* Anointing of the Sick 1	▪ *Only ordained priests can, through the Holy Spirit, change the bread and wine into the body and blood of Christ.* [CCC 1411] ▪ *Bishops confer Holy Orders by "laying on of hands" and prayer of consecration.* [CCC 1597; 1600] ▪ *God calls bishops and priests to continue the leadership of Jesus in his Church.* [CCC 1536] ▪ *Jesus's love for his people is the model of love for all married people.* [CCC 1661] ▪ *The Christian home is normally the place where children first hear about God's plan of love for them.* [CCC 1666] ▪ *Anointing of the Sick is for those who are frail, seriously sick, or in danger of death.* [CCC 1527] ▪ *The sacrament of anointing gives graces to the sick and dying.* [CCC 1527]

GRADES 5, 6, 7

	THEMES	TIME OF YEAR	TOPICS
The Holy Spirit continues to make Christ present through us.		AUGUST / SEPTEMBER	Moral Formation; Prayer
	Focus Solemnity: Pentecost.	OCTOBER	Social Justice; Example of Mary & Saints

GRADE 5	GRADE 6	GRADE 7	DOCTRINAL CONTENT
Moral Formation Revise Grace and Courtesy Procedures Re-establish classroom chores Set up Classroom Procedures for the Year *Repeat:* Maxims of Jesus Moral Parables *Add:* 10 Commandments	**Moral Formation** Revise Grace and Courtesy Procedures Re-establish classroom chores Set up Classroom Procedures for the Year *Repeat:* Maxims of Jesus; Moral Parables 10 Commandments *Add:* The Virtues	**Moral Formation** Revise Grace and Courtesy Procedures Re-establish classroom chores Set Up Classroom Procedures for the Year *Repeat:* Maxims of Jesus; Moral Parables; 10 Commandments; Virtues *Add:* Beatitudes	▪ *In Baptism we receive three theological virtues (faith, hope and love) and four moral virtues (prudence, justice, temperance and fortitude).* [CCC 1833–34; 1839–40] ▪ *The virtues are habits that help us to do what is good.* [CCC 1833–34] ▪ *The virtue of faith enables us to believe in God and all that He has revealed.* [CCC 1842] ▪ *The virtue of hope enables us to trust in God's future promise of eternal life.* [CCC 1843] ▪ *The virtue of charity enables us to love God above all things and to love our neighbour as ourself.* [CCC 1844] ▪ *The virtue of prudence enables us to discover our true good and helps us to choose this:* [CCC 1835] ▪ *The virtue of justice enables us to give to God and our neighbour what is due to them.* [CCC 1836] ▪ *The virtue of fortitude enables us to be strong and courageous in doing what is right and good.* [CCC 1837] ▪ *The virtue of temperance enables us to use the pleasures of this world as God intended.* [CCC 1838]
Prayer Set up prayer table*., Establish prayer routine*., Memorize formal prayers. See chart. Lectio Divina: Praying with the Scriptures	**Prayer** Set up prayer table*., Establish prayer routine*., Memorize formal prayers. See chart. Lectio Divina: Praying with the Scriptures	**Prayer** Set up prayer table*., Establish prayer routine*., Memorize formal prayers. See chart. Lectio Divina: Praying with the Scriptures	▪ *The Holy Spirit helps us to pray.* [CCC 2661] ▪ *We pray to Jesus among us in the Eucharist.* [CCC 1418] ▪ *Lord's Prayer shows us how to pray to the Father.* [CCC 2799] ▪ *There are various kinds of prayer.* [CCC 2644] ▪ *Self-denial is an important part of Christian prayer.* [CCC 2015]

GRADE 5	GRADE 6	GRADE 7	DOCTRINAL CONTENT
Christian Anthropology *Introduce:* Every human being is loved by God.	**Christian Anthropology** *Repeat:* Every human being is loved by God. *Add:* Human person is created in the image of God.	**Christian Anthropology** *Repeat:* Every person is loved by God and created in the image of God. *Add:* Our obligation to love others. We should be willing to embrace life.	▪ *"A New Commandment I give to you; love one another as I have loved you."* [JOHN 13:34] ▪ *God calls me to discover his plan for my life.* [CCC 2253]
Christian Social Ethics *Introduce:* Honesty is the basic condition for all human relationships. Introduce the Commandments.	**Christian Social Ethics** *Repeat:* Honesty is the basic condition for all human relationships. Commandments *Add:* Justice is the recognition of the rights of each individual.	**Christian Social Ethics** *Repeat:* Honesty is the basic condition for all human relationships. Justice is the recognition of the rights of each individual. Commandments. *Add:* The goods of the earth are gifts of God, and are not the privilege of some individuals or groups.	▪ *"A New Commandment I give to you; love one another as I have loved you."* [JOHN 13:34] ▪ *The commandments call us to love God and our neighbour as we journey towards Heaven.* [CCC 1983; 1051–54] ▪ *The Beatitudes express Christ's plan for our happiness in this world and the next.* [CCC 1725–26]
Christian Community Life *Introduce:* Christian community life requires a spirit of simplicity and humility. (Mt 18, 3)	**Christian Community Life** *Repeat:* Christian community life requires a spirit of simplicity and humility. (Mt 18, 3) *Add:* Christian community life requires particular care for those who are alienated. (Mt 18, 12)	**Christian Community Life** *Repeat:* Christian community life requires a spirit of simplicity and humility (Mt 18, 3) and particular care for those who are alienated. (Mt 18,12) *Add:* Fraternal love embraces all these attitudes. (Jn 13, 34)	▪ *We believe in one, holy, catholic and apostolic Church.* [CCC 866–69; 938]
Ecclesiology *Introduce:* Belonging to the Church has obvious consequences for life, for apostolate, and for a Christian vision of the world.	**Ecclesiology** *Repeat:* Belonging to the Church has obvious consequences for life, for apostolate, and for a Christian vision of the world.	**Ecclesiology** *Repeat:* Belonging to the Church has obvious consequences for life, for apostolate, and for a Christian vision of the world.	▪ *The Church is a Communion of Saints.* [CCC 960–62] ▪ *All members of the Church (lay and ordained) are called to use their own gifts and talents in building up the Church.* [CCC 900] ▪ *Jesus is the Head of the Church. The Pope is the Vicar of Christ on earth.* [CCC 936; 2050] ▪ *We believe in one, holy, catholic and apostolic Church.* [CCC 866–69; 938] ▪ *In the liturgy, the Holy Spirit helps us to recall the saving work of the Father and the Son. In this way, the Holy Spirit is the living memory of the Church.* [CCC 1091–92]

GRADE 5	GRADE 6	GRADE 7	DOCTRINAL CONTENT
The Scriptures Allow time for free reading of the Bible Typology of Creation Typology of the Fall (*See Salvation History*)	**The Scriptures** Allow time for free reading of the Bible Typology of Abraham (*See Paschal Narratives*)	**The Scriptures** Allow time for free reading of the Bible Typology of the Exodus (*See Paschal Narratives*)	▪ *Through Sacred Tradition the Church interprets the Sacred Scriptures.* [CCC 80; 137–38] ▪ *The Catholic Church recognizes a special link with the Jewish people.... God chose them before all others to receive his Word.* [COMPENDIUM 179]

GRADES 5, 6, 7

THEMES	TIME OF YEAR	TOPICS
Death and Everlasting Life	EARLY NOVEMBER	**Human Person; Family; The Last Things; Eschatology**

GRADE 5	GRADE 6	GRADE 7	DOCTRINAL CONTENT
The Last Things *Introduce:* The last judgment points to an eternal destiny which each of us merits through our own works.	**The Last Things** *Repeat:* The last judgment points to an eternal destiny which each of us merits through our own works. *Add:* We are personally responsible in everything we do, because we must render an account to God.	**The Last Things** *Repeat:* The last judgment points to an eternal destiny which each of us merits through our own works. We are personally responsible in everything we do, because we must render an account to God. *Add:* Christian hope in our ultimate destiny offers comfort in life's difficulties.	▪ *Those who die in God's grace and friendship live forever with Christ.* [CCC 1023] ▪ *Faith is necessary for us to be saved.* [CCC 183] ▪ *Purgatory prepares those not ready for heaven; it is a state of purification and hope.* [CCC 1054] ▪ *God's mercy is shown to those in Purgatory, for whom we should pray and offer the Eucharist.* [CCC 1054–55] ▪ *Only those who have rejected God completely are deprived of Him forever in hell. We don't know how many people make this choice.* [CCC 1056–57] ▪ *At death, my soul is separated from my body.* [CCC 1005] ▪ *Jesus will come again at the end of time to judge the living and the dead.* [CCC 1038–41; 1059] ▪ *We believe in the Resurrection of the body at the end of time.* [CCC 1016; 1059] ▪ *I only die once because in this world, I only have one life.* [CCC 1013]

GRADES 5, 6, 7

THEMES	TIME OF YEAR	TOPICS
God Prepares the World to receive His Son	MID-NOVEMBER / DECEMBER	Salvation History; Infancy Narratives; Advent; Christmas

GRADE 5	GRADE 6	GRADE 7	DOCTRINAL CONTENT
Salvation History *Introduce:* Plan of God	**Salvation History** *Repeat:* Plan of God *Add:* Creation Typology	**Salvation History** *Repeat:* Plan of God; Creation Typology *Add:* The Fall Typology	▪ *In the liturgy, the Holy Spirit helps us to recall the saving work of the Father and the Son. In this way, the Holy Spirit is the living memory of the Church.* [CCC 1091–92]
Infancy Narratives *Introduce:* Prophecies of the Coming of Christ	**Infancy Narratives** *Repeat:* Prophecies of the Coming of Christ *Add:* Art synthesis of the Infancy Narratives: Find related Scripture passages. Create Nativity scenes based on Scripture passages.	**Infancy Narratives** *Repeat:* Prophecies of the Coming of Christ *Add:* Art synthesis of the Infancy Narratives: Find related Scripture passages. Create Nativity scenes based on Scripture passages. *Add:* Joyful Mysteries of the Rosary *Focus:* Mary is ever virgin; Mother of God.	▪ *During Advent, we remember the people of Old Testament times who waited for the Saviour, Jesus Christ.* [CCC 524] ▪ *During Advent, we try to become more like Jesus by making changes in the way we live our lives.*

GRADES 5, 6, 7

	THEMES	TIME OF YEAR	TOPICS
	Life of Christ	JANUARY	Biblical Geography; Gospel Narratives
	Focus Solemnity: Easter	EARLY FEBRUARY	Lent; Parables; Miracles
	Paschal Mystery	PRIOR TO EASTER BREAK	Paschal Mystery; Holy Week

GRADE 7	DOCTRINAL CONTENT
Biblical Geography *Repeat:* Land of Israel*; City of Jerusalem* *Add:* Flag Maps of Israel*	▪ *The Gospels tell us about the life and teachings of Jesus.* [CCC 68; 561]
Lent *Repeat:* Making Burying the Alleluia*; Changing the prayer tablecloth to purple.*; Temptation of Christ (Christ is human)	▪ *Lent is the season of forty days. We prepare to celebrate the death and Resurrection of the Lord Jesus.* ▪ *In Lent, the Church calls us to pray more, to make sacrifices and to give to the poor.* ▪ *Jesus was fully human. We call this mystery the Incarnation.* [CCC 479; 483]
Life of Jesus *Repeat:* Miracles of Jesus: Bartimaeus*, Son of the Widow of Nain* *Add:* Miracles of Jesus: Miracle of the Loaves*, Cure of Peter's mother-in- law*, Art Synthesis of the Life of Jesus: Deeds & Miracles of Christ *Focus:* Historical Fact of the Resurrection; Christ the Priest	▪ *We call Jesus "the Christ," which means "the anointed one of God."* [CCC 453] ▪ *Jesus is true God. He is the second person of the Blessed Trinity.* [CCC 464; 480] ▪ *Jesus Christ is true man. He was born of the Virgin Mary. We call this mystery the Incarnation.* [CCC 464] ▪ *Jesus was like us in all things except that he did not sin.* [CCC 480]

GRADE 5	GRADE 6
Biblical Geography *Introduce:* Land of Israel*	**Biblical Geography** *Repeat:* Land of Israel* *Add:* City of Jerusalem*
Lent *Introduce:* Making sacrifices to be ready for Easter Burying the Alleluia*; Changing the prayer tablecloth to purple. * *Add:* Stations of the Cross	**Lent** *Repeat:* Making sacrifices to be ready for Easter Burying the Alleluia*; Changing the prayer tablecloth to purple. * *Add:* Christ Reveals the Mysteries of God
Life of Jesus *Introduce:* Art Synthesis: Life of Jesus; Luminous Mysteries of the Rosary; Find Scripture Verses in support. *Focus:* Jesus is teacher.	**Life of Jesus** *Add:* Art Synthesis: Life of Jesus; Miracles of Jesus: Bartimaeus*, Son of the Widow of Nain*; *Focus:* Deeds & Miracles of Christ; Sorrowful Mysteries of the Rosary *Focus:* Jesus is Savior (Christ; Messiah)

GRADE 5	GRADE 6	GRADE 7	DOCTRINAL CONTENT
Mary and the Saints *Introduce:* Art Synthesis: Life of Mary *Focus:* Role of Mary in the Mission of Christ; Joyful Mysteries of the Rosary *Focus:* Role of Mary in Mission of Christ; Christ is divine	**Mary and the Saints** *Repeat:* Art Synthesis: Life of Mary *Add:* Glorious Mysteries of the Rosary *Focus:* Mary Immaculate; Mary Assumed into Heaven	**Mary and the Saints** *Repeat:* Art Synthesis: Life of Mary *Add: Focus:* Because Mary is the mother of Jesus, she is the mother of God.	▪ *Mary is the mother of God and our mother. She prays for us in heaven.* [CCC 495; 969–70; 975] ▪ *Mary continues to be honoured through her feast days.* [CCC 971] ▪ *Saints can help us come closer to God.* [CCC 957] ▪ *Mary is the model disciple for all believers.* [CCC 2030] ▪ *The Church recalls and 'celebrates Mary's faithfulness to God in the Magnificat.* [CCC 971] ▪ *Mary was conceived free from original sin.* [CCC 508; 491] ▪ *Mary was assumed body and soul into Heaven.* [CCC 974] ▪ *Mary had no other children except Jesus.* [CCC 501]
Christian Anthropology *Introduce:* The redeemed human person is present in all the truths of faith. *Focus:* The liturgy presents the mystery of God's plan of salvation for all humanity.	**Christian Anthropology** *Repeat:* Christ died to save human beings. *Add:* The redeemed human person is a member of Christ's Body: the Church.	**Christian Anthropology** *Repeat:* Christ died to save human beings. The redeemed human person is a member of Christ's Body: the Church.	▪ *Jesus Christ rose in the same human body that suffered on the cross.* [CCC 645] ▪ *Christ's resurrected body was changed for a new life, no longer limited by earthly time and space. This change will also happen to us when we rise from the dead at the end of time.* [CCC 646]
Paschal Narratives Easter Triduum: Palm Sunday *Revise:* Last Supper*; Revise Resurrection (Mt 28:1–8)*	**Paschal Narratives** *Repeat:* Resurrection (Matthew 28:1–8)*, Last Supper: Origin of the Eucharist*; Art Synthesis of the Paschal Narratives *Add:* Typology: Abraham*	**Paschal Narratives** *Repeat:* Resurrection (Mt 28:1–8)*, Last Supper: Origin of the Eucharist*; Art Synthesis of the Paschal Narratives *Add:* Typology: Moses; Passover, Crossing of Red Sea; Manna in the Desert.*	▪ *By His sacrifice on the cross, Jesus overcame sin and death. We celebrate his sacrifice in the Eucharist.* [CCC 629] ▪ *The most important days of Holy Week are Palm Sunday, Holy Thursday, Good Friday and Easter Sunday.* ▪ *His body was changed for a new life, no longer limited by earthly time and space.* [CCC 646]

GRADES 5, 6, 7

THEMES	TIME OF YEAR	TOPICS
The Holy Spirit continues to make Christ present through the Sacraments. Focus Solemnity: Pentecost.	APRIL	Ascension; Pentecost; Baptism
	MAY	Eucharist; Reconciliation
	JUNE	Holy Orders; Marriage; Anointing of the Sick

DOCTRINAL CONTENT

- *After his Resurrection, Jesus ascended into heaven to prepare a place for us.* [CCC 666]
- *Jesus Christ will come again at the end of time.* [CCC 682]

- *All the baptised receive a special mission from God.* [CCC 1279]
- *In baptism, we receive the theological virtues (faith, hope and charity) and are helped to live the moral virtues (prudence, justice, temperance and fortitude).* [CCC 1266]
- *Through baptism we share in the life, death and Resurrection of Jesus.* [CCC 2017; 2020]
- *Baptism places a spiritual mark (character) on the soul.* [CCC 1317]

GRADE 5	GRADE 6	GRADE 7
Major Feasts: *Repeat:* Ascension; Pentecost;* Sacred Heart *Add:* Trinity Sunday	**Major Feasts:** *Repeat:* Ascension; Pentecost;* Sacred Heart, Trinity Sunday *Add:* St. John the Baptist	**Major Feasts:** *Repeat:* Ascension; Pentecost;* Sacred Heart, Trinity Sunday; St. John the Baptist *Add:* Sts. Peter & Paul
Baptism *Repeat:* Baptism Introduction*, Baptism, the Rite* *Add:* Baptismal Mystagogy: Pictures	**Baptism** *Repeat:* Baptism Introduction*, Baptism, the Rite*; Baptismal Mystagogy: Pictures *Add:* Baptismal Mystagogy: Scriptures	**Baptism** *Repeat:* Baptism Introduction*, Baptism, the Rite*; Baptismal Mystagogy: Pictures; Baptismal Mystagogy: Scriptures *Add:* Baptismal Mystagogy: Personal project (search the scriptures for other instances).

GRADE 5	GRADE 6	GRADE 7	DOCTRINAL CONTENT
Reconciliation *See also: Moral Formation* Briefly revise all relevant parables. The True Vine *Add:* Examination of Conscience; Preparation for participation in sacrament	**Reconciliation** *See also: Moral Formation* Briefly revise all relevant parables. The True Vine *Add:* Scriptural Examination of Conscience; Preparation for participation in sacrament	**Reconciliation** *See also: Moral Formation* Briefly revise all relevant parables. The True Vine *Add:* Scriptural Examination of Conscience; Preparation for participation in sacrament	■ *God always wants us to turn back to him after we have sinned.* [CCC 1847; 1870] ■ *A mortal sin destroys God's life in a person. God's mercy is shown to those who repent; usually in the sacrament of Penance.* [CCC 1855–56; 1489; 1493; 1497] ■ *The sacrament of Reconciliation gives us the grace to overcome sins.* [CCC 1458; 1875; 1876] ■ *The sacrament of Reconciliation involves conversion, repentance, confession, reconciliation and forgiveness.* [CCC 1490–93] ■ *The sacrament of Reconciliation brings the forgiving love of our Father and the grace of the Holy Spirit.* [CCC 1496] ■ *Jesus's teachings bring home to us God's immense love and joy at our turning away from sin.* [CCC 1443] ■ *People can always return to God during their lifetime through the Sacrament of Penance.* [CCC 1426]
Eucharist *Repeat:* Synthesis of the Mass*, The Mystery of Faith* *Add:* Structure of the Mass	**Eucharist** *Repeat:* Structure of the Mass* *Add:* Memorial	**Eucharist** *Repeat:* Structure of the Mass*, Memorial * *Add:* Full Missal*	■ *Communion with the body and blood of Christ:* ■ *Increases our union with Christ and with one another* ■ *Forgives venial sins and preserves from grave sins* ■ *Strengthens the whole Church.* [CCC 1416] ■ *We adore Jesus, really present in the Eucharist.* [CCC 1378] ■ *In the Eucharist, Jesus offers to all the gift of redemption.* [CCC 1410] ■ *The Eucharist is the source and summit of Christian life.* [CCC 1407] ■ *The celebration of the Eucharist is called the Mass. It makes present the sacrifice of Jesus, offered for the living and the dead.* [CCC 1414]
Gestures of the Mass *Repeat:* The Offering*; Synthesis of Epiclesis and Eucharistic Presence*; The Lamb of God	**Gestures of the Mass** *Repeat:* The Offering;* The Lamb of God; Synthesis of Epiclesis and Eucharistic Presence* *Add:* Propers of the Mass*	**Gestures of the Mass** *See* "Full Missal"*	■ *In the liturgy, the Holy Spirit enables the assembly to encounter Christ.* [CCC 1112] ■ *Communion with the body and blood of Christ:* ■ *Increases our union with Christ and with one another* ■ *Forgives venial sins and preserves from grave sins* ■ *Strengthens the whole Church.* [CCC 1416]

GRADE 5	GRADE 6	GRADE 7	DOCTRINAL CONTENT
Other Sacraments *Repeat:* Holy Orders: The Rite 1; Marriage: The Rite 1 *Add:* Anointing of the Sick	**Other Sacraments** *Repeat:* Anointing of the Sick* *Add:* Holy Orders: The Rite 2; Marriage: The Rite 2	**Other Sacraments** *Add:* The Holy Trinity and Marriage (very advanced)	**Anointing of the Sick** ■ *Anointing of the Sick brings strength, peace and courage to endure suffering in a Christian manner.* [CCC 1532] ■ *Anointing of the Sick sometimes restores the person to health if this is for their good.* [CCC 1532] ■ *Anointing of the Sick can only be given by a priest.* [CCC 1530] ■ *Brief study of the Rite of Anointing.* [CCC 1517–25] **Holy Orders** ■ *Bishops and priests serve us in the name and person of Christ.* [CCC 1549; 1591] ■ *Holy Orders gives sacred power to a priest: to teach, to sanctify and to lead the faithful.* [CCC 1592] ■ *Deacons assist bishops and priests in the ministry of the word and the sacraments.* [CCC 1570; 1596] ■ *Only baptised men can be ordained.* [CCC 1598] ■ *Through the ministerial priesthood, bishops and priests share in the one priesthood of Christ.* [CCC 1591] **Marriage** ■ *The Sacrament of Marriage is between a man and a woman. It is a covenant based on God's love, help, and forgiveness.* [CCC 1662] ■ *The Sacrament of Marriage was instituted by God. It is exclusive and for life.* [CCC 1646–47] ■ *The sacrament of Marriage is the union in love of a woman and a man. It signifies the union of Christ and the Church.* [CCC 1661] ■ *The couple give each other the sacrament of marriage. The priest is the Church's witness.* [CCC 1630]

GRADE 5	GRADE 6	GRADE 7	DOCTRINAL CONTENT
Confirmation	**Confirmation**	**Confirmation**	▪ *By our Confirmation the Holy Spirit strengthens us to live a holy life to love and respect one another, proclaim the Gospel, and serve others as Jesus did.* [CCC 1319]
Select elements of the Confirmation program if suitable.	Elements of a Confirmation Program ▪ *Review the other sacraments of initiation, Baptism and Eucharist.* ▪ *Articles and gestures used in the Rite of Confirmation* ▪ *Explanation of the Gifts of the Spirit; Fruit of the Spirit* ▪ *Explanation of the Rite of Confirmation* ▪ *Service Project — offering some practical service to others on behalf of the Church* ▪ *Research life of a saint as a model for living out of the faith*	Select elements of the Confirmation program if suitable.	▪ *Confirmation gives us the special strength of the Holy Spirit to spread and defend the faith by word and action. We are helped in this task by the gifts of: wisdom, understanding, counsel, fortitude, knowledge, piety, and fear of the Lord.* [CCC 1316; 1845] ▪ *Like Baptism, Confirmation places a spiritual mark (character) on the soul.* [CCC 1317] ▪ *The Rite of Confirmation (studied as part of Confirmation preparation).* [CCC 1320]

PRAYER DEVELOPMENT CHART

KINDERGARTEN – YEAR 1	GRADE 2 – GRADE 4	GRADE 5 – GRADE 8
Introduce one at a time. Have the children pray with you as you are reciting these prayers aloud. Parents should be encouraged to train their children to *repeat* these prayers as part of their home routine – Morning and Evening.	*Repeat:*	*Repeat:*
	▪ Sign of the Cross	▪ Sign of the Cross
▪ Sign of the Cross	▪ Our Father	▪ Our Father
▪ Our Father	▪ Hail Mary	▪ Hail Mary
▪ Hail Mary	▪ Glory Be	▪ Glory Be
▪ Glory Be	▪ Simple Grace	▪ Simple Grace
▪ Simple Grace	▪ Angel of God	▪ Angel of God
▪ Angel of God	▪ Glory Be	▪ Glory Be
▪ Glory Be	▪ Grace Before Meals	▪ Grace Before Meals
▪ Grace Before Meals	▪ Psalms	▪ Psalms
▪ Psalms	▪ Church Visits	▪ Church Visits
▪ Church Visits	▪ Simple Stations of the Cross	▪ Simple Stations of the Cross
▪ Simple Stations of the Cross	▪ Personal Prayer	▪ Personal Prayer
▪ Personal Prayer	▪ Hymns	▪ Hymns
▪ Hymns	▪ Psalms (Selected Verses)	▪ Psalms (Selected Verses)
▪ Psalms (Selected Verses)		▪ Morning Offering
	Add:	▪ Short Acts of Faith, Hope, and Charity
	▪ Morning Offering	▪ Act of Contrition
	▪ Short Acts of Faith, Hope, and Charity	
	▪ Act of Contrition	*Add:*
	▪ Prayer for the Dead	▪ Prayer for the Dead
	▪ Psalms	▪ Psalms
	▪ Personal Prayer	▪ Personal Prayer
	▪ Hymns and Carols	▪ Hymns and Carols
	▪ Psalms	▪ Psalms
	▪ Prayers before and after Communion	▪ Prayers before and after Communion
	▪ Responses to the Mass	▪ Responses to the Mass
	▪ Apostles Creed	▪ Apostles Creed
	▪ The Rosary	▪ The Rosary
	▪ The Angelus	▪ The Angelus
		Add:
		▪ Memorare
		▪ Hail Holy Queen
		▪ Divine Praises
		▪ Aspirations
		▪ Nicene Creed

FEAST DAY	DOCTRINAL CONTENT
St. Patrick	▪ *Saints can help us come closer to God.* [CCC 957] ▪ *Saints can pray and intercede for us.* [CCC 956]
St. Joseph	▪ *All proper authority comes from God.* [CCC 1921] ▪ *The family is a community of life and love.* [CCC 2204–06]
Annunciation	▪ *Mary is the mother of God and our mother. She prays for us in heaven.* [CCC 495; 969–70; 975] ▪ *In Jesus Christ, God became man. We call this mystery the Incarnation.* [CCC 479; 483]
Help of Christians	▪ *Mary is the model disciple for all believers.* [CCC 2030] ▪ *The Church recalls and celebrates Mary's faithfulness to God in the Magnificat.* [CCC 971]
Ascension	▪ *After his Resurrection, Jesus ascended into heaven to prepare a place for us.* [CCC 666] ▪ *On this day, the visible presence of Christ on earth passes into the sacraments.* [ST. LEO THE GREAT: SERMON FOR THE ASCENSION]
Pentecost	▪ *The Holy Spirit gives us the grace to help our faith to grow.* [CCC 684] ▪ *Jesus asked God his Father to send the Holy Spirit to be with us always.* [CCC 689] ▪ *The Holy Spirit is sent by the Father and the Son to give the life of grace to all God's people.* [CCC 689] ▪ *The Holy Spirit builds up and unites the Christian community, especially through the Liturgy and prayer.* [CCC 797; 813; 1112]
Trinity Sunday	▪ *God the Father is our Creator; God the Son is our Redeemer; God the Holy Spirit is our Sanctifier.* [CCC 238; 267] ▪ *The Trinity is the central mystery of our faith, revealed to us by Jesus and by the Holy Spirit.* [CCC 228; 230; 234; 249; 261] ▪ *Jesus is true God. He is the second person of the Blessed Trinity.* [CCC 464; 480] ▪ *Jesus Christ is true man. He was born of the Virgin Mary.* [CCC 464] ▪ *God alone is to be worshipped.* [CCC 2096–97] ▪ *God is infinite, perfect, and powerful, and all loving.* [CCC 320]
Corpus Christi	▪ *We adore Jesus, really present in the Eucharist.* [CCC 1378] ▪ *The Eucharist is the source and summit of the Christian life.* [CCC 1407]
Sacred Heart	▪ *"A New Commandment I give to you; love one another as I have loved you."*
Sts. Peter and Paul	▪ *Jesus is the Head of the Church. The Pope is the Vicar of Christ on earth.* [CCC 936; 2050]
Assumption	▪ *Mary was honoured by the first Christian communities.* [CCC 496; 971] ▪ *Mary continues to be honoured through her feast days.* [CCC 971] ▪ *Mary is honoured in Christian Communities throughout the world.* [CCC 971] ▪ *Mary was assumed body and soul into Heaven.* [CCC 974]
Holy Souls	▪ *Purgatory prepares those not ready for Heaven; it is a state of purification and hope.* [CCC 1054] ▪ *God's mercy is shown to those in Purgatory, for whom we should pray and offer the Eucharist.* [CCC 1054–55] ▪ *I only die once because in this world, I only have one life.* [CCC 1013]
Immaculate Conception	▪ *Mary was conceived free from original sin.* [CCC 508; 491] ▪ *Mary had no other children except Jesus.* [CCC 501]
Parish Feast Day	▪ *The Church tries to proclaim the Gospel to people in their language and culture.* [CCC 806] ▪ *All members of the Church (lay and ordained) are called to use their own gifts and talents in building up the Church.* [CCC 900]

SOME COMMENTS, RE: CATECHESIS OF THE GOOD SHEPHERD

 * Items marked with an asterisk indicate that this is a work used in Catechesis of the Good Shepherd. This excellent program, devised by Sofia Cavalletti and Gianna Gobbi, focused on the needs of children at various age groups, using a Montessori methodology. This outline shows how readily the Catechesis of the Good Shepherd can cover most of the doctrinal ground required for an organic presentation of the Catholic faith. Those who have easy access to a Catechesis of the Good Shepherd program should be encouraged to use it, based on its outstanding results and the deep commitment of its many fine catechists.

THERE IS ONE CAVEAT...

Cavalletti and Gobbi, together with their current collaborators throughout the world, would not permit any activity in their program that the children did not find captivating. They also follow the Montessori view that children should not be subjected to "assessment" or testing. Nevertheless, these less attractive elements are strongly recommended by the Church and so they are included here in this outline.

In a conversation I had with Cavalletti in 2009, she generously agreed that all of her material should be available widely to whoever found it useful. "The Shepherd's voice," she said "should be heard as widely as possible." The one stipulation she placed on the use of her materials was that it should not be called *Catechesis of the Good Shepherd* unless it was being used in a properly designated program. I understand her and have respected her wishes — she desired only the best for children, and wanted to give them the finest fruits of her labor — a job worth doing is worth doing well. My own view is a little different. I am concerned that the perfect can be the enemy of the good. I prefer, in this matter to follow the line of G.K. Chesterton: "A job worth doing is worth doing badly!" That is, I don't want to "do nothing" for fear that it might not be perfect. I have not used any copyrighted material in this text, but I freely acknowledge my debt to Cavalletti and her collaborators in listening to them and presenting their ideas in my own words.

Appendix B:

*Organization of Content
in Liturgical Spiral Curriculum,
Kindergarten–Gr. 7
(Australian Schools)*

THEMES	TIME OF YEAR	TOPICS
	TERM 1	
Life of Christ Focus Solemnity: Easter	FEBRUARY	Prayer; Biblical Geography; Gospel Narratives
	MARCH	Lent; Parables; Miracles
Paschal Mystery	TWO WEEKS PRIOR TO EASTER BREAK	Paschal Mystery; Holy Week
	EASTER BREAK	
	TERM 2	
The Holy Spirit continues to make Christ present through the Sacraments. Focus Solemnity: Pentecost	APRIL	Ascension; Pentecost; Baptism
	MAY	Eucharist; Reconciliation
	JUNE	Holy Orders; Marriage; Anointing of the Sick
	JULY HOLIDAYS	
	TERM 3	
The Holy Spirit continues to make Christ present through us. Focus Solemnity: Pentecost	JULY / EARLY AUGUST	Moral Formation; Prayer
	LATE AUGUST / SEPTEMBER	Social Justice; Example of Mary & Saints
	SEPTEMBER HOLIDAYS	
	TERM 4	
Death and Everlasting Life	EARLY NOVEMBER	Human Person; Family; The Last Things; Eschatology
God Prepares the World to receive His Son Focus Solemnity: Christmas	FROM MID-NOVEMBER TO MID-DECEMBER	Salvation History; Infancy Narratives; Advent; Christmas
	CHRISTMAS BREAK	

TERM 1: KINDERGARTEN, GRADE 1

	THEMES	TIME OF YEAR	TOPICS
	Life of Christ Focus Solemnity: Easter	FEBRUARY	Setting Up Procedures; Prayer; Moral Formation; Biblical Geography
		MARCH	Gospel Narratives; Lent
	Paschal Mystery	TWO WEEKS PRIOR TO EASTER BREAK	Paschal Mystery; Holy Week

GRADE 1	DOCTRINAL CONTENT
Prayer Set up prayer table See Prayer Development Chart	▪ *Prayer is loving, speaking, listening and singing to God.* [CCC 2590] ▪ *We also pray at Mass, with our families and at school.* [CCC 2694] ▪ *The Bible has a central place in personal and community prayer.* [CCC 2653; 2662] ▪ *Jesus promises that when we gather in his name, he is there with us.* [CCC 1373] ▪ *Jesus wants us to pray often, at any time and in any place.* [CCC 2757] ▪ *The Holy Spirit helps us to pray.* [CCC 741] ▪ *God speaks to us in the Bible, which is the Church's book.* [CCC 141] ▪ *God speaks to us through his Church.* [CCC 100]
Moral Formation *Repeat:* Grace Courtesy Procedures*; Setting up of Response Tools*; Practical Life Activities* *Repeat:* Dusting; Watering Plants; Flower Arranging; Cleaning Surfaces; Sweeping; Rolling a Mat *Add:* Leaf Washing; Polishing	▪ *God helps us to do good.* [CCC 2003] ▪ *When we sin, we are not living the way Jesus taught us. We make choices that are not good, and hurt others and ourselves.* [CCC 1745; 1871] ▪ *Jesus wants us to share our good things with others.* [CCC 1926]

KINDERGARTEN
Prayer Set up prayer table*; See Prayer Development Chart
Moral Formation *Introduce:* Grace Courtesy Procedures*; Setting up of Response Tools:*; Drawing; Watercolor Painting; Collage & Pasting; Playdough Modelling; Writing/ Modelling in Damp Sand. **Practical Life Activities*** Dusting; Watering Plants; Flower Arranging; Cleaning Surfaces; Sweeping; Rolling a Mat

KINDERGARTEN	GRADE 1	DOCTRINAL CONTENT
Biblical Geography Creation: Gifts of God*; Globe: Locate Israel*; Raised Map of Israel*	**Biblical Geography** *Repeat:* Raised Map of Israel* *Add:* City of Jerusalem*; Puzzle Map of Israel*; Tracing Maps*; Coloring Maps*	※ *God made the world to show his love.* [CCC 315] ※ *God made us.* [CCC 44; 45; 315] ※ *God loves us and his work is good.* [CCC 319] ※ *God makes us to be different from one another. Each of us is special.* [CCC 353]
Life of Jesus *Introduce:* Annunciation*; Good Shepherd*	**Life of Jesus** *Repeat:* Annunciation*; Good Shepherd* *Add:* Found Sheep*; Good Shepherd and the Wolf*	※ *Mary was asked to be the mother of Jesus, who is God.* [CCC 495; 509] ※ *Angels are God's messengers.* [CCC 329–32] ※ *Jesus loves us and shows this through those who care for us.* [CCC 383] ※ *Jesus gives his life for his sheep.* [CCC 754] ※ *Jesus the Good Shepherd loves us.* [CCC 764]
Lent: Making Promises: Remembering Jesus in the desert Mystery of Life & Death: Planting Seeds*; Burying the Alleluia*	**Lent:** Making Promises Burying the Alleluia Mystery of Life & Death: Planting Seeds*	※ *During Lent, the Church reflects on the meaning of Christ's 40 days in the desert.* [CCC 540]
Paschal Narratives *Introduce:* Last Supper (Cenacle)*; Resurrection (Empty Tomb)*	**Paschal Narratives** *Repeat:* Last Supper (Dramatize); Resurrection (Dramatize) *Add:* Palm Sunday (Dramatize); Stations of the Cross and Crucifixion (Dramatize)	※ *At the Last Supper, Jesus taught us to celebrate the Eucharist.* [CCC 1340] ※ *On Good Friday, Jesus died for our sins.* [CCC 623] ※ *On Easter Sunday, Jesus rose from the dead to a new and everlasting life.* [CCC 656–58]

TERM 2: KINDERGARTEN, YEAR 1

THEMES	TIME OF YEAR	TOPICS
The Holy Spirit continues to make Christ present Part 1:	APRIL / MAY	Ascension; Pentecost; Baptism
Sacraments	JUNE	Eucharist
Focus Solemnity: Pentecost		

KINDERGARTEN	GRADE 1	DOCTRINAL CONTENT
Major Feasts: *Introduce:* Pentecost; Ascension; Our Lady Help of Christians	**Major Feasts:** *Repeat:* Pentecost; Ascension ; Our Lady Help of Christians *Add:* Sacred Heart; Corpus Christi	■ At the Ascension, Jesus went back to Heaven to prepare a place for us. [CCC 2177] ■ At Pentecost, Jesus sent the Holy Spirit to Mary and the Apostles and to stay always with the Church. [CCC 731–32]
Baptism *Introduce:* Spreading the Light of Christ: Baptism*; Baptism Introduction*	**Baptism** *Repeat:* Spreading the Light of Christ: Baptism*; Baptism Introduction* *Add:* Baptism Collage*; Baptism Articles & Gestures Chart*	■ The Holy Spirit was given to us at our Baptism. [CCC 1266] ■ At Baptism, we are welcomed into God's family, the Church. [CCC 804] ■ In Baptism, we receive God's life (grace). [CCC 1277; 2017; 2023] ■ By the grace given at Baptism, we can live forever in Heaven. [CCC 1212; 1987]
Eucharist *Introduce:* Eucharistic Presence of the Good Shepherd*; Last Supper* **Mass Moments** *Introduce:* Preparing the Chalice (Water and Wine)*; Epiclesis*; Consecration Offering (Doxology)*	**Eucharist** *Repeat:* Eucharistic Presence of the Good Shepherd* **Mass Moments** *Repeat:* Preparing the Chalice (Water and Wine)*; Epiclesis*; Offering (Doxology)*; Consecration *Add:* Sign of Peace*; Washing of Hands (Lavabo)*	■ Jesus is present with us when we celebrate the Eucharist (Presence of the Good Shepherd). [CCC 1418] ■ On Sunday, Catholics go to Mass. [CCC 1193] ■ At the Last Supper, Jesus taught us to celebrate the Eucharist. [CCC 1340] ■ Jesus gives himself to us in the Eucharist. [CCC 1406]

TERM 3: KINDERGARTEN, YEAR 1

THEMES	TIME OF YEAR	TOPICS
The Holy Spirit continues to make Christ present: Part 2	JULY / EARLY AUGUST	**Liturgy 1**
Focus Solemnity: Pentecost	LATE AUGUST / SEPTEMBER	**Liturgy 2; Parables**

KINDERGARTEN	YEAR 1	DOCTRINAL CONTENT
Liturgical Gestures, Colors *Introduce:* Sign of the Cross (+ Holy Water)*; Liturgical Colors – Chasuble stands*	**Liturgical Gestures, Colors** *Repeat:* Sign of the Cross (+ Holy Water)*; Liturgical Colors – Chasuble stands* *Add:* Liturgical Calendar*; Genuflection*; Kneeling*	▪ *God is the Father, the Son (Jesus) and the Holy Spirit. We show this in the sign of the cross.* [CCC 261]
Liturgical Furniture, Vessels and Linen *Introduce:* Altar; Altar Cloth; Crucifix; Candles*; Chalice; Cruets; Purificator; Corporal*; Lectern, Lectionary; Tabernacle; Ciborium*	**Liturgical Furniture, Vessels and Linen** *Repeat:* Altar; Altar Cloth; Candles*; Chalice; Cruets; Purificator; Corporal*; Lectern, Lectionary; Tabernacle; Ciborium* *Add:* Finger Bowl; Finger Towel*; Bell; Sanctuary Lamp*	▪ *Every item used in the liturgy reminds us of something important that Jesus did or taught.* [CCC 1075]
Ecclesiology: Kingdom Parables *Introduce:* Mustard Seed*; Leaven*	**Ecclesiology: Kingdom Parables** *Repeat:* Mustard Seed*; Leaven*; Treasure in a Field* *Add:* Pearl of Great Price*	▪ *Jesus taught us about God's Kingdom using parables.* [CCC 546; 2607]

TERM 4: : KINDERGARTEN, YEAR 1

THEMES	TIME OF YEAR	TOPICS
God Prepares the World to receive His Son **Focus Solemnity: Christmas**	FROM MID-NOVEMBER TO MID-DECEMBER	**Infancy Narratives; Advent; Christmas**

KINDERGARTEN	YEAR 1	DOCTRINAL CONTENT
Advent *Introduce:* Advent Procession*; Prophecy of the Young Women*; Prophecy of the Town*; Prophecy of the Star and the Scepter*	**Advent** *Repeat:* Advent Procession*; Prophecy of the Young Women*; Prophecy of the Town*; Prophecy of the Star and the Scepter*	▪ *God spent many years gradually preparing His people for the coming of Jesus.* [CCC 69]
Infancy Narratives *Introduce:* Annunciation*; Visitation*; Birth of Jesus: Shepherds and Angels*; Birth of Jesus: Visit of the Magi*; Presentation in the Temple*; Christmas Pageant	**Infancy Narratives** *Repeat:* Annunciation*; Visitation*; Birth of Jesus: Shepherds and Angels*; Birth of Jesus: Visit of the Magi*; Presentation in the Temple*; Christmas Pageant *Add:* Flight into Egypt*	▪ *Mary was asked to be the mother of Jesus, who is God.* [CCC 495; 509] ▪ *Angels are God's messengers.* [CCC 329, 330, 332] ▪ *Jesus, Mary and Joseph were a family.* [CCC 488] ▪ *God made human beings to live in families. Families can help us to know God better.* [CCC 383]

Revision
By this time of year, the children will have experienced a wide variety of materials and presentations.
They should be free to select any of these as part of their experiences.

TERM 1: YEARS 2, 3, 4

THEMES	TIME OF YEAR	TOPICS
Life of Christ / Focus Solemnity: Easter	FEBRUARY	**Biblical Geography; Gospel Narratives**
	MARCH	**Lent; Parables; Miracles**
Paschal Mystery	TWO WEEKS PRIOR TO EASTER BREAK	**Paschal Mystery; Holy Week**

DOCTRINAL CONTENT

- *"Through Christ our Lord" we pray to the Father.* [CCC 2664]
- *Prayer allows us to listen and respond to God.* [CCC 2590]
- *We are meant to pray often; every day.* [CCC 2720]
- *All our prayers bring our minds and hearts to God, or ask for good things from Him.* [CCC 2590]
- *We grow in relationship with Jesus through prayer.* [CCC 2565]
- *Jesus prayed often to his Father: by himself and publicly.* [CCC 2599]
- *In the Our Father, Jesus taught us how to pray.* [CCC 2763]

- *The Gospels tell us about the life and teachings of Jesus.* [CCC 68; 561]

- *Jesus loved us so much that he died for our sins.* [CCC 629]
- *The Gospels tell us about the life and teachings of Jesus.* [CCC 68; 561]
- *Jesus is our Saviour. He has won for us the life of grace.* [CCC 1715; 2020]

YEAR 2	YEAR 3	YEAR 4
Prayer *Introduce:* Set up prayer table*; Establish prayer routine*; Study Our Father each week, phrase by phrase in prayer time. Memorize formal prayers *See Prayer Development Chart*	**Prayer** *Repeat:* Set up prayer table*; Establish prayer routine *Add:* Introduce praying with icons *See Prayer Development Chart*	**Prayer** *Repeat:* Set up prayer table*; Establish prayer routine*; Praying with icons *Add:* Continue memorizing formal prayers *See Prayer Development Chart*
Biblical Geography *Introduce:* Land of Israel*	**Biblical Geography** *Repeat:* Land of Israel* *Add:* City of Jerusalem*	**Biblical Geography** *Repeat:* Land of Israel*; City of Jerusalem* *Add:* Flag Maps of Israel*
Life of Jesus *Introduce:* Art Synthesis: Life of Jesus Luminous Mysteries of the Rosary *Focus:* Jesus is teacher.	**Life of Jesus** *Repeat:* Art Synthesis: Life of Jesus; Sorrowful Mysteries of the Rosary *Add:* Biblical Charts of key events in the life of Jesus. (Children should read the Bible for themselves.) *Focus:* Jesus is Savior (Christ; Messiah)	**Life of Jesus** *Repeat:* Art Synthesis: Life of Jesus; Biblical Charts of key events in the life of Jesus. *Add: Focus:* Jesus is God and man.

YEAR 2	YEAR 3	YEAR 4	DOCTRINAL CONTENT
Mary and the Saints *Introduce:* Art Synthesis: Life of Mary*	**Mary and the Saints** *Repeat:* Art Synthesis: Life of Mary* *Add: Focus:* Role of Mary in Mission of Jesus	**Mary and the Saints** *Repeat:* Art Synthesis: Life of Mary* *Add: Focus:* Because Mary is the mother of Jesus, she is the mother of God.	▪ *Mary said "yes" to God by doing as he asked.* [CCC 973] ▪ *Mary is mother of the Church and our mother.* [CCC 975] ▪ *Mary continues to work through the Church in leading us to Jesus.* [CCC 975] ▪ *Angels are spirits who serve God and act as his messengers.* [CCC 350]
Lent *Introduce:* Making sacrifices to be ready for Easter; Burying the Alleluia*; Changing the prayer table cloth to purple*	**Lent** *Repeat:* Making sacrifices to be ready for Easter; Burying the Alleluia*; Changing the prayer table cloth to purple* *Add:* Temptation of Christ	**Lent** *Repeat:* Making sacrifices to be ready for Easter; Burying the Alleluia*; Changing the prayer table cloth to purple; Temptation of Christ *Add:* Typology: The Passover*	▪ *During Lent and Holy Week, we try to do something in our lives to bring us closer to Jesus.* ▪ *During Lent and Holy Week, we remember that Jesus suffered and died for our sins. He rose from the dead on Easter Sunday.* ▪ *During Lent, we come closer to God through prayer, fasting, almsgiving and making sacrifices.*
Paschal Narratives *Introduce:* Easter Triduum: Palm Sunday Revise Last Supper*; Revise Resurrection (Mt 28:1–8)*	**Paschal Narratives** *Repeat:* Resurrection Account (Mt 28:1–8) *Add:* Last Supper: Origin of the Eucharist*; Art Synthesis of the Paschal Narratives	**Paschal Narratives** *Repeat:* Resurrection Account* (Mt 28:1–8); Last Supper: Origin of the Eucharist*; Art Synthesis of the Paschal Narratives *Add:* Glorious Mysteries of the Rosary	▪ *Through Jesus's life, death, and Resurrection, we have new life.* [CCC 1016]
Christian Anthropology The human person is present in all the truths of faith. *Focus:* Christ died to save human beings.	**Christian Anthropology** *Repeat:* Christ died to save human beings. *Add:* The redeemed human person is elevated by God to the dignity of a child of God.	**Christian Anthropology** *Repeat:* Christ died to save human beings. The redeemed human person is elevated by God to the dignity of a child of God. *Add:* The human person is affected by original sin, but redeemed by Christ.	▪ *Jesus is our Lord and Saviour because he gained for us the new life of grace.* [CCC 455; 620–21] ▪ *Jesus Christ is the first to rise forever from the dead. He promised that we too will rise again.* [CCC 655; 658]

TERM 2: GRADES 2, 3, 4

THEMES	TIME OF YEAR		TOPICS
The Holy Spirit continues to make Christ present through the Sacraments.	APRIL		Ascension; Pentecost; Baptism
Focus Solemnity: Pentecost	MAY		Eucharist; Reconciliation
	JUNE		Holy Orders; Marriage; Anointing of the Sick

DOCTRINAL CONTENT	GRADE 4	GRADE 3	GRADE 2
※ The Holy Spirit gives us grace to guide and strengthen us during life. [CCC 733; 735–36; 747] ※ We celebrate the coming of the Holy Spirit at Pentecost. [CCC 731] ※ On the solemnity of the Ascension, we remember that the "visible presence of Christ on earth has now passed into the sacraments." [ST LEO THE GREAT] ※ We worship Jesus who is present in the Eucharist. We call this the "real presence." [CCC 1377–78; 1418] ※ On the feast of the Sacred Heart, we recall God's great love for us. [CCC 68]	**Major Feasts:** *Repeat:* Ascension; Pentecost* *Add:* Sacred Heart	**Major Feasts:** *Repeat:* Ascension; Pentecost* *Add:* Corpus Christi	**Major Feasts:** *Introduce:* Ascension; Pentecost*
※ Baptism gives us the new life of grace, forgiveness of sin, and the gifts of faith, hope and love. [CCC 1266; 1279; 1842–44] ※ Baptism is the first and chief sacrament of the forgiveness of sins. [CCC 985] ※ Baptism, Confirmation and Eucharist are the sacraments of Christian initiation. [CCC 1212]	**Baptism** *Repeat:* Baptism Introduction*; Gestures*; Symbols and Objects of Baptism* *Add:* Baptism: The Rite*	**Baptism** *Repeat:* Baptism Introduction*; Gestures* *Add:* Symbols and Objects of Baptism*	**Baptism** *Introduce:* Baptism Introduction* *Add:* Gestures*
※ Jesus gave the Church the power to forgive sins. [CCC 986] ※ To receive God's forgiveness in the Sacrament of Penance we must be sorry for our sins and want to avoid them in the future. We must tell our sins to God through the priest. ※ The priest absolves us from our sins and gives us a penance to do. [CCC 1490–91; 1494–95] ※ Forgiveness brings peace. [CCC 1468]	**Reconciliation** *See also:* Moral Formation Briefly revise all relevant parables* *Repeat:* The True Vine*; Rite of Reconciliation Cards* *Add:* Preparation and participation in the sacrament.	**Reconciliation** *See also:* Moral Formation Briefly revise all relevant parables* *Repeat:* The True Vine* *Add:* Rite of Reconciliation Cards*	**Reconciliation** *See also:* Moral Formation Briefly revise all relevant parables *Add:* The True Vine*

GRADE 2	GRADE 3	GRADE 4	DOCTRINAL CONTENT
Eucharist *Introduce:* Origin of the Eucharist*	**Eucharist** *Repeat:* Origin of the Eucharist* *Add:* Synthesis of the Mass	**Eucharist** *Repeat:* Origin of the Eucharist* , Synthesis of the Mass* *Add:* First Missal*	▪ *Jesus is present when the Scriptures are read and the Eucharist is celebrated at Mass.* [CCC 1101; 1408; 1373] ▪ *The Eucharist is the greatest sacrament of Christian initiation.* [CCC 1322; 1407] ▪ *We call the celebration of the Eucharist the Mass. It is the thanksgiving sacrifice of Jesus, offered for the living and the dead.* [CCC 1414] ▪ *The Eucharist is the great memorial of Jesus's sacrifice on the cross.* [CCC 1356; 1358; 1365; 1366]
Gestures of the Mass *Introduce:* The Offering*, Synthesis of Epiclesis and Eucharistic Presence *	**Gestures of the Mass** *Repeat:* The Offering*; Synthesis of Epiclesis and Eucharistic Presence* *Add:* Lamb of God	**Gestures of the Mass** *Repeat:* The Offering*; Synthesis of Epiclesis and Eucharistic Presence*; Lamb of God *Add:* The Mystery of Faith*	▪ *The stories and actions of Jesus are remembered and lived out in the liturgy.* [CCC 1111] ▪ *The Eucharist is the centre of Christian liturgy.* [CCC 1193] ▪ *Through the liturgy, we worship God in our actions and words.* [CCC 1110]
Other Sacraments *Introduce:* Holy Orders	**Other Sacraments** *Repeat:* Holy Orders *Add:* Marriage: The Rite 1	**Other Sacraments** *Repeat:* Holy Orders; Marriage: The Rite 1 *Add:* Anointing of the Sick 1	▪ *Only ordained priests can, through the Holy Spirit, change the bread and wine into the body and blood of Christ.* [CCC 1411] ▪ *Bishops confer Holy Orders by the "laying on of hands" and a prayer of consecration.* [CCC 1597; 1600] ▪ *Bishops and priests have been called by God to continue the leadership of Jesus Christ in his Church.* [CCC 1536] ▪ *The sacrament of Marriage gives special blessings to married people.* [CCC 1660] ▪ *Jesus's love for his people is the model of love for all married people.* [CCC 1661] ▪ *The Christian home is normally the place where children first hear about God's plan of love for them.* [CCC 1666] ▪ *Anointing of the Sick is for those who are frail, seriously sick or in danger of death.* [CCC 1527] ▪ *The sacrament of anointing gives graces to the sick and dying.* [CCC 1527]

TERM 3: GRADES 2, 3, 4

THEMES	TIME OF YEAR	TOPICS
The Holy Spirit continues to make Christ present through us.	JULY / EARLY AUGUST	Moral Formation; Prayer
Focus Solemnity: Pentecost	LATE AUGUST / SEPTEMBER	Social Justice; Example of Mary & Saints

GRADE 2	GRADE 3	GRADE 4	DOCTRINAL CONTENT
Moral Formation Introduce: Maxims of Jesus*; Moral Parables: The insistent Friend*	**Moral Formation** Repeat: Maxims of Jesus*; The insistent Friend Add: Moral Parables: The Sower*; The Pharisee and the Tax Collector*;	**Moral Formation** Repeat: Maxims of Jesus*; The insistent Friend; The Sower*; The Pharisee and the Tax Collector* Add: Moral Parables: The Debtors*	■ The commandments call us to love God and our neighbour. [CCC 1983] ■ I have the power to choose. [CCC 1733]
Christian Social Ethics Introduce: Parables of Mercy: Forgiving Father*; Social Parables: Good Samaritan*; Scripture: The First Christian Community (Acts 2:44–45); Practical: Identify acts of service that can be done for others	**Christian Social Ethics** Repeat: Good Samaritan*; Forgiving Father*, The First Christian Community (Acts 2:44–45) Add: Lost Coin*; Practical: Identify acts of service that can be done for others	**Christian Social Ethics** Repeat: Good Samaritan*; Forgiving Father*, Lost Coin Add: Centurion's Servant*; The Great Commission; Practical: Identify acts of service that can be done for others	■ Our problems and troubles can bring us closer to God. [CCC 1508; 1521] ■ God wants us to turn back to him after we have sinned. This is called "Repentance." [CCC 1490] ■ Many scripture stories show that Jesus loved and forgave sinners who asked to be forgiven. ■ Jesus asks us to love one another as he has loved us. [CCC 1970]
Christian Anthropology Introduce: Every human being is loved by God	**Christian Anthropology** Repeat: Every human being is loved by God Add: The obligation of human persons to love others	**Christian Anthropology** Repeat: Every human being is loved by God; The obligation of human persons to love others Add: The capacity to be an active and creative agent	■ The commandments call us to love God and our neighbour. [CCC 1983] ■ By loving God and our neighbour, we journey towards Heaven. [CCC 1051; 1054]

GRADE 2	GRADE 3	GRADE 4	DOCTRINAL CONTENT
Ecclesiology *Introduce:* Baptism makes us members of the Church; The True Vine*	**Ecclesiology** *Repeat:* Baptism makes us members of the Church; The True Vine* *Add:* Parables of the Kingdom: Pearl of Great Price*	**Ecclesiology** *Repeat:* Baptism makes us members of the Church; The True Vine*; Pearl of Great Price* *Add:* Parables of the Kingdom: Treasure in the Field	▪ *The Church helps us to know Jesus, and to make him known to others.* [CCC 851] ▪ *The Holy Spirit lives in the Church.* [CCC 797–98] ▪ *We share God's life and love (grace).* [CCC 2021] ▪ *Grace has been given to us by the Holy Spirit.* [CCC 1999]
Christian Community Life *Introduce:* Care for the least among the brethren (Mt 18, 6)	**Christian Community Life** *Repeat:* Care for the least among the brethren (Mt 18, 6) *Add:* Christian life requires common prayer (Mt 18, 19)	**Christian Community Life** *Repeat:* Care for the least among the brethren (Mt 18, 6); Christian life requires common prayer (Mt 18, 19) *Add:* The need for mutual forgiveness (Mt 18, 22)	▪ *Jesus teaches that whatever we do for the poor and disadvantaged, we do to him.* [CCC 1932; MT 25:40] ▪ *The Our Father teaches us to forgive others as we have been forgiven ourselves.* [MT 6:12]
The Scriptures *Introduce:* The Books of the Bible*	**The Scriptures** *Repeat:* The Books of the Bible* *Add:* Bible Charts*	**The Scriptures** *Repeat:* The Books of the Bible*; Bible Charts* *Add:* Free Reading of the Bible	▪ *The Holy Spirit inspired the writers of the Bible.* [CCC 81; 136] ▪ *The Bible comprises the books of the Old and the New Testaments.* [CCC 138]

TERM 4: GRADES 2, 3, 4

	THEMES	TIME OF YEAR	TOPICS
	Death and Everlasting Life	EARLY NOVEMBER	**Human Person; Family; The Last Things; Eschatology**
	God Prepares the World to receive His Son **Focus Solemnity: Christmas**	FROM MID-NOVEMBER TO MID-DECEMBER	**Salvation History; Infancy Narratives; Advent; Christmas**

YEAR 2	YEAR 3	YEAR 4	DOCTRINAL CONTENT
Christian Anthropology *Introduce:* Every human person has a destiny that is immortal.	**Christian Anthropology** *Repeat:* Every human person has a destiny that is immortal.	**Christian Anthropology** *Repeat:* Every human person has a destiny that is immortal. *Add:* The redeemed human person is destined to eternal life.	▪ *God created us with a body and a soul . . . the hand guided by intelligence.* [CCC 362–68; 382] ▪ *Our immortal soul is a spirit, created directly by God.* [CCC 382]
The Last Things *Introduce:* Reflection on the "Last Things" using the story of Dives and Lazarus (Jn 11:25–27).	**The Last Things** *Repeat:* Reflection on the "Last Things" using the story of Dives and Lazarus (Jn 11:25–27). *Add:* Those who have died are not separated from us. They, with us, form the one Church, the People of God, united in the "communion of saints."	**The Last Things** *Repeat:* Those who have died are not separated from us. They, with us, form the one Church, the People of God, united in the "communion of saints." *Add:* The good or evil done to each human being is as if done to Christ.	▪ *God brings to heaven those who die in his love.* [CCC 1051] ▪ *The sacraments strengthen and comfort the dying.* [CCC 1525] ▪ *We continue to pray for those who have died.* [CCC 1032] ▪ *By loving God and our neighbour, we journey towards Heaven.* [CCC 1051 1054] ▪ *Jesus will come again at the end of time.* [CCC 1060] ▪ *Through Jesus's life, death, and resurrection, we have new life.* [CCC 1016]
Salvation History *Introduce:* Three Moments Chart: Creation; Redemption, Parousia*, Advent Procession*, Advent Prophecies*	**Salvation History** *Repeat:* Three Moments Chart*, Advent Procession*, Advent Prophecies*, Advent Prophecies* *Add:* Timeline Ribbon — Major events of Salvation History*	**Salvation History** *Repeat:* Three Moments Chart*, Advent Procession*, Advent Prophecies*, Timeline Ribbon* *Add:* Creation to Parousia Timeline*	▪ *God's creation is good.* [CCC 299; 315] ▪ *Sin came into our world when our first parents disobeyed God.* [CCC 390; 415–17] ▪ *The Old Testament introduces the stories of God's Chosen People.* ▪ *God send prophets to guide and form his people.* [CCC 64] ▪ *The New Testament reveals the Good News of Jesus Christ to all.*

YEAR 2	YEAR 3	YEAR 4	DOCTRINAL CONTENT
Infancy Narratives Revise Infancy Narrative directly from the Scriptures: Annunciation*; Visitation*; Birth of Jesus*; Shepherds Angels*; Visit of the Magi* *Add:* Flight into Egypt*	**Infancy Narratives** *Repeat:* Individual revision of Infancy Narratives from the Scriptures. Select own response *Add:* Art synthesis of the Infancy Narratives. Provide images*	**Infancy Narratives** *Repeat:* Individual revision of Infancy Narratives from the Scriptures. Select own response. *Add:* Joyful Mysteries of the Rosary; Art synthesis of the Infancy Narratives. Students search for images.	▪ *Like the shepherds and the magi, we must "kneel" humbly before Jesus, born in a stable in Bethlehem.* [CCC 563] ▪ *The Presentation in the Temple reminds us that Jesus was born to be the promised savior.* [CCC 529] ▪ *The Flight into Egypt reminds us that Jesus lived his whole life under the sign of persecution.* [CCC 530] ▪ *Jesus lived most of his life doing ordinary things.* [CCC 531]

TERM 1: YEARS 5, 6, 7

	THEMES	TIME OF YEAR	TOPICS
	Life of Christ	FEBRUARY	**Prayer; Biblical Geography; Gospel Narratives**
	Focus Solemnity: Easter	MARCH	**Lent; Parables; Miracles**

YEAR 5	YEAR 6	YEAR 7	DOCTRINAL CONTENT
Prayer Set up prayer table*; Establish prayer routine*; Memorize formal prayers See chart Lectio Divina: Praying with the Scriptures	**Prayer** Set up prayer table*; Establish prayer routine*; Memorize formal prayers See chart Lectio Divina: Praying with the Scriptures	**Prayer** Set up prayer table*; Establish prayer routine*; Memorize formal prayers See chart Lectio Divina: Praying with the Scriptures	■ *The Holy Spirit helps us to pray.* [CCC 2661] ■ *We pray to Jesus among us in the Eucharist.* [CCC 1418] ■ *The Lord's Prayer shows us how to pray to the Father.* [CCC 2799] ■ *Various kinds of prayer: blessing, petition, intercession, thanksgiving and praise.* [CCC 2644] ■ *Self-denial is an important part of Christian prayer.* [CCC 2015]
Biblical Geography *Introduce:* Land of Israel*	**Biblical Geography** *Repeat:* Land of Israel* *Add:* City of Jerusalem*	**Biblical Geography** *Repeat:* Land of Israel*; City of Jerusalem* *Add:* Flag Maps of Israel*	■ *The Gospels tell us about the life and teachings of Jesus.* [CCC 68; 561]
Life of Jesus *Introduce:* Art Synthesis: Life of Jesus; Luminous Mysteries of the Rosary; Find Scripture Verses in support. *Focus:* Jesus is teacher	**Life of Jesus** *Add:* Art Synthesis: Life of Jesus; Miracles of Jesus: Bartimaeus*, Son of the Widow of Nain* *Focus:* Deeds & Miracles of Christ; Sorrowful Mysteries of the Rosary *Focus:* Jesus is Savior (Christ; Messiah)	**Life of Jesus** *Repeat:* Miracles of Jesus: Bartimaeus*; Son of the Widow of Nain* *Add:* Miracles of Jesus: Miracle of the Loaves*, Cure of Peter's mother-in-law*; Art Synthesis of the Life of Jesus: Deeds & Miracles of Christ *Focus:* Resurrection; Christ the Priest	■ *We call Jesus "the Christ" — "anointed of God."* [CCC 453] ■ *Jesus is true God. He is the second person of the Blessed Trinity.* [CCC 464; 480] ■ *Jesus Christ is true man. He was born of the Virgin Mary. We call this mystery the Incarnation.* [CCC 464] ■ *Jesus was like us in all things except sin.* [CCC 480]

YEAR 5	YEAR 6	YEAR 7	DOCTRINAL CONTENT
Mary and the Saints Introduce: Art Synthesis: Life of Mary Focus: Role of Mary in the Mission of Christ; Joyful Mysteries of the Rosary; Christ is divine	**Mary and the Saints** Repeat: Art Synthesis: Life of Mary Add: Glorious Mysteries of the Rosary Focus: Mary Immaculate; Mary Assumed into Heaven	**Mary and the Saints** Repeat: Art Synthesis: Life of Mary Add: Focus: Because Mary is the mother of Jesus, she is the mother of God.	▪ Mary is the mother of God and our mother. She prays for us in heaven. [CCC 495; 969–70; 975] ▪ Mary continues to be honoured through her feast days. [CCC 971] ▪ Saints can help us come closer to God. [CCC 957] ▪ Mary is the model disciple for all believers. [CCC 2030] ▪ The Church recalls and celebrates Mary's faithfulness to God in the Magnificat. [CCC 971] ▪ Mary was conceived free from original sin. [CCC 508; 491] ▪ Mary was assumed body and soul into Heaven. [CCC 974] ▪ Mary had no other children besides Jesus. [CCC 501]
Lent Introduce: Making sacrifices to be ready for Easter; Burying the Alleluia*; Changing the prayer tablecloth to purple.* Add: Stations of the Cross	**Lent** Repeat: Making sacrifices to be ready for Easter; Burying the Alleluia*; Changing the prayer tablecloth to purple.* Add: Christ Reveals the Mysteries of God	**Lent** Repeat: Making sacrifices to be ready for Easter; Burying the Alleluia*; Changing the prayer tablecloth to purple*; Temptation of Christ (Christ is human)	▪ Lent is the season of forty days when we prepare to celebrate the death and Resurrection of the Lord Jesus during Holy Week and Easter. ▪ In Lent, the Church calls us to pray more, to make sacrifices and to give to the poor. ▪ Jesus was fully human. We call this mystery the Incarnation. [CCC 479; 483]
Paschal Narratives Introduce: Easter Triduum: Palm Sunday Revise: Last Supper*, Resurrection (Mt 28:1–8)*	**Paschal Narratives** Repeat: Resurrection (Mt 28:1–8)*; Last Supper: Origin of the Eucharist*; Art Synthesis of the Paschal Narratives Add: Typology: Abraham*	**Paschal Narratives** Repeat: Resurrection (Mt 28:1–8)*; Last Supper: Origin of the Eucharist*; Art Synthesis of the Paschal Narratives Add: Typology: Moses - Passover, Crossing of Red Sea; Manna in the Desert.*	▪ By His sacrifice on the cross, Jesus overcame sin and death. We celebrate his sacrifice in the Eucharist. [CCC 629] ▪ The most important days of Holy Week are Palm Sunday, Holy Thursday, Good Friday and Easter Sunday. ▪ His body was changed for a new life, no longer limited by earthly time and space. [CCC 646]
Christian Anthropology Introduce: The redeemed human person is present in all the truths of faith. Focus: The Liturgy presents the mystery of God's plan of salvation for all humanity.	**Christian Anthropology** Repeat: Christ died to save human beings. Add: The redeemed human person is a member of Christ's Body: the Church.	**Christian Anthropology** Repeat: Christ died to save human beings. The redeemed human person is a member of Christ's Body: the Church.	▪ Jesus Christ died to save human beings that suffered on the cross. [CCC 645] ▪ Christ's resurrected body was changed for a new life, no longer limited by earthly time and space. This change will also happen to us when we rise from the dead at the end of time. [CCC 646]

TERM 2: YEARS 5, 6, 7

THEMES	TIME OF YEAR	TOPICS
The Holy Spirit continues to make Christ present through the Sacraments. **Focus Solemnity: Pentecost**	APRIL	Ascension; Pentecost; Baptism
	MAY	Eucharist; Reconciliation
	JUNE	Holy Orders; Marriage; Anointing of the Sick

YEAR 5	YEAR 6	YEAR 7	DOCTRINAL CONTENT
Major Feasts: *Repeat:* Ascension; Pentecost*, Sacred Heart *Add:* Trinity Sunday	**Major Feasts:** *Repeat:* Ascension; Pentecost*, Sacred Heart Trinity Sunday *Add:* St John the Baptist	**Major Feasts:** *Repeat:* Ascension; Pentecost*, Sacred Heart Trinity Sunday; St John the Baptist *Add:* Sts. Peter & Paul	■ After his Resurrection, Jesus ascended into heaven to prepare a place for us. [CCC 666] ■ Jesus Christ will come again at the end of time. [CCC 682]
Baptism *Repeat:* Baptism Introduction*, Baptism, the Rite* *Add:* Baptismal Mystagogy: Pictures	**Baptism** *Repeat:* Baptism Introduction*, Baptism, the Rite*; Baptismal Mystagogy: Pictures *Add:* Baptismal Mystagogy: Scriptures	**Baptism** *Repeat:* Baptism Introduction*, Baptism, the Rite*; Baptismal Mystagogy: Pictures Baptismal Mystagogy: Scriptures *Add:* Baptismal Mystagogy: Personal project (search the Scriptures for other instances).	■ All the baptised receive a special mission from God. [CCC 1279] ■ In Baptism, we receive the theological virtues (faith, hope and charity) and are helped to live the moral virtues (prudence, justice, temperance and fortitude). [CCC 1266] ■ Through Baptism we share in the life, death and Resurrection of Jesus. [CCC 2017; 2020] ■ Baptism places a spiritual mark (character) on the soul. [CCC 1317]

YEAR 5	YEAR 6	YEAR 7	DOCTRINAL CONTENT
Reconciliation *See also:* Moral Formation Briefly revise all relevant parables; The True Vine *Add:* Examination of Conscience; Preparation for participation in sacrament	**Reconciliation** *See also:* Moral Formation Briefly revise all relevant parables; The True Vine *Add:* Scriptural Examination of Conscience; Preparation for participation in sacrament	**Reconciliation** *See also:* Moral Formation Briefly revise all relevant parables; The True Vine *Add:* Scriptural Examination of Conscience; Preparation for participation in sacrament	▪ *God always wants us to turn back to him after we have sinned.* [CCC 1847; 1870] ▪ *A mortal sin destroys God's life in a person. God's mercy is shown to those who repent; usually in the sacrament of Penance.* [CCC 1855–56, 1489; 1493; 1497] ▪ *The sacrament of Reconciliation gives us the grace to overcome sins.* [CCC 1458; 1875–76] ▪ *The sacrament of Reconciliation involves conversion, repentance, confession, reconciliation and forgiveness.* [CCC 1490–93] ▪ *The sacrament of Reconciliation brings the forgiving love of our Father and the grace of the Holy Spirit.* [CCC 1496] ▪ *Jesus's teachings bring home to us God's immense love and joy at our turning away from sin.* [CCC 1443] ▪ *People can always return to God during their lifetime through the Sacrament of Penance.* [CCC 1426]

Eucharist
Repeat: Synthesis of the Mass*, The Mystery of Faith*
Add: Structure of the Mass
	Eucharist
	Repeat: Structure of the Mass*
	Add: Memorial
		Eucharist
		Repeat: Structure of the Mass*, Memorial *
		Add: Full Missal*
			▪ *Communion with the body and blood of Christ:*
			   ▪ *Increases our union with Christ and with one another*
			   ▪ *Forgives venial sins and preserves from grave sins*
			   ▪ *Strengthens the whole Church.* [CCC 1416]
			▪ *We adore Jesus, really present in the Eucharist.* [CCC 1378]
			▪ *In the Eucharist, Jesus offers to all the gift of redemption.* [CCC 1410]
			▪ *The Eucharist is the source and summit of Christian life.* [CCC 1407]
			▪ *The celebration of the Eucharist is called the Mass. It makes present the sacrifice of Jesus, offered for the living and the dead.* [CCC 1414]

Gestures of the Mass
Repeat: The Offering*; Synthesis of Epiclesis and Eucharistic Presence*; The Lamb of God
	Gestures of the Mass
	The Offering*; The Lamb of God
	Synthesis of Epiclesis and Eucharistic Presence*
	Add: Propers of the Mass*
		Gestures of the Mass
		See "Full Missal"*
			▪ *In the liturgy, the Holy Spirit enables us to encounter Christ.* [CCC 1112]
			▪ *Communion with the body and blood of Christ:*
			   ▪ *Increases our union with Christ and with one another*
			   ▪ *Forgives venial sins and preserves from grave sins*
			   ▪ *Strengthens the whole Church.* [CCC 1416]

YEAR 5	YEAR 6	YEAR 7	DOCTRINAL CONTENT
Other Sacraments *Repeat:* Holy Orders: The Rite 1; Marriage: The Rite 1 *Add:* Anointing of the Sick	**Other Sacraments** *Repeat:* Anointing of the Sick* *Add:* Holy Orders: The Rite 2; Marriage: The Rite 2	**Other Sacraments** *Add:* The Holy Trinity and Marriage (very advanced)	**Anointing of the Sick** • Anointing of the Sick brings strength, peace and courage to endure suffering in a Christian manner. [CCC 1532] • Anointing of the Sick sometimes restores the person to health if this is for their good. [CCC 1532] • Anointing of the Sick can only be given by a priest. [CCC 1530] **Holy Orders** • Bishops and priests serve us in the name and person of Christ. [CCC 1549; 1591] • Holy Orders gives sacred power to a priest: to teach, to sanctify and to lead the faithful. [CCC 1592] • Deacons assist bishops and priests in the ministry of the word and the sacraments. [CCC 1570; 1596] • Only baptised men can be ordained. [CCC 1598] • Through the priesthood, bishops and priests share in the one priesthood of Christ. [CCC 1591]
Other Sacraments *Repeat:* Holy Orders: The Rite 1; Marriage: The Rite 1 *Add:* Anointing of the Sick	**Other Sacraments** *Repeat:* Anointing of the Sick* *Add:* Holy Orders: The Rite 2; Marriage: The Rite 2	**Other Sacraments** *Add:* The Holy Trinity and Marriage (very advanced)	**Marriage** • Marriage was instituted by God. It is exclusive and for life. [CCC 1646–47] • Marriage is the union in love of a woman and a man. It signifies the union of Christ and the Church. [CCC 1661] • The couple give each other the sacrament of marriage. The priest is the Church's witness. [CCC 1630]
Confirmation Select elements of the Confirmation program if suitable.	**Confirmation** Elements of a Confirmation Program • Review the other sacraments of initiation, Baptism and Eucharist • Articles and gestures used in the Rite of Confirmation • Explanation of the Gifts of the Spirit; Fruit of the Spirit • Explanation of the Rite of Confirmation • Service Project: offering some practical service to others on behalf of the Church • Research life of a saint as a model for living out of the faith	**Confirmation** Select elements of the Confirmation program if suitable.	• By our Confirmation the Holy Spirit strengthens us to live a holy life to love and respect one another, proclaim the Gospel, and serve others as Jesus did. [CCC 1319] • Confirmation gives us the special strength of the Holy Spirit to spread and defend the faith by word and action. We are helped in this by the gifts of the Spirit. [CCC 1316; 1845] • Like Baptism, Confirmation places a spiritual mark (character) on the soul. [CCC 1317] • The Rite of Confirmation (studied as part of Confirmation preparation). [CCC 1320]

TERM 3: YEARS 5, 6, 7

	THEMES	TIME OF YEAR	TOPICS
	The Holy Spirit continues to make Christ present through us. **Focus Solemnity: Pentecost.**	JULY / EARLY AUGUST	**Moral Formation; Prayer**
		LATE AUGUST / SEPTEMBER	**Social Justice; Example of Mary & Saints**

YEAR 5	YEAR 6	YEAR 7	DOCTRINAL CONTENT
Moral Formation *Revise:* Grace and Courtesy Procedures; Re-establish classroom chores; Set Up Classroom Procedures for the Year *Repeat:* Maxims of Jesus; Moral Parables *Add:* 10 Commandments	**Moral Formation** *Revise:* Grace and Courtesy Procedures; Re-establish classroom chores; Set Up Classroom Procedures for the Year *Repeat:* Maxims of Jesus; Moral Parables; 10 Commandments *Add:* The Virtues	**Moral Formation** *Revise:* Grace and Courtesy Procedures; Re-establish classroom chores; Set Up Classroom Procedures for the Year *Repeat:* Maxims of Jesus; Moral Parables; 10 Commandments; Virtues *Add:* Beatitudes	■ In Baptism we receive the three theological virtues and the four moral virtues. [CCC 1833–34; 1839–40] ■ The virtues are habits that help us to do what is good. [CCC 1833–34] ■ The virtue of faith enables us to believe in God and all that He has revealed. [CCC 1842] ■ The virtue of hope enables us to trust in God's future promise of eternal life. [CCC 1843] ■ The virtue of charity enables us to love God above all things and to love my neighbour as myself. [CCC 1844] ■ The virtue of prudence enables us to discover our true good and helps us to choose this. [CCC 1835] ■ The virtue of justice enables us to give to God and our neighbour what is due to them. [CCC 1836] ■ The virtue of fortitude enables us to be strong and courageous in doing what is right and good. [CCC 1837] ■ The virtue of temperance enables us to use the pleasures of this world as God intended. [CCC 1838] ■ When we put the virtues into practice, they become stronger.
Christian Social Ethics *Introduce:* Honesty is the basic condition for all human relationships. Introduce the Commandments.	**Christian Social Ethics** *Repeat:* Honesty is the basic condition for all human relationships. Commandments *Add:* Justice is the recognition of the rights of each individual	**Christian Social Ethics** *Repeat:* Honesty is the basic condition for all human relationships. Justice is the recognition of the rights of each individual. Commandments *Add:* The goods of the earth are gifts of God, and are not the privilege of some individuals or groups while others are deprived of them.	■ "A New Commandment I give to you; love one another as I have loved you." [JOHN 13:34] ■ The commandments call us to love God and our neighbour as we journey towards Heaven. [CCC 1983; 1051–54] ■ The Beatitudes express Christ's plan for our happiness in this world and the next. [CCC 1725–26] [CCC 2070–74]

YEAR 5	YEAR 6	YEAR 7	DOCTRINAL CONTENT
Christian Anthropology *Repeat:* Every human being is loved by God	**Christian Anthropology** *Repeat:* Every human being is loved by God *Add:* Human person is created in the image of God.	**Christian Anthropology** *Repeat:* Every human being is loved by God; The obligation of human persons to love others *Add:* Human persons should have a willingness to embrace life.	▪ *"A New Commandment I give to you; love one another as I have loved you."* [JOHN 13:34] ▪ *God calls me to discover his plan for my life.* [CCC 2253]
Ecclesiology *Introduce:* Belonging to the Church has obvious consequences for life, for apostolate, and for a Christian vision of the world.	**Ecclesiology** *Repeat:* Belonging to the Church has obvious consequences for life, for apostolate, and for a Christian vision of the world.	**Ecclesiology** *Repeat:* Belonging to the Church has obvious consequences for life, for apostolate, and for a Christian vision of the world.	▪ *The Church is a Communion of Saints.* [CCC 960–62] ▪ *All members of the Church are called to use their own gifts in building the Church.* [CCC 900] ▪ *Jesus is the Head of the Church. The Pope is the Vicar of Christ on earth.* [CCC 936; 2050] ▪ *We believe in one, holy, catholic and apostolic Church.* [CCC 866–69; 938] ▪ *In the liturgy, the Holy Spirit recalls the work of the Father and Son. He is the living memory of the Church.* [CCC 1091–92]
Christian Community Life *Introduce:* Christian community life requires a spirit of simplicity and humility (Mt 18, 3)	**Christian Community Life** *Repeat:* Christian community life requires a spirit of simplicity and humility (Mt 18, 3) *Add:* Christian community life requires particular care for those who are alienated (Mt 18,12)	**Christian Community Life** *Repeat:* Christian community life requires a spirit of simplicity and humility (Mt 18, 3). Christian community life requires particular care for those who are alienated (Mt 18, 12) *Add:* Fraternal love embraces all these attitudes (Jn 13, 34)	▪ *We believe in one, holy, catholic and apostolic Church.* [CCC 866–69; 938]
The Scriptures Allow time for free reading of the Bible Typology of Creation Typology of the Fall (See Salvation History)	**The Scriptures** Allow time for free reading of the Bible Typology of Abraham (See Paschal Narratives)	**The Scriptures** Allow time for free reading of the Bible Typology of the Exodus (See Paschal Narratives)	▪ *Through Sacred Tradition the Church interprets the Sacred Scriptures.* [CCC 80; 137–38]

TERM 4: YEARS 5, 6, 7

THEMES	TIME OF YEAR	TOPICS
Death and Everlasting Life	EARLY NOVEMBER	Human Person; Family; The Last Things; Eschatology
God Prepares the World to receive His Son Focus Solemnity: Christmas	FROM MID-NOVEMBER TO MID-DECEMBER	Salvation History; Infancy Narratives; Advent; Christmas

YEAR 5	YEAR 6	YEAR 7	DOCTRINAL CONTENT
The Last Things *Introduce:* The last judgment points to an eternal destiny which each of us merits through our own works.	**The Last Things** *Repeat:* The last judgment points to an eternal destiny which each of us merits through our own works. *Add:* We are personally responsible in everything we do, because we must render an account to God.	**The Last Things** *Repeat:* The last judgment points to an eternal destiny which each of us merits through our own works. We are personally responsible in everything we do, because we must render an account to God. *Add:* Christian hope in our ultimate destiny offers comfort in life's difficulties.	▪ *Those who die in God's grace live forever with Christ.* [CCC 1023] ▪ *Faith is necessary for us to be saved.* [CCC 183] ▪ *Purgatory prepares those not ready for Heaven.* [CCC 1054] ▪ *God's mercy is shown to those in Purgatory, for whom we should pray.* [CCC 1054–55] ▪ *Only those who have rejected God completely are deprived of Him forever in hell.* [CCC 1056–57] ▪ *Jesus will come again at the end of time to judge the living and the dead.* [CCC 1038–41; 1059] ▪ *We believe in the Resurrection of the body at the end of time.* [CCC 1016; 1059] ▪ *I only die once because in this world, I only have one life.* [CCC 1013]
Salvation History *Introduce:* Plan of God	**Salvation History** *Repeat:* Plan of God *Add:* Creation Typology	**Salvation History** *Repeat:* Plan of God; Creation Typology *Add:* The Fall Typology	▪ *In the liturgy, the Holy Spirit helps us to recall the saving work of the Father and the Son. In this way, the Holy Spirit is the living memory of the Church.* [CCC 1091–92]
Infancy Narratives *Introduce:* Prophecies of the Coming of Christ	**Infancy Narratives** *Repeat:* Prophecies of the Coming of Christ *Add:* Art synthesis of the Infancy Narratives: Find related Scripture passages. Create Nativity scenes based on Scripture passages.	**Infancy Narratives** *Repeat:* Prophecies of the Coming of Christ *Add:* Art synthesis of the Infancy Narratives: Find related Scripture passages. Create Nativity scenes based on Scripture passages. *Add:* Joyful Mysteries of the Rosary *Focus:* Mary is ever virgin; Mother of God	▪ *During Advent, we remember the people of Old Testament times who waited for the Saviour, Jesus Christ.* [CCC 524] ▪ *During Advent, we try to become more like Jesus by making changes in the way we live our lives.*

PRAYER DEVELOPMENT CHART

KINDERGARTEN – YEAR 1	GRADE 2 – GRADE 4	GRADE 5 – GRADE 8
Introduce one at a time.	*Repeat:*	*Repeat*
Have the children pray with you as you are reciting these prayers aloud.	▪ Sign of the Cross	▪ Sign of the Cross
Parents should be encouraged to train their children to	▪ Our Father	▪ Our Father
Repeat these prayers as part of their home routine:	▪ Hail Mary	▪ Hail Mary
Morning and Evening.	▪ Glory Be	▪ Glory Be
	▪ Simple Grace	▪ Simple Grace
	▪ Angel of God	▪ Angel of God
▪ Sign of the Cross Grace Before Meals	▪ Glory Be	▪ Glory Be
▪ Our Father Psalms	▪ Grace Before Meals	▪ Grace Before Meals
▪ Hail Mary Church Visits	▪ Psalms	▪ Psalms
▪ Glory Be Simple Stations of the Cross	▪ Church Visits	▪ Church Visits
▪ Simple Grace Personal Prayer	▪ Simple Stations of the Cross	▪ Simple Stations of the Cross
▪ Angel of God Hymns	▪ Personal Prayer	▪ Personal Prayer
▪ Glory Be Psalms (Selected Verses)	▪ Hymns	▪ Hymns
	▪ Psalms (Selected Verses)	▪ Psalms (Selected Verses)
		▪ Morning Offering
	Add:	▪ Short Acts of Faith, Hope and Charity.
	▪ Morning Offering	
	▪ Short Acts of Faith, Hope and Charity.	*Repeat*
	▪ Act of Contrition	▪ Act of Contrition
	▪ Prayer for the Dead	▪ Prayer for the Dead
	▪ Psalms	▪ Psalms
	▪ Personal Prayer	▪ Personal Prayer
	▪ Hymns and Carols	▪ Hymns and Carols
	▪ Psalms	▪ Psalms Prayers before and after Communion
	▪ Prayers before and after Communion	▪ Responses to the Mass
	▪ Responses to the Mass	▪ Apostles Creed
	▪ Apostles Creed	▪ The Rosary
	▪ The Rosary	▪ The Angelus
	▪ The Angelus	
		Add:
		▪ Memorare
		▪ Hail Holy Queen
		▪ Divine Praises
		▪ Aspirations
		▪ Nicene Creed

MAJOR FEAST DAYS
(To Be Celebrated on the Day)

FEAST DAY	DOCTRINAL CONTENT
St. Patrick	▪ *Saints can help us come closer to God.* [CCC 957] ▪ *Saints can pray and intercede for us.* [CCC 956]
St. Joseph	▪ *All proper authority comes from God.* [CCC 1921] ▪ *The family is a community of life and love.* [CCC 2204–06]
Annunciation	▪ *Mary is the mother of God and our mother. She prays for us in heaven.* [CCC 495; 969–70; 975] ▪ *In Jesus Christ, God became man. We call this mystery the Incarnation.* [CCC 479; 483]
Help of Christians	▪ *Mary is the model disciple for all believers.* [CCC 2030] ▪ *The Church recalls and celebrates Mary's faithfulness to God in the Magnificat.* [CCC 971]
Ascension	▪ *After his Resurrection, Jesus ascended into heaven to prepare a place for us.* [CCC 666] ▪ *On this day, the visible presence of Christ on earth passes into the sacraments.* [ST. LEO THE GREAT: SERMON FOR THE ASCENSION]
Pentecost	▪ *The Holy Spirit gives us the grace to help our faith to grow.* [CCC 684] ▪ *Jesus asked God his Father to send the Holy Spirit to be with us always.* [CCC 689] ▪ *The Holy Spirit is sent by the Father and the Son to give the life of grace to all God's people.* [CCC 689] ▪ *The Holy Spirit builds up and unites the Christian community, especially through the Liturgy and prayer.* [CCC 797; 813; 1112]
Trinity Sunday	▪ *God the Father is our Creator; God the Son is our Redeemer; God the Holy Spirit is our Sanctifier.* [CCC 238; 267] ▪ *The Trinity is the central mystery of our faith, revealed to us by Jesus and by the Holy Spirit.* [CCC 228; 230; 234; 249; 261] ▪ *Jesus is true God. He is the second person of the Blessed Trinity.* [CCC 464; 480] ▪ *Jesus Christ is true man. He was born of the Virgin Mary.* [CCC 464] ▪ *God alone is to be worshipped.* [CCC 2096–97] ▪ *God is infinite, perfect, and powerful, and all loving.* [CCC 320]
Corpus Christi	▪ *We adore Jesus, really present in the Eucharist.* [CCC 1378] ▪ *The Eucharist is the source and summit of the Christian life.* [CCC 1407]
Sacred Heart	▪ *"A New Commandment I give to you; love one another as I have loved you."*
Sts. Peter and Paul	▪ *Jesus is the Head of the Church. The Pope is the Vicar of Christ on earth.* [CCC 936; 2050]
Assumption	▪ *Mary was honoured by the first Christian communities.* [CCC 496; 971] ▪ *Mary continues to be honoured through her feast days.* [CCC 971] ▪ *Mary is honoured in Christian Communities throughout the world.* [CCC 971] ▪ *Mary was assumed body and soul into Heaven.* [CCC 974]
Holy Souls	▪ *Purgatory prepares those not ready for Heaven; it is a state of purification and hope.* [CCC 1054] ▪ *God's mercy is shown to those in Purgatory, for whom we should pray and offer the Eucharist.* [CCC 1054–55] ▪ *I only die once because in this world, I only have one life.* [CCC 1013]
Immaculate Conception	▪ *Mary was conceived free from original sin.* [CCC 508; 491] ▪ *Mary had no other children except Jesus.* [CCC 501]
Parish Feast Day	▪ *The Church tries to proclaim the Gospel to people in their language and culture.* [CCC 806] ▪ *All members of the Church (lay and ordained) are called to use their own gifts and talents in building up the Church.* [CCC 900]

Bibliography

Anatrella, Tony. "Disappearing Fathers, Destabilized Families." *Communio International Catholic Review* (Summer, 2009): 307–28.

Aronson, E. "Building Empathy, Compassion, and Achievement in the Jigsaw Classroom." In J. J. Aronson (ed.) *Improving Academic Achievement: Impact of Psychological Factors in Education*. San Diego: Academic Press, 2002.

Azmitia, M. and K. Crowley. "The Rhythms of Thinking: The Study of Collaboration in an Earthquake Microworld." In K. Crowley, C. D. Schunn, and T. Okada (eds.), *Designing for Science: Implications for Everyday, Classroom, and Professional Settings*. Mahawa, NJ: Lawrence Earlbaum, 2001.

Bandura, A., D. Ross, and S. A. Ross. "Imitation of Film-mediated Aggressive Models." *Journal of Abnormal and Social Psychology*. 66 (1) (1963).

Benedict XVI. *Address to Catholic Religion Teachers*. Vatican City: Libreria Editrice Vaticana, 2009.

—. *Light of the World: The Pope, the Church, and the Signs of the Times, a Conversation with Peter Seewald*. Trans. Michael J. Miller and Adrian J. Walker. San Francisco: Ignatius Press, 2008.

—. *Deus Caritas Est*. Vatican City: Libreria Editrice Vaticana, 2005.

—. *Sacramentum Caritatis*. Vatican City: Vaticana Editrice, 2007.

Bennett, E. de Corte and H. F. Friedrich (eds.), *Learning and Instruction: European Research in an International Context*. Vol. 2. London: Pergamon, 1989.

Bushnell, Horace. *Christian Nurture*. New Haven: Yale University Press, 1847.

Cameron, J., K. M. Banko, and W. D. Pierce. "Pervasive Negative Effects of Rewards on Intrinsic Motivation: The Myth Continues." *Behaviour Analyst*, 24 (1) (2001): 1–44.

Carlson, S. M., L. J. Moses, and H. R. Hicks. "The Role of Inhibitory Processes in Young Children's Difficulties with Deception and False Belief." *Child Development* 69 (1998): 184–98.

Carpenter, M., N. Akhtar, and M. Tomasello. "Fourteen through 18-month-old Infants Differentially Imitate Intentional and Accidental Actions." *Infant Behaviour and Development*, 21 (1998): 315–30.

Catechism of the Catholic Church. Vatican City: Libreria Editrice Vaticana, 1997.

Cavalletti, Sofia. *The History of the Kingdom of God. From Creation to Parousia. Part 1*. Chicago: Catechesis of the Good Shepherd Publications, 2012.

—.*The Religious Potential of the Child*. Chicago: LTP. Revised Edition, 1992.

Chartrand, T. L., and J. A. Bargh. "The Chameleon Effect: The Perception-Behaviour Link and Social Interaction." *Journal of Personality and Social Psychology*, 76 (1999): 893–910.

Chesterton, G. K. *Orthodoxy*. London: Bodley Head, 1909.

Clark, R. E. "When Teaching Kills Learning: Research on Mathematics." in H. N. Mandl, N. Bennett, E. de Corte, and H. F. Friedrich (eds.). *Learning and Instruction:*

European Research in an International Context. (London: Pergamon, 1989), 1–22.

Cohen, R. L. "Memory for Action Events: The Power of Enactment." *Educational Psychology Review*, 1 (1) (1989): 57–80.

Compendium of the Catechism of the Catholic Church. Strathfield, NSW: St. Paul's, 2006.

Congregation for Catholic Education. *Circular Letter to the Presidents of Bishops' Conferences on Religious Education in Schools* (2009).

—. *Educating to Intercultural Dialogue in Catholic Schools: Living in Harmony for a Civilization of Love* (2013).

—. *Educating Together in Catholic Schools: A Shared Mission between Consecrated Persons and the Lay Faithful*. Vatican City: Libreria Editrice Vaticana, 2007.

—. *The Catholic School*. Vatican City: Libreria Editrice Vaticana, 1977.

—. *The Catholic School on the Threshold of the Third Millennium*. Vatican City: Libreria Editrice Vaticana, 1997.

—. *The Religious Dimension of Education in a Catholic School*. Vatican City: Libreria Editrice Vaticana, 1988.

Congregation for the Clergy. *The General Directory of Catechesis*, 1997.

Cornelius-White, J. "Learner-Centred Teacher-Student Relationships are Effective: A Meta-analysis." *Review of Educational Research*, 77 (1) (2007): 113–43.

Cumberland-Li, A., N. Eisenberg, and M. Reiser. "Relations of Young Children's Agreeableness and Resiliency to Effortful Control and Impulsivity." *Social Development*, 13 (2) (2004): 193–212.

Deci, E. L., R. Koestner, and R. M. Ryan. "A Meta-analytical Review of Experiments Examining the Effects of Extrinsic Rewards on Intrinsic Motivation." *Psychological Bulletin*, 125 (1999): 627–68.

Engelkamp, J., H. D. Zimmer, G. Mohr, and O. Sellen. "Memory of Self-performed Tasks: Self-performing during Recognition." *Memory and Cognition*, 22 (1) (1994): 34–39.

Fantuzzo, J. and M. Ginsburg-Block. "Reciprocal Peer Tutoring: Developing and Testing Effective Peer Collaborations for Elementary School Students." In K. Topping & S. Ehly (eds.). *Peer-assisted Learning*. Mahawa, N.J.: Lawrence Earlbaum, 1998: 121–44.

Flavell, J. H. "Cognitive Development: Children's Knowledge about the Mind." *Annual Review of Psychology*, 50 (1999): 21–45.

Francis I. *Evangelii Gaudium*. Vatican City: Libreria Vatican Editrice, 2013.

—. *Lumen Fidei*. Vatican City: Vaticana Editrice, 2013.

Fuchs, L. S. and D. Fuchs. "Effects of Systematic Formative Evaluation: A Meta-analysis." *Exceptional Children*, 53 (3): 199–208.

Gauvain, M. *The Social Context of Cognitive Development*. London: Guilford, 2001.

Gauvain, M. and B. Rogoff. "Collaborative Problem Solving and Children's Planning Skills." *Developmental Psychology*, 25 (1) (1989): 139–51.

Gergely, G., H. Bekkering, and I. Kiraly. "Rational Imitation in Pre-verbal Infants." *Nature*, 415 (6873) (2002): 755.

Glasersfeld, E. von. "Environment and Education." In L. P. Steffe and T. Wood (eds.). *Transforming Children's Mathematics Education: International Perspectives*. Hillsdale, NJ: Lawrence Erlbaum, 1990.

Glenberg and Kaschak. "Grounding Language in Action." *Psychonomic Bulletin and*

Review, 9 (3) (2002): 36–41.

Gobbi, Gianna. *Listening to God with Children.* Loveland OH: Treehaus Communications, 1998.

Grazzini, Camillo. "The four planes of development." *The NAMTA Journal* 21, no. 2 (1996): 208–41.

Greenwood, C. R., B. Terrey, C. A. Utley, D. Montagna, and D. Walker. "Achievement, Placement and Services: Middle School Benefits of Classwide Peer Tutoring Used at the Elementary School." *School Psychology Review,* 22 (3) (1993): 497–516.

Hattie, John. *Visible Learning: A Synthesis of over 800 Meta-analyses Relating to Achievement.* New York: Routledge, 2009.

Held, R. and A. Hein. "Movement Produced Stimulation in the Development of Visually Guided Behaviour." *Journal of Comparative and Physiological Psychology,* 56 (5) (1963): 872–76.

Iyengar, S. S. and M. R. Lepper. "Rethinking the Value of Choice: A Perspective on Intrinsic Motivation." *Journal of Personality and Social Psychology,* 76 (1999): 349–66.

—. "When Choice is De-motivating: Can One Desire too much of a Good Thing?" *Journal of Personality and Social Psychology,* 79 (6) (2000): 995–1006.

John Paul II. *Angelus Address:* Sunday 6th August, 1995.

—. *Catechesi Tradendae.* Vatican City: Libreria Vatican Editrice, 2013.

—. *Familiaris Consortio.* Vatican City: Libreria Editrice Vaticana, 1981.

—. *Letter to Archbishop Vincent Nichols on the Occasion of the Second Centenary of the Birth of Newman,* 22 January, 2001, in Chavasse, Paul. "John Henry Newman: A Saint for Our Times." *Newman Studies Journal* 1, no. 1 (2004): 29–41.

—. *Ecclesia in Oceania.* Vatican City: Libreria Editrice Vaticana, 2001.

Kanselaar, G. "Constructivism and Socio-constructivism." University of Utrecht: Open Access, 2002.

Kirschner, P. A., J. Sweller, and R. E. Clark. "Why Minimal Guidance during Instruction Does Not Work: An Analysis of the Failure of Constructivist, Discovery, Problem-based, Experiential and Inquiry-based Teaching." *Educational Psychologist* 41 (2) (2006): 75–86.

Kraus and Hadar. "The Role of Speech Related Arm/Hand Gestures in Word Retrieval." In L. S. Messing and R. Campbell (eds.). *Gesture, Speech and Sign.* New York: Oxford University Press, 1999: 93–116.

Kuncel, N. R., M. Crede, and L. L. Thomas. "The Validity of Self-reported Grade-point Averages, Class Ranks, and Test Scores: A Meta-analysis and Review of the Literature." *Review of Educational Research,* 75 (1) (2005).

Laird, J. D., J. J. Wagener, M. Halal, and M. Szegda. "Remembering What You Feel: Effects of Emotion on Memory." *Journal of Personality and Social Psychology,* 42 (4) 1982): 646–57.

Lepper, M. R., D. Greene, and R. E. Nisbett. "Undermining Children's Intrinsic Interest with Extrinsic Reward: A Test of the 'Overjustification' Hypothesis." *Journal of Personality and Social Psychology,* 28 (1) (1973): 129–37.

Lillard, Angeline Stoll, *Montessori: The Science behind the Genius.* New York: Oxford University Press, 2005.

Lubac, Henri de. "Internal Causes for the Weakening and Disappearance of the Sense of the Sacred." Re-published in *Josephinum Journal of Theology*, 18, 1 (2011): 37–50.

Lundeberg, M. A, "Metacognitive Aspects of Reading Comprehension: Studying Understanding in Legal Case Analysis." *Reading Research Quarterly*, 61 (1): 94–106.

Macmurray, J. *Persons in Relation*. London: Harper and Harper, 1961.

Markus, H. R. and S. Kitayama. "Culture and the Self: Implications for Cognition, Emotion and Motivation." *Psychological Review*, 98 (1991): 224–53.

Mazza, Enrico. *Mystagogy*. New York: Pueblo, 1989.

McCain, M. and F. Mustard. *Reversing the Real Brain Drain: The Early Years Study. Final Report*. Toronto: Ontario Children's Secretariat. 1999.

McNeill, D. *Hand and Mind*. Chicago: University of Chicago Press, 1992.

Metcalf, K. K. "Laboratory Experiences in Teacher Education: A Meta-analytical Review of Research." Paper presented at the Annual Meeting of the American Educational Research Association, San Francisco, CA, 1995.

Montessori, Maria. *From Childhood to Adolescence: Including 'Erdkinder' and the Functions of the University*. New York: Schocken, 1987.

Naglieri, J. A., and J. P. Das. "Intelligence Revised: The Planning, Attention, Simultaneous, Successive (PASS) Cognitive Processing Theory." R. F. Dillon (ed.). *Handbook on Testing* (36–163). Westport: CT, Greenwood Press, 1997.

Newman, John Henry. *The Grammar of Assent: An Essay on the Development of Christian Doctrine*. London: Longmans, Green and Co., 1903.

Noice, H., T. Noice, and C. Kennedy. "Effects of Enactment by Professional Actors at Encoding and Retrieval." *Memory*, 8 (6) (2000): 353–63.

Ochs, E., P. Gonzales, and S. Jacoby. "Collaborative Discovery in a Scientific Domain." *Cognitive Science*, 21 (2) (1996): 109–46.

Oliner, Samuel and Pearl M. Oliner. *The Altruistic Personality: Rescuers of Jews in Nazi Europe*. Chicago: University of Chicago Press, 1990.

Paul VI. *Address to the International Congress of Montessori Educators on the Centenary of the Birth of Maria Montessori*. Vatican City: Libreria Editrice Vaticana, 1970.

Phillips, N. B., C. L. Hamlett, L. S. Fuchs, and D. Fuchs. "Combining Classwide Curriculum-based Measurement and Peer Tutoring to Help General Educators Provide Adaptive Education." *Learning Disabilities Research and Practice*, 8 (3) (1995): 148–56.

Pontifical Council for Justice and Peace. *Compendium of the Social Doctrine of the Catholic Church*. Vatican City: Libreria Editrice Vaticana, 2004.

Ratzinger, Joseph. *Pilgrim Fellowship of Faith*. San Francisco: Ignatius, 2005.

Rogoff, B., L. Bartlett and C. G. Turkanis. "Lessons about Learning as Community." In B. Rogoff, C. G. Turkanis, and L. Bartlett (eds.) *Learning Together: Children and Adults in a School Community*. New York: Oxford University Press, 2001.

Rorty, R. *Philosophy and the Mirror of Nature*. Princeton: Princeton University Press, 1979.

Rosenshine, B. and C. Meister. "Reciprocal Teaching: A Review of the Research." *Review of Educational Research*, 64 (4) 1994): 479–530.

Ruff, H. A. and M. K. Rothbart. *Attention in Early Development: Themes and Variations*. New York: Oxford University Press, 1996.

Ryan, R. M. and D. L. Deci. "Self-determination Theory and the Facilitation of Intrinsic Motivation, Self-development, and Well-being." *American Psychologist,* 55 (1) (2000): 68–78.

Samuelstuen, M. S., and I. Braten. "Examining the Validity of Self-reports on Scales Measuring Students' Strategic Processing." *British Journal of Educational Psychology,* 77 (2) (2000): 351–78.

Schwartz, B. *The Paradox of Choice.* New York: Harper Collins, 2004.

Sergiovanni, T. *Building Community in Schools.* San Francisco: Jossey-Bass, 1994.

Small, R. "A Fallacy in Constructivist Epistemology." *Journal of Philosophy of Education,* 37 (3) (2003): 483–502.

Spry, G. and J. Graham. *School Community Leadership: The Perspective of Primary School Principal.* Melbourne, Australia: Australian Association for Research in Education, 2007.

Standing, E. M. *Maria Montessori: Her Life and Work.* New York: Plume Books, 1998.

Sweller, John. "Cognitive load theory and the use of educational technology." *Educational technology* 48, no. 1 (2008): 32–35.

Tönnies, F. *Community and Society.* C. Loomis, ed. and trans. East Lansing: Michigan State University Press, 1957.

Vaillant, George E. *Triumphs of Experience: The Men of Harvard.* Harvard: Harvard University Press, 2012.

Vatican Council II. *Gaudium et Spes.* Vatican City: Libreria Vaticana Editrice, 1965.

—. *Gravissimum Educationis.* Vatican City: Libreria Editrice Vaticana, 1965.

—. *Lumen Gentium.* Vatican City: Libreria Editrice Vaticana, 1964.

Whetstone, J. "Personalism and Moral Leadership: The Servant Leader with a Transformational Vision." *Business Ethics: A European Review,* 11 (4), (2002): 385–92.

ABOUT THE AUTHOR

Gerard O'Shea is Professor of Religious Education and assistant dean of the School of Education at the University of Notre Dame, Australia (Sydney campus). His professional experience spans every level of religious education: as a father in a family; a catechist in the parish; a teacher in Catholic schools; a lecturer in undergraduate teaching programs; and a supervisor of doctoral dissertations. He spent over thirty years as a teacher and principal in Catholic schools before taking up an academic position. The combination of practical experience underpinned by academic research is a key characteristic of his published work. Gerard is fully trained in Sofia Cavalletti's Catechesis of the Good Shepherd and was one of the lead writers for the Australian religious education text series "To Know, Worship and Love." He has consulted widely in the field of religious education for Australian Catholic dioceses and recently recorded eight sessions for the Catechetical Institute of the Franciscan University of Steubenville. His handbook for training parents to educate their own children in a Christian vision of sexuality, "As I Have Loved You," has been very well received and is being used throughout the English-speaking world. Gerard and his wife Anne have five adult children and nine grandchildren. They served a five-year term as president couple for the National Association of Catholic Families, and were sent as Australian delegates to the World Meeting of Families in Mexico City, 2008.

Made in United States
Orlando, FL
22 February 2022

15061030R00174